Sydney's Passion
Tested to the Limits

Susie Wright

This book and series are purely a work of fiction. Any names, characters, places, events of anything that happens here within these pages is strictly from the creative imagination of the author. Any resemblance to actual people or events is completely coincidental.

Sydney's Passion is a continuous series. There are five planned books currently. The previous book was Sydney's Passion. The next book to follow this one is Sydney's Passion Tomorrow Isn't Promised. Enjoy and please leave reviews so other readers may know your experience while reading this book.

Contents

CHAPTER 1
The Grand Donation

"Get out!"

"*Please*...let me explain! It's not what you think!"

"I said get out! I don't care where you go but get out!" She says as she trembles with fear. "Take your things and just go! I will call you when I am ready to talk with you again. But for the love of God, just go."

"But please, I don't wanna go. I love you. You are my whole world."

"Look, either you go, or I will, but I want you gone! I need some time to think," she says, waiting for him to make his move. "Okay, it looks like you are going to make this harder than it has to be. So fine, I will be the one to leave. When I return, I expect you to be gone." She grabs her purse, and she walks out the front door, letting it slam behind her.

He decides to get his things and leave to give her the space she needs and asked for.

Buzz. Buzz.

The radio announcer is saying, "Good morning, Lexington! It's a beautiful eighty-five degrees outside today! Traffic is steady, and in other news today: Won't you stop by Ivy's Boutique today to donate money to the cancer society? They have a goal they want to smash! So, please stop by, donate, and save 25% on all merchandise while supplies last. They do have a limit on certain items. Be sure to stop by and fill up on your necessities..." Sydney hits the alarm to turn it off.

"Ugh, what a dream!"

"Sydney!" Emma shouts up to her room. "Are you up? It's a big day today. We have to get going."

"Yes, Em, I'm up and moving. Give me a few minutes. Can you make me a waffle to eat, please?" Sydney yells down to Emma.

"Okay, I'm on it. But hurry up, young lady."

A few minutes later, Sydney makes her way to the kitchen, where Emma stands waiting for her.

"Waffle?" Sydney asks in a hurry.

"Yes, ma'am, here ya go." Emma hands her the waffle as she grabs her purse and keys.

"Thanks! Okay, let's go, Em. I'm so excited to see how everything goes today."

"Do we need to get Sophie?" Emma checks with Sydney.

"Let me ask her."

> *Sydney:* Hey, bestie, you and Liz need a ride?

> *Sophie:* Mom said she would drop us off. We should be leaving here soon. See you in a bit. ♡U.

Sydney: Okay, ♡U2, bestie.

"She's getting dropped off and is leaving in a few minutes. So, let's get rolling Em," Sydney states with excitement.

"Okay, I'm out the door right after you. Just want to grab a bottle of water."

They get in the car and head out the driveway. On their way out, they pass Parker coming in the lane. Emma stops to chat quickly with Parker.

"Good morning, Parker. Wow, you are up early. Everything okay?" Emma asks with concern.

"Yes, ma'am. All is good. I just went for a drive. Are y'all headed to the shop?"

"Yes. I'm hoping it's a good day," Emma states.

"I heard our little commercial on the radio this morning. I hope we have a great sale and raise a bunch of money and smash our goal for cancer today," Sydney chimes in.

"Okay, sounds great, ladies, but I have to get back and take care of these fine equines. I will leave y'all to go raise some money! Be safe, have a great day, and I love you ladies so much."

"I love you too, Dad!"

"Will do, Parker. Will you be stopping by later?"

"Emma, I don't wanna make any promises, but I will do my best to try to get there."

"Okay, Parker. If you can, we will see ya then. Have a great day. We are gonna be late unless we head out now." She waves as she drives away.

Parker nods and heads for the ranch. As he nears the barn, he parks, jumps out, and hollers for Obee. "Obee? Are you out here yet?" As he walks near the stables to let the horses out to the pasture, he only hears silence.

"Good morning, SOT. How are you this morning, young lady?" Parker says as he hooks the lead rope and unlocks the stall door. As he walks SOT to the pasture, he rubs her neck and tells her how beautiful she is.

He finishes putting all the rest of the horses out, and by this time, Obee comes around the corner.

"Hey, Parker, I'm sorry. Am I late this morning?"

"Nah, Obee. I was just up super early this morning. So, I just thought I would let them out."

"Is everything okay? Did you have a bad dream?" Obee asks with concern.

"No, I just woke up and felt I needed to go for a drive. Everything is all good, though," Parker reassures Obee.

"Well, that's good. I know you are all good, but I still worry sometimes. I mean you are family," Obee says with heart. "Hey, isn't this the day that Sydney is doing the cancer fundraiser at the boutique?"

"Yes, it is. The ladies have already headed out this morning. So, I am guessing that we have to fend for ourselves for breakfast. You wanna go see if there is anything?" Parker suggests.

"Sure," Obee says as his stomach growls. "See, even my stomach agrees!" Obee laughs.

They go inside to check for breakfast, not expecting to find anything, but much to their surprise, there is breakfast sitting on the counter, smelling amazing, covered, and just waiting to be devoured.

"Well, Emma, still amazes me every day. Talk about someone needing sleep," Parker chuckles as he grabs forks and the pre-made plates breakfast and hands one to Obee. "I was not gone that long this morning and she was still asleep when I left this morning, but she still found some time to make all this."

"I honestly don't know what we would do without her here. We should do something special for her," Obee suggests.

"Obee, what a great idea. Let's put our heads together and see what we can get or do for her."

"Okay, let me think about it and get back to ya. But for now, it's time for me to get back to work," Obee says as he excuses himself from the table.

"Okay, sounds good. I will be out in a bit," Parker states.

Meanwhile in town at the Boutique

"Thank you, ma'am. Please come again," Sydney tells a customer.
The customer nods and takes their merchandise and leaves the store.
"Sophie, can you please come wait on our customers?" Sydney politely asks.

"Yes, ma'am, on my way," Sophie says as she makes her way to the register.

"I rang up their items so all that you need to do is take their money. Thanks, Sophie," Sydney says gratefully.

"Sure." Sophie gets the money and continues to ring up the customers.

Sydney goes to check on Eliza and see how she's doing with the customers' children.

"Hey, Liz. How's everything going? Do you need anything?"

"Nope. All good, Syd. Guess what?" Eliza asks.

"What's up, Liz?" Sydney wonders.

"I made some new friends today," she says excitedly.

"Oh really? That's awesome, I am so glad!" Sydney says with excitement. "Okay then. Let me know if you need anything."

Sydney makes her way to Lucas.

"Lucas? How are you today? Are you getting many donations?" Sydney asks.

"Sydney, hey! I am good now," he starts blushing and looks away quickly. "Ah, yes. I am getting some donations. It's truly amazing how many people care about cancer and finding a cure," Lucas shockingly states.

"Yeah, cancer is the second leading cause of death. It hits home with many people. It's something like one in every one or two people that will have cancer. Most everyone knows someone who has or had cancer at one point in time or another."

"Well, I don't know anyone yet. But I want to donate something to the cause," Lucas says with heart.

"Well, my grandmom did. So, it really hits home for our family. I appreciate your donation. I hope we do well today," wishes Sydney. "Is everyone signing a card to hang up on the wall showing that they donated today?"

"Yes, ma'am!" Lucas states excitedly. "And those who don't want their names up, I talked them into either putting up a name anonymously or maybe someone whom they knew either that had or has cancer. It seems to be working well."

"Well, great. Just keep pushing the limits, gently of course! Just be polite and friendly and you should do just great! In the end, we want people to not feel bugged or nagged but that they are helping for a great cause! Also please remind them that they will get 25% off their purchase today," Sydney shares.

"I agree wholeheartedly! I am and that also has been helping to get some donations," Lucas says cheerfully. "So, what are you up to later today? When we're done here."

"I am not sure yet. I have to wait to see how today goes. Why? What are you thinking?" Sydney wonders.

"Well, I was wondering if you might want to go riding with me?" Lucas asks with hesitation.

"Riding with you? Like at my ranch?" She asks curiously.

"Well, yes. I mean that's where Loads of Luck is, silly girl." Lucas hopes with anticipation that she says yes.

"Well, yeah, sure! If we get done here early enough, then yeah, sure!" Sydney says with excitement.

"Okay, well, is there anything I can do to help us to get outta here earlier?" Lucas asks with high anticipation of getting out earlier with his help.

"Well, when we close, just straighten up so there's less we have to do when the money's counted. Also, can you please make sure that the doors are wiped down and the floors are swept? I'm sorry to make it seem like you are doing everything because you won't be, but those are the things that will need to be done to get outta here after we close. I will ask Sophie to help too," Sydney instructs.

"Oh, Sydney, that's fine. I can get those things done. I don't mind at all! Anything I can do to help," Lucas states with enthusiasm.

"Okay, well, I have to make my rounds and check on some customers and do a little stocking of low items." Sydney winks as she walks away.

Lucas catches Sydney's wink and gets even more excited. He proceeds to watch Sydney as the day goes on. He begins to daydream about them riding together later at the farm.

As the day continues, customers keep coming into the boutique in big bands of people. As the day nears the end, people are still coming in, but Sydney lets people come in till she has to lock the door. Once she locks the door, she makes an announcement: "Hello. Good evening, everyone. We are officially closed for the day, but please feel free to shop till you have filled all your needs today. Please just let Sophie or Lucas know, and they will be more than happy to let you out. Thank you, everyone. Please enjoy your shopping experience here at Ivy's Boutique. The only thing I have to ask is if you are donating to the cancer society, can you please make your donations here so we may close the donation container? Thank you."

Sydney waits for anyone who wants to come to donate before she closes down the donation box then heads to the back room to count the donations.

Sophie closes out the last of the customers and shows them to the door. She thanks them and welcomes them back.

"Syd! Can we have some tunes? I left the last customer out," Sophie asks.

From the back room, Sydney yells, "Sure thing!" as she turns up the radio.

Lucas tries to get done the small list that Sydney asked him to do.

Sophie tries to help Lucas get things done too. She ends up doing more of the restocking to get it finished.

Sydney gets the donation box and the cash register counted and all the paperwork taken care of.

"Okay, my awesome co-workers, are you ready?"

"Ready for what?" Lucas asks like he doesn't have a clue.

"Lucas, really? She wants to know if we want to know what we raised today," Sophie states to Lucas with an "as if" attitude.

"Yeah, I know. I was trying to play dumb. But yes, please lay it on us!" Lucas comically says to try to get a laugh from the others.

"Okay, I had Em recount to be sure I counted correctly, and with that said, drumroll please," Sydney says as she points to Lucas.

Lucas starts drum-rolling on a cardboard box nearby.

"Okay, my friends. I am super excited to announce that we had sales of $25,254.88 cents today. Which means as per Mom's wishes, we raised $5,050.98 from sales today. And continue the drumroll please, Lucas," she instructs him.

He nods and keeps playing but with a slightly different beat.

Sophie is so impatient she yells out, "Come on, just tell us already!"

"Okay, bestie. I am, just chill! Okay now, ladies and gents. Our donation total is...are you ready?" Sydney tries to prolong the anticipation.

"Yes, now would you just tell us already?" Sophie blurts out.
"Okay, our donation box had $8,848.52!" They all start screaming and yelling.
Sydney continues, "So our grand total to give to the cancer society is $13,899.50!"

"Wow, Syd, that's a lot!" Sophie says in shock.

"Yeah, really! Wow, that's something awesome," Lucas adds. "So now what?"

"Well, now we get a hold of the cancer society and get them a check," Sydney shares.

"Syd, I know that I have already gave some money, but could I please do one more donation?" Lucas asks.

"Umm sure that would be great!" Sydney said graciously. "But if you already, did you really don't need to."

"Well, we are so close to $14,000.00 I think it would be great to send them an even amount," Lucas shares. "It's just a difference of $100.50."

"I would do a donation too!" Sophie adds.

"Sure, I'd be glad to share in building it up too," Sydney shares smiling. "Since I am the technically the owner per se I will step up and do $34.50 if you can both do $33?"

"Sounds good to me," Sophie says as she gets money from her purse.

"I'm on it!" Lucas gladly pulls his wallet from his pocket and gives Sydney the money.

"Okay great! I will make the check out for $14,000.00!" She adds their money to the collection and puts it into an envelope and into the safe for the bank deposit.

"Now what kids?" Emma asks.

"Well, there's a little time left in the day, how about we all go for a ride back at the ranch? I have something I want to ask you two, and I have to show you to be able to ask you," Sydney says to Sophie and Lucas.

"Wait, what about me?" Eliza asks.

"Well, this time, let me take your sister, and she can ask your mom for the next time, okay?"

"Oh, okay, you promise?" Eliza says as he hangs her head.

"Yes, ma'am, okay. Let's get going. It's gonna be dark soon before we know it," Sydney says.

"Eliza, how about we make some cookies together? Would you like that, sweetheart?" Emma asks to make her feel like she's not missing out.

"Oh, could we? That would be just awesome," Eliza says.
"Yes, ma'am, we can. For the rest of you, if we are done here, let's get going. I have cookies to make with my baker pal Eliza," Emma states as she tries to wrangle everyone to hurry out the door.

They all hurry out the door and get into the car as Sydney locks up and joins them. Then they head off to the ranch.

CHAPTER 2
Camp Survival

They get back to the ranch with about two hours to spare before dark. Sydney has something amazing planned for her friends. She doesn't want to do this special event till the fall, but she thinks now is a great time inform her friends. She just hopes that they love it as much as she does.

"Well, here we are. Would anyone like some dinner?" Emma asks.

"Actually, Em, I have something I would like to do so can we get a basket packed with a few things. I will explain in a little bit. But right now, it's a surprise," Sydney excitedly states.

"Sure, sweetheart, just let me know what all you need."

"Thanks, Em! You are the best!" Sydney praises.

Sophie and Lucas look confused. Sydney doesn't know if they can see the excitement on her face, but she is beyond excited.

"Sophie, are you okay?" Sydney wonders.

"I think so, bestie. What do you have up your sleeve?" Sophie asks with a very puzzled look on her face.

"Well, I need you two to please call your parents and ask them if you may spend the night here at the ranch. I have something cool and fun I would love to share with you guys. Once I know that you both will be able to stay, I will be happy to give you more details. So please message your parents, and then we can let the fun begin. Sophie, can you please make sure that it's okay for Eliza to stay too?" Sydney informs Lucas and Sophie.

"But she will be with Em making cookies."

"Sure thing, bestie," Sophie agrees.

"Ah, Sydney, can I get a few minutes with you while I message my mom?" Lucas asks, hoping she agrees.

"Sure, Lucas, what's up?" Sydney says as though she is paying close attention but in reality, is too wrapped up in her surprise to pay attention.

"Well, when I asked you earlier to go riding, I meant you and I," Lucas says with slight disappointment.

"Yeah, I know, but I thought, 'What better time than now for me to do this special thing with you and my bestie?' It means so much to me to include the two most important people in my life with me on this cool excursion," Sydney states with the utmost sincerity.

"Oh." Lucas pauses for a moment then continues, "Okay, I guess I understand."

"Lucas, is everything okay? You seem distracted or like something is wrong," Sydney asks with empathy.

"Nah, I'm all good, just excited to see what you have planned for us," he says with a different tone that Sydney picks up on.

"Okay, well, if you need anything, just let me know," Sydney says, knowing that Lucas seems to be hiding something. But she will have to work on what that is later.

Lucas thinks to himself, *Sydney, I was trying to talk to you, but it can wait*, as he smiles in curiosity as to what she has planned.

"Okay, guys, I will be right back. I have to get some supplies. Just wait here by the stables for me to return." Sydney turns to take off toward the house, skipping along the way. She's gone for about 10 minutes when Lucas sees her coming back out.

"Sophie here comes Syd. Did your mom and dad say you could stay?" Lucas asks, hoping they said no so he could have Sydney all to himself.

"Yep! My parents love Sydney, so I am always allowed to stay anytime I want. So, I don't have to ask... I just have to let them know so that they don't worry. Did your mom say it was okay for you to stay?" Sophie asks, hoping that Claire would say no.

"Yes, she did. I told her that Sydney had something special she wanted to share with you, and I and she said to have a great time. So, I intend to have a great time," Lucas says, trying to make Sophie jealous that he too is going to be along for the fun.

"Wow, you two, what's up? Are you coming along for the trip or what?" Sydney asks as she senses the tension between Sophie and Lucas.

"Yep! You know I'm gonna be there, bestie! Like always! Till the end of time!" Sophie says as she makes a "nah nah boo boo" face sticking her tongue out toward Lucas before Sydney sees her taunting Lucas.

"Yeah, Sydney, my mom said to have fun. I told her that I intend to," Lucas says as he wrinkles up his face right back at Sophie. But he wasn't so lucky for Sydney not to see.

"Lucas, what was that face for? I thought you intended on having fun?" Sydney says with confusion.

"It's nothing. I was just playing," he says as Sophie makes a face back at him behind Sydney's back, but this time, Sydney catches her out the corner of her eye.

"Sophie!" Sydney screams. "What is up with you two? I can cut the tension between you two with a chainsaw! Now suck it up, and let's go get this party on. I wanted to wait till this fall to do this with y'all, but when Lucas mentioned riding today, I thought what better time than now to do it. So, I really hope y'all can put on your big girl and boy panties and have a great time. I used to do this with my grandad. We would have a great time. So, we need to find Obee. Did you guys see him anywhere?" Sydney asks as she looks around trying to see Obee close by.

"Nope," they both say simultaneously.

"Okay, give me a few more minutes. Fight nice till I return please, or better yet, how about y'all kiss and make up till I get back," Sydney says as she walks away, shouting out for Obee.

"Thanks again, Lucas!" Sophie snickers.

"For what? She caught you making the face! I didn't make you do it," Lucas says with an attitude firing right back at Sophie.

"Well, Syd isn't just my friend—she's my best friend—and I don't want you hurting her. So, you best watch yourself," Sophie says with jealousy.

"I'm just here to have fun. So back off, would you?" He advises Sophie sternly.

"Are you threat—" Sophie gets interrupted when she hears Syd coming. Then before Sydney can see her actions, she takes her fingers and signs to Lucas that she's watching him. Lucas smirks back like he doesn't care.

"Okay, I see that y'all haven't kissed and made up, but you also haven't killed each other yet either, so Obee is coming to help us hook up a carriage as I saddle up SOT, then we will be on our way," Sydney professes with excitement.

"Can I be of any help, Syd?" Sophie asks.

"Actually, yes, can you please come with me and get PB Cup and Lucas? Can you please come get Loads of Luck? We are taking the bigger carriage, and we need two horses for that one. Hey, there's Obee!" Sydney waves to Obee.

"Hey, kiddos, let's get y'all hooked up. Syd, you want me to hook up Black Boots and ride out with ya too?" Obee happily suggests.

"That would be great, Obee, if you don't mind? Just so you know where we are," Sydney says with sincerity.

"Sure thing. I will saddle him up," Obee says as he turns to retrieve Black Boots's saddle.

Once they get the carriage hooked up with Loads of Luck and PB Cup; and Black Boots and SOT are saddled up, they head out to the lake.

It isn't long before Sophie realizes that they are not headed toward the part of the lake she is used to going to. "Syd, I thought you said we were headed to the lake? This isn't how we get to the lake," Sophie states with confusion.

"Yeah, I know. I'm taking y'all out to a special place that I used to go out with Grandad too. It's been a little while, and I have been wanting to go, and I wanted to share it with you Sophie." Sophie looks at Lucas and gives him a huge "I won" smile.

"But when Lucas wanted to ride today, I thought it would be awesome if I can get both of my friends out here together. What fun that could be. So, I decided to ask you both back to this special place." Lucas nods at Sophie and winks like "Yep! That's what I was talking about!" Sophie crosses her arms, gives Lucas the evil eye, and turns to look away.

It takes about thirty minutes to get to the part of the lake that Sydney wants to take her friends to. Once they arrive, she stops SOT and shouts, "Surprise! Welcome to Camp Survival! This is where Granddad taught me how to live off the land and to survive like the pioneers did on the wagon trains. What do you think, guys?" Sydney excitedly exclaims.

"Wow, Sydney, this is so cool. So, like, are we gonna live off the land for...how long did you say we were gonna be out here?" Lucas wonders.

"Syd, please tell me that we are not gonna eat critters, bugs, and grass out here!" Shrieks Sophie.

"Lucas, just a night but don't wander too far—you will get lost! And, Sophie, we can but we don't have to. I have yum fixings from back at the house in this here basket!" Sydney reassures Sophie.

"Come on, guys, let's get set up for some camping fun." Sydney tries to hurry them along.

"Oh, okay, if you say so, bestie," Sophie reluctantly agrees.
"I'm excited, guys. I think we can have some real fun. Thank you, Syd, for inviting us," Lucas states with enthusiasm. "This is something I have always wanted to do with my dad before he passed." Lucas hangs his head for a moment while trying not to cry.

"Okay, kiddos, I am headed back to the ranch. If you need anything, just text me," Obee states as he turns to get ready to mount Black Boots.

"Thanks, Obee, for everything!" Sydney says with appreciation.

"Anytime, Syd." Obee mounts Black Boots and waves as he rides off into the distance.

"Okay, Syd, is there anything I can do to help?" Lucas asks.
"Actually, yes! Would you mind gathering some wood to make a fire with? See if you can find some kindling and some bigger pieces to burn for a while," Sydney instructs Lucas.

"Sure, I'm on it!" Lucas takes off looking for wood and kindling.
"Now, bestie, let's talk. What is going on with you?" Sydney asks, concerned.

Sophie looks away and hangs her head. "Nothing. I am good. Things are just great," Sophie says, trying to district from Sydney from figuring anything out.

Sydney puts her hand on Sophie's shoulder. "Bestie, we have been friends for a long time, and I can tell when something's up. So come on, spill it! Something is working on you. You can tell me. I will listen," she reassures Sophie.

"Really? Because I beg to differ," Sophie says with a slight angry tone.

"Sophie, yes, come out with it! I want to get over whatever it is that's bothering you. I wanted to come out here to have a good time with my friends."

"It's Lucas! He's just rubbing me the wrong way. It's like he doesn't want me here," she says with jealousy.

"Sounds like you are a bit jealous too when there is absolutely no need to be! We are all just friends here! So can you just forget about whatever is eating you up with Lucas, and I will talk with him too. Please, for me, bestie?" Sydney pleads.

"I'm sorry. I know I have nothing to worry about, and I will do my best for you. So, what can I do to help?" Sophie asks to try to distract Sydney and change the subject.

"How about you grab some water from the stream just over that way before it gets into the lake?" Sydney states as she points in the direction of the spring-fed stream.

By now, Lucas has returned with wood. "How's this, Syd?" he says as he's looking around for Sophie. "Where's Sophie?"

"I sent her for some water. So, what's up with you two anyways? I'm getting a strange vibe from you two," Sydney asks. "I am a bit concerned. I wanted to have a great time and don't want any issues out here."

"You think there's something up? What gave you that impression? I'm just excited to be lucky enough for you to have invited me out here and that you consider me a friend," Lucas says, trying to throw Sydney off track.

"Okay, Lucas. I will take your word for it for now, but let's get a fire started," Sydney states as she watches Lucas's face out the corner of her eye as they start the fire.

Lucas works with Sydney to get the fire going. As Sophie is coming back from the stream when she sees Lucas and Sydney trying to get the fire going. So, she lags back to see what happens next.

Lucas watches Sydney and waits for just the right time to talk with her. When he gets up his nerve, he clears his throat and tries to speak.

"Sydney, since it's just you and I here, can I ask you something?" Lucas shyly and quietly asks so Sophie can't hopefully hear if she comes back unexpectedly.

"Lucas, you can ask me anything you want. So, what's up?" Sydney hopes it'll help solve what's up with Lucas and Sophie.

"So, I have been wanting to ask you for quite some time now, but I've been afraid of what you may say, and well, now I will ask you." He's interrupted by Sophie's return.

While Sophie is hanging back, she can barely hear what was being said, but she has a good feeling what is up, so she takes it upon herself to interrupt them. At the very most, it will hopefully postpone what he wants to ask her.

"Hey, guys, how's the fire coming? I have the water you wanted, Syd. I'm so hungry, so what's for dinner?" Sophie says with excitement.

"Oh, great, thanks. Sophie, let's just sit the water over here next to the side of the little cabin."

"Sorry, it's not much," Sophie says.

"Oh, but we should be just fine. We can get more if need be. As far as dinner is concerned, how about some roasted weenies over the fire? And we can do mountain pies or S'mores for dessert?" Sydney suggests.

"Oh, awesome. Sounds like fun. Do we have weenie sticks?" Sophie asks, not seeing any anywhere nearby.

"No, we don't need weenie sticks. We just go grab a small branch from a tree and strip off the bark. Would you like to go grab one for each of us?" Sydney asks Sophie.

"Sure, I will be right back." Sophie runs to look for three sticks for cooking the weenies.

"Sydney, now where was I?" Lucas tries to continue with his question.

"Lucas, can we just have this conversation later? I'm sorry I have to get things together for dinner, and before it gets dark, I have to get everything set up."

"Sure, Sydney. I've waited this long so I can wait a little longer. It's not super important anyway," Lucas says, disappointed he couldn't ask Sydney what he wanted to.

Sophie comes back with three twigs for weenie sticks. "How are these, Syd?"

"They are perfect! Okay, you can each pick a stick and peel your bark off and slide on your weenies and start cooking them. Are you guys okay with sleeping out here under the stars?"

"Sure, Syd, sounds like fun," Lucas says eagerly.

"What about bugs and critters?" Sophie asks.

"Nah, we will be fine, bestie."

"Oh, okay. If you are cool with it, Syd, then I will give it a try," Sophie says as she is a little unsure as to what she signed up for.

"Okay, I will get the sleeping bags out of the little cabin. Be right back."

"This is so fun, dontcha think, Sophie?" Lucas asks.

"Yeah, I guess so. I've never done anything like this. I'll let you know in the morning how I feel about it," Sophie states with a little bit of fear in her voice.

"Okay, so here's a sleeping bag for each of us. We can lay here on the ground next to the fire. Just don't get too close. We don't need any sparks lighting us up." Sydney chuckles as she looks at the fear on Sophie and Lucas's faces.

"Seriously, Syd! That's not funny. Did you bring us out here to eliminate us?" Sophie says seriously at first then starts to laugh.

"Never! You guys are my best friends. What would I do without y'all?" Sydney asks with an evil laugh.

"I know, Syd. I love you too, bestie." Sophie smiles as she reaches out for a hug from Sydney.

"Wow, I've been upgraded to best friend? How cool is that?" Lucas states happily.

When their weenies are cooked, they pull them off the sticks and eat them up. Sydney teaches them how to make mountain pies. They tell some jokes and have a great time before they lie down to count the stars, and Sydney shows them all the constellations she can find.

Just before they all fall asleep Sydney fills them in on what they may be doing tomorrow.

Chapter 3
Best Catches

"**L**isten, woman, I am the one in charge! You don't do anything without my permission!" he screams as he smacks her across the face.

Lucas and Sophie are awakened by Sydney screaming in her sleep.

"Sydney, wake up! Sydney? Are you okay?" Sophie says as she tries to wake up Sydney.

"Please stop shaking me, Sophie! You are gonna make me sick," Sydney exclaims.

"Sorry, but you were screaming in your sleep. Are you okay? What were you dreaming about?" Sophie sternly asks Sydney.

"I don't remember what I was dreaming about. But my heart is racing. It must have been bad," Sydney replies, breathing heavily.

"Well, duh, you were screaming! While you get your breath back, are you ready for today?" Sophie wonders as she changes the subject.

Sydney tries to remember her dream and then thinks about the day. "Well, like I said last night, we can go fishing, or we can go for a trail ride. Whatever y'all would like to do," Sydney suggests.

"I'm good with any of the ideas you said, so I guess we just need to see what Sophie would like to do?" Lucas suggests.

"We can go fishing. But the rods are at the cottage," Sophie sadly reports.

"Nope, there are some here in this little cabin. We just have to look for bait," Sydney says cheerfully.

"Look for bait?" Sophie says with hesitation. "Syd, do I even want to know how we are gonna look for bait?"

"Well, there are all kinds of ways, but mainly just lift logs, sticks, leaves, rocks, or whatever is laying around and see what's under there. We can use crickets, grasshoppers, sow bugs, pill bugs, worms—just depends on what's around. Let's look and see what we find," Sydney states excitedly.

"Eww, Syd, I don't do bugs! You know that! I'm suddenly not feeling so well," Sophie says, rubbing her belly.

"Come on, wuss. I thought you, my bestie, were an adventurer and wanted to try new things? Bugs aren't all that bad. Beside you are just touching them it's not like you are going to eat them," Sydney states to try to encourage Sophie to just do it.

"Sydney! Sophie! Look, I found some worms! And these little bugs that are rolled up in a ball," Lucas screams with excitement. "Whoo-hoo! Now what do I do with them?" he asks, puzzled.

"Hold on, Lucas. Let me get a bait pail for you to put them in." Sydney opens the door on the little cabin and shouts out from inside, "Those little rolled-up critters are called pill bugs or, as Grandad used to call 'em, Rolly Pollies. They are good for trout! The worms work for mostly everything else. We have all kinds of fish stocked up in there. And with the size of this lake, you just never know what you will fish out." Sydney grabs the pail and heads out to let Lucas. "Here ya go! Let's see what else we can find."

"Syd! *Agh!*"

"What did ya find, Sophie?" Sydney tries to see before she gets to Sophie.

"I do not know what it is, but it is definitely ugly. It's long and flat, except for its head. It has tiny legs on the butt, about six longer legs on the head and body area, and looks like pincers on the head," Sophie describes.

"Sounds like a hellgrammite. Don't touch it. Those pincers up front of it will put you in a bit of pain if it gets you. What color is it?" she asks as she gets closer.

"Black."

"Yep, that's a hellgrammite. Good job, Sophie. That is good for some smallmouth bass. You wanna use it?"

"Nope, I'm good. I will just stick with a worm," Sophie says as she shudders like she just got chills and walks away.

"Ah, Sydney, can I give it a shot?" Lucas asks eagerly.

"Ah, yeah, sure, so listen—here's what you have to do. Pick it up by the hard collar there in the middle of it just before the flat, then hook it from the bottom up through the collar to its head. You will want to keep it drifted with current toward the top of the water. You should try to use a tiny split shot and cast into that school of fish right out there. Watch your line, and don't let it sink because the hellgrammite will try to grab a rock. And if you do everything just right, you should be able to get a bass," Sydney instructs Lucas.

"Okay, so hold it on the collar. Put the hook up through to the head," Lucas repeats out loud as he tries to secure the bait. "Oops, I came out before the head, Syd."

"That's okay. If you have most of it, you should be just fine. Now just put on the little sinker and cast out," Sydney instructs Lucas.

"Okay, sinker is on and now casting out." Lucas gets a good cast out. "Wow, just over the—oh, I got a bite!" he screams.

"Quick, set your hook! Give it a quick jerk up!" Sydney quietly screams.

"Ah, I think it's on!" Lucas states with excitement.

"Reel! Reel! Easy, not too fast. It looks like a feisty one. Stop! Let it calm down a bit when it does reel again." Sydney tries to coach Lucas to land the fish.

"Good luck!" Sophie says while clapping and jumping up and down.

"You got it! Good job, Lucas. Now just reel it in. I'll get the net!" Sydney gets the net and scoops it up. They take it away from the water's edge to get the hook out and weigh and measure it. "Nice one, Lucas—it's like 16 and ¾ pounds and about 24 inches long! That's definitely a record for our lake for smallmouth!"

"Lucas, look here. I will get a picture of you with it!" Sophie says quickly before they throw it back in the lake. "Smile!"

"Thanks, Sophie! I'll give you my number later so you can text me a pic of it," Lucas says, smiling from ear to ear.

"Yeah, bestie. Send me a pic too, and we will put it here in the cabin so that we have proof of his catch! Lucas, would you like to come in here and carve your measurements on the wall, and then we just have to add your picture when I get them printed off. Put your name too!" Sydney asks Lucas.

"Okay, sure, Syd. But I wanna see Sophie catch something, so can you wait till I come back out to cast in, Sophie?" he says as he sees her putting a worm on her hook.

"Sure, I will wait for you, Lucas, but hurry up—I don't want my worm to dry up," she says, laughing out loud.

"Sophie, you are a trip!" Sydney laughs.

"What!"

"Because your worm won't dry up, silly goose!" laughs Sydney.

"Well, you never know. I mean, he has to carve it into the wood," Sophie says cluelessly.

"It will be okay, bestie!" Sydney says, shaking her head at Sophie's silliness.

Lucas returns after a few minutes. "Okay, give it all you got, Sophie!"

She casts out and does her normal let it sit and reel again and again. Then she lets it sit and waits.

Sydney prepares her hook with a worm, while Lucas looks close by for more bait.

"Okay, Sophie, watch over the top. I'm casting out and don't wanna catch you." Sydney casts out really far and just lets it sit.

"Oooh, I got a nibble!" Sophie whispers.

"Just wait for the hard hit!" Sydney whispers back.

"Ohh, yeah! There it is!" Sophie yells as she sets her hook. At just about the same time, Sydney gets a bite too.

"Get ready, Lucas! We're bringing in a double! Oooh, this one is a fighter!" Sydney says excited that she caught a fish and that they are all working well together and having fun.

"Mine too, Syd! Wow, they must be hungry without anyone out here trying to catch 'em!" Sophie states excitedly.

"Just keep calm and reel when it slows down. Stop and let it play out before reeling again," Sydney instructs Sophie.

"Yeah, I know, bestie! I got this! I'm just excited to see what it is!" Sophie proudly exclaims.

"Me too!" Just as Sydney agrees with Sophie, her fish jumps outta the water. "Oh nice, did you see the size of that bass?" She exclaims.

"Yeah, that's awesome, Syd!" Lucas chimes in.

As they wrangle their catches into land, Lucas is ready to net them. Sydney gets hers in first. She catches a largemouth bass.

"Keep going, Sophie. I'm gonna weigh and measure mine," Sydney proudly states.

"Okay, I'm trying. But this one's strong!" Sophie says, breathing hard. "It's giving me a workout for sure!"

"Nice. Mine is 5 1/4 pounds and 20 inches long. Another record for here! They are all gonna be huge cause this lake is barely fished at anymore. Let's see what you got, Sophie." Sydney says as she rushes over to help Lucas with Sophie's catch.

"Sydney, look here—let's get a picture." Sydney smiles at Lucas and releases her fish just after he takes the picture.

"Yes! Grab the net, Lucas. She's got a big cat!" Sydney quickly states to Lucas.

"A big cat?" he asks.

"Yep, a flathead!" Sydney says while looking at the confusion on Lucas's face. "A flathead catfish!"

"Oh, nice, Sophie, that's one big flathead catfish! Do we wanna make bets to see who's closer to guessing it right?" Sydney suggests.

"Sure! I think 23 inches and 23 pounds," Lucas proudly states.

"I think its 25 inches and about 30 pounds," states Sophie with her fingers crossed she guessed right.

"Well, I would have to guess 28 inches and 42 pounds," Sydney chimes in.

"Well, let's get to measuring, ladies." Lucas gets the scale and the tape measure and starts.

"Sophie, yours is 45 pounds and 24 inches. Looks like we were close with one measurement or another," Lucas states.

"I can't tell if that's any kind of record or not, but let's get a picture anyways so we document today's fun!" Sydney says.

"Sydney, yours is 26 inches and 10 pounds for your largemouth bass," Lucas says.

"Nice! That possibly could be a record, but either way, let's get some pictures and carve our info on the wall with Lucas's."

After they carve their names and info on the wall, they decided to go on a trail ride.

CHAPTER 4
The Trail Ride

They saddle up their rides and grab a bottle of water and mount their horses.

"Okay, guys, we have a few trails to pick from. We have the lake trail, which goes around the lake. We have the perimeter trail, which goes around the perimeter. Then there are the front and back trails. The one goes from front side of the lake to the corner of the property, and the other goes from the back side of the lake to the back corner of the property. So, which would y'all like to do?"

"Sydney, I would love to do the lake trail," Sophie states. Lucas agrees.

"Okay, guys, let's go. There are a few streams that feed into and exit the lake, so PB Cup and SOT are experienced with crossing water. But Loads of Luck? I'm afraid you are gonna end up finding out, Lucas, but if you take it easy, he should do just fine.

Well, let's go, y'all!" Sydney says with excitement as she takes SOT from a walk to a trot. "Come on, guys. See if you can keep up."

Lucas looks at Sophie and shrugs. "Are we gonna take that from her?" Lucas asks Sophie.

"Nah, let's give her a run for her money!" Sophie says as she gently kicks her heels off PB Cup's sides and takes off to a gallop.

Lucas is hot on her tail.

"Hey! I thought I was leading?" Sydney screams ahead.

"Didn't you say that this was the lake trail and that it went around the lake?" Sophie states as she starts to pull ahead and away from Sydney with Lucas hot on her tail.

"Yeah, I did, but Lucas won't be ready for the streams, and he could have some fun getting over them if Loads of Luck has a fear of water," she shouts ahead.

"How bad could it be?" Sophie yells back over her shoulder.

Sydney says and laughs to herself, *Ha ha ha, you will see soon enough.*

And right at about that time, there is a hidden creek almost of a marsh consistency that Sophie and PB Cup go right through. But Lucas is not quite as lucky. When Loads of Luck realizes that there is water in that grass, he stops dead, and Lucas goes flying up over his head and lands in the swampy wet grass face first.

"Ugh," Lucas says while trying to sit up and spitting out grass and muddy water. "Not again!"

"Again? So, this happened to you before today?" Sydney asks as she walks her and SOT up to Lucas to help him up.

"Whoops, sorry. I should have warned ya, Lucas," Sophie says, chuckling as she returns to the scene of the horse dumping.

"Umm, yeah, this happened before. To be honest, it was at this very lake," Lucas says with his head hanging down.

"Please do tell!" Sydney says while she places her hands on her hips.

"Yeah, inspiring young minds need to know!" Sophie adds. "Because you never told me Syd that you had Lucas out here! So, what's up with that, bestie?"

"Because I didn't!" Sydney says abruptly.

"It wasn't Syd!" Lucas shouts quickly to divert a bigger fight between the girls. They both stop speaking and turn to look at him.

Simultaneously, they both say, "Then who did?"

"It was your dad, Sydney," Lucas states as he wipes his face.

"My dad? When? Where was I?" Sydney asks.

"It was after the one big fight we had in school. He went to talk to my mom and arranged for me to come over. Then right after is when I got Loads of Luck."

"Oh, nice!" Sydney laughs.

"Yeah, your dad is sneaky, Syd!" Sophie chuckles.

"Yeah, guess I will have to have a chat with him," Sydney laughs.

"Well, now that we know, let's try walking Loads of Luck around through here to get him more used to it and see how it goes from here," Sydney suggests.

"Yeah, okay, sounds like a plan," Lucas adds.

After they feel that Loads of Luck is ready to go, they take off again.

As they are riding along, they come across another more visible stream.

"Okay, so up ahead is another stream. Just follow me and let's see how this goes," Sydney says to the others.

She gets SOT to take off and jumps the creek. Sophie follows with PB Cup, and she jumps the creek.

"Come on, Lucas, you can do it! Just run and jump him!" Sydney advises him.

Lucas gets Loads of Luck to take off running, and he jumps and clears the creek. "Yee haw! That was awesome!" Lucas yells.

As they are riding, Lucas tries to start up a conversation.

"Ladies, do you mind me asking y'all a question?" Lucas shyly asks.

"Shoot, Lucas," Sydney says while curiously waiting to hear the question.

"So, I know neither of you have a boyfriend right now, but have you ever?"

"Nope," they both say simultaneously.

"Why do you ask?" Sophie asks while looking at Sydney and winking.

Sydney reaches across and smacks Sophie with one of her rein straps.

"Ouch!" Sophie shrieks.

"Oh, I'm sorry. I didn't see you there," Sydney says laughing.

"Never mind," Lucas says as he looks away.

"Never mind what?" Sophie asks.

"Y'all aren't interested in what I have to ask," he said sadly.

"Lucas, we are sorry. We're just girls being girls. So why do you ask?" Sydney questions him.

"Yeah, we are all friends here, so you can ask us anything," Sophie adds.

Lucas mumbles under his breath, "That's just what I need," and hangs his head and gently shakes it.

"What was that you said, Lucas?" Sydney asks.

"Nothing. I'm glad I have you two as my friends," he says sadly.

"Well, if that's so, then why do you sound so sad?" Sydney asks him.

"Yeah, anyways, we are some of the nicest girls you will ever meet," Sophie adds.

"For sure!" Sydney says, agreeing with Sophie and trying to reassure Lucas.

"No, it's not that. I know you girls are super nice, and I don't even know why y'all even give me the time of day because after the way I treated you two, I seriously don't deserve your forgiveness," Lucas reluctantly states.

"Lucas, everyone deserves a second chance. It's what you do with it that matters. If you continue to be rotten or bad and don't change, then you don't deserve forgiveness. But so far, you seem to have changed and that's all that matters. You are using your second chance well!" Sydney explains.

"Well, I appreciate that. I am trying to do very well compared to how I was. But I just want a girl to go steady with. I am just afraid that the girl I like doesn't feel that way back."

"So have you said anything to her about how you feel?" Sophie asks to see if she can figure out if it's Sydney.

"I mean yes and no. I have in a roundabout way asked her or at least let her know how I feel."

"Okay, Lucas, I still hear a *but* there," Sophie points out. "Yeah, Sophie, there is a big but," Lucas agrees.

"Well, what's stopping you from asking her?" Sydney asks.

"Fear! Fear of rejection, fear of acceptance. Fear of what my mom and friends would say. Fear that it won't work out, fear that it will! Fear that the girl I like doesn't even think of me in a way that she would even consider herself to be my girlfriend." Lucas spills out his thoughts, making himself feel very vulnerable.

"Lucas, if I had to live my life being afraid of anything and everything, I would never leave my room! Especially when we were going to school and having to deal with you and your friends bullying us. But I did it anyways. Now I'm in charge of my mom's boutique, and I have awards and trophies for racing. It just keeps getting better with each new thing I stand up to and conquer. Trust me, you will think the same thing when you just stand up to your fears and face 'em head on. Plus, have you ever really put yourself in a situation where you are able to give subtle hints as to your feelings for this special girl? Or like give her little handmade goodies and notes to show her your appreciation for her. I can guarantee that when she figures out what you are up to, you will be a couple before you know it!" Sydney pleasantly reports.

"Do you really think so, Sydney?" Lucas asks with tons of hope.

"Yes, I do, Lucas! Check up on her a couple of times a day and leave little things for her to find like little love notes, little doodle drawings, little things you made special just for her. I can promise you if you do those little things, she will fall for you head over heels," Sydney says, hoping it helps Lucas loosen up and come out of his shell.

"Thank you, Sydney. I will give that a try and see how it goes. So now enough with my petty self. Let's get back to riding. How far have we made it, Sydney?" Lucas asks out of curiosity.

"Well, we have a ways to go, Lucas. We have only just begun. But now that we know you can handle streams and water, let's race to feel the wind in our hair and see who can get to the cottage first. Ready, get set," Sydney says when Lucas interrupts her.

Lucas shouts, "Go!" and takes off, and Sophie catches on and is hot on his tail. It takes Sydney a little bit longer to get with the party, but when she does, she takes off and catches up to them as quickly as they took off.

"It's about time you decided to join us!" Lucas shouts over to Sydney as she gets up beside them.

"Ha! Y'all think you are hilarious, I see!" Sydney says as she devises her own plan, and with that, she is off. "Ha, losers, see if ya can catch me!" She yells back over her shoulder as she gains speed and pulls away from them.

They frolic and play along with each other for most of the afternoon as they make their way around the lake to the cottage.

"Aha, we finally made it!" Sophie points out.

"Sophie, has anyone ever told you that you are a freaking genius?" Sydney says, heckling Sophie.

"Sydney, did anyone ever tell you how much of an art smass you are?" Sophie fires back as she starts laughing.

"Aww, you finally figured that out. I mean we've only been friends like forever!" Sydney laughs so hard.

"Yeah, well, it's okay because I still love ya!" Sophie says while making a heart with her fingers to Sydney.

"As do I, bestie!" Sydney smiles as she catches a glimpse of Lucas looking at her with a very different look. At first, she wonders if what Sophie has been saying is true! *Nah*, she thinks to herself, *it's just my imagination*.

"Okay, Syd, how much further back to the little cabin from the carriage?" Sophie wonders.

"Why? Are you in a hurry to get back, bestie?" Sydney asks.

"No, I was just curious. It's so beautiful out here," Sophie states, admiring all the beauty.

"Well, it's just about as much time as we took to get here. So, we better get stepping. I will text Obee and let him know where we are and let him know he can come out to meet us," Sydney tells Sophie and Lucas.

So, Sydney messages Obee and lets him know they are at the cottage and headed back to the little cabin and to meet them there so they can hook up and get back.

By the time they get back to the little cabin, Obee is coming up the trail right behind them.

"That was good timing, Obee," Sydney happily says to him.

"Well, you messaged me at just the right time, Syd," Obee replies.

As he helps them hook up the carriage, he asks, "So how was your night of camping out and your day today? Did y'all have a good time? What all did you do?"

"Well, sure! We had an amazing time, Obee! We had a campfire, cooked out, slept out under the stars, and counted constellations, fished, and did some trail riding." Sydney lists off all the fun stuff they did.

"Yeah, we kinda made it a spa day out here today too!" Sophie chuckles.

"Oh, really, how's that?" Obee curiously asks.

"Loads of Luck stopped dead in his tracks and threw me off into the swampy area of the back side of the lake," Lucas says with embarrassment.

"Well, that would explain why you are all wet!" Obee tries not to laugh. "At first, I thought maybe that the girls tried to push you into the lake."

Lucas chuckles and says, "If they would have tried that I would have grabbed them and taken 'em with me," he laughs.

"Wow, remind me not to try anything crazy against you, Lucas, but sounds like y'all had a ball! Okay, well, are y'all ready to head back?" Obee asks.

"Yes! Yes, sir, we are. Till we all meet again, Mother Nature!" Sydney says.

"Yes, I will definitely come back, bestie," Sophie agrees.

"For sure I would absolutely love to come back again, Sydney. If you wouldn't mind," Lucas tells Sydney.

"Sounds like an awesome game plan, besties. Now let's get back before dark!" Sydney instructs.

CHAPTER 5
The Big Blowup

They get back to the ranch just before dark. Everyone works together to get the horses unhitched and unsaddled, fed, and watered, and brushed and put away for the night.

"Thanks, kids, for helping me get the horses cleaned up and put away for the night. I'm off to my cottage. I will see you kiddos later." Obee graciously thanks the kids and turns to walk away.

"Sure thing, Obee! Thanks for riding out with us and then coming back out! We shall see ya tomorrow morning," Sydney quickly responds before Obee gets too far away.

"Anytime, sweetheart. Good night, y'all," Obee says as he walks away to his cottage seemingly very tired.

"Okay, what do y'all wanna do now?" Sydney asks.

"Well, bestie, can I ask to stay the night?" Sophie politely asks.

"Sure, sounds like fun! But what about Eliza?" Sydney wonders.

"Yeah, she can stay too! If it's okay with y'all?" Sophie says with hesitation.

"Oh, without a doubt she can stay! Dad and Em would love for y'all to be here! But what about you, Lucas? Are you ready to go home, or would you like to get into anything else before you leave?" Sydney thoughtfully asks.

"Well, I..." Lucas stops to think for a minute. "You know what? yeah, I think I am ready to go home," he says with a somber tone.

"Are you sure? Because it kinda sounds like you had something else in mind," Sophie asks like she is curious about what he wanted to do.

"No, yeah, I'm sure. I really have to get some rest for tomorrow. I think your dad wanted me to stop by and do some practice with Loads of Luck before I went to the boutique with y'all," Lucas says to try to throw off Sophie.

"Oh, okay. Yeah, I will ask if someone can give ya a ride home. Be right back." Sydney leaves to look for Emma or her dad.

"So really, between you and I, Lucas, what did you really want to do?" Sophie asks all dreamy-eyed.

"Well, if you promise to keep it between us," Lucas says with hesitation.

"Cross my heart, and it'll be just like Vegas. What gets said between us stays between us! Pinky swear!" Sophie sticks out her pinky and waits for Lucas to respond with his pinky.

He hesitates for a minute and then sticks out his pinky.

"So, spill it, Lucas! What were you wanting to do?" Sophie almost demands.

"Okay! Okay, wow, you are awful bossy!" Lucas tries to play off as being a jerk but then bursts out laughing.

Sophie gets frustrated and smacks Lucas on the arm and tries not to laugh because she doesn't think it's funny. She ends up smiling and says, "Seriously, Lucas. Come on before Syd comes back."

"Why is it so important that you know what it is? Especially before Syd comes back?" he wonders.

"No reason. I'm just curious is all," she quickly says, hoping he answers as quickly.

Lucas senses that Sophie is up to no good but responds to her anyway. "I was gonna ask to spend the night but…"

Sophie rudely interrupts him, "Seriously!" Sophie is noticeably irritated. "Why would you even ask that? Just where do you think that you would even sleep?" She snaps.

"Well, I don't know!" Lucas says with some attitude like why it should even matter to her because it's not even her house.

"Look, jock, don't go getting cocky with me! I'm just watching out for my friend!" Sophie says like she's the boss.

"I'm sorry, but Syd is my friend too! When are you gonna wake up and realize that?" Lucas reminds Sophie.

"Yeah, but I was first!" She states with stern jealousy.

Sydney hears Lucas and Sophie going at it, as she makes her way towards them in a bit of a hurry before Sophie breaks out the claws.

"Hey! Hey! Hey! You two chill out please! Sophie, put the claws away and relax! Lucas, step back and breathe," Sydney instructs them.

"He started it!" Sophie quickly shouts out like she is three years old again.

Lucas just stands there like, *what is happening right now?* As he just looks at Sydney to see what her next move is.

"Sophie, it doesn't matter who started what! There still is no reason for this! Lucas, are you okay? Did you still wanna go home?" Sydney asks with concern.

"Yes, please, I would like to go home," he says while glaring at Sophie. "There's no need for me to be staying here," Lucas mumbles under his breath.

"What was that, Lucas?" Sophie rudely asks.

"Nothing!" Lucas snaps back. "I wasn't even talking to you, Sophie!"

"Sophie!" Sydney snaps to quickly intervene.

Sophie just glares at Sydney like a toddler who just got punished.

"Okay, let me go see if Em can take ya, Lucas. I will be right back! Can you two please try not to kill each other till I return?" She asks kindly as she takes a deep breath.

"Sure thing, Syd," Lucas says.

Sophie just nods with a bit of attitude.

Sydney walks away to find Emma.

Lucas just stands there watching Sophie. She stands with attitude and her arms crossed as she hears the door and Emma talking with Sydney as they walk toward her and Lucas, with Eliza hot on Emma's heels.

"Okay, kiddos, who is riding with me to take Lucas home?" Emma wonders.

"If it's okay, Em, I would just like to stay here and wait for y'all to get back," Sophie states.

"I will wait with my sis," Eliza adds as she takes Sophie's hand.

"Okay. If it's okay with you, Sophie, I am gonna ride with Em to take Lucas home," Sydney asks.

"Sure, Sydney, whatever you wanna do," Sophie says like she doesn't care either way.

Emma, Lucas, and Sydney get into Emma's car and head out the driveway and disappear into the darkness.

Sophie gets out her phone and proceeds to message her mom.

> *Sophie*: Mom?
>
> *Allison:* Is everything OK Sophie?
>
> *Sophie:* Sure. Can you please come get Eliza and I?
>
> *Allison*: Sure, I was just fixing to head out to the store I can swing by and pick you girls up.
>
> *Sophie*: Will you please get us first?
>
> *Allison*: I can.
>
> *Sophie*: Ok great cause I would love to get some snacks.
>
> *Allison*: Ok see you in a bit.
>
> *Sophie*: Ok love you mom

"Okay, Liz. Mom is on her way. Do you have all your things?" Sophie quickly and quietly asks.

"No, but why are we leaving? I wanna stay!" Eliza says pouting.

"No! We are going home!" Sophie demands.

"But I don't wanna!" Eliza screams as she stomps her feet. "But why can't we stay?"

"Just go get your things quickly and quietly. Mom will be here soon!" Sophie orders Eliza.

Eliza stomps away as she starts bawling her eyes out.

"Liz!" Sophie calls to her.

"What! I'm going!" Liz shouts back while sobbing uncontrollably.

"I said quietly!" Sophie quietly yells.

Liz turns and stomps away more quietly while Sophie thinks to herself about her and Sydney's friendship over the years and how they never left a boy come between them before.

Meanwhile in Emma's car

"I'm so sorry, Syd, for that situation back at your house," apologizes Lucas.

"It's okay, Lucas. I just knew it was getting late, and I really didn't feel like dealing with a bunch of BS, and I didn't think you did either. So maybe by tomorrow, whatever that was will be all cleared up and dealt with before we all end up at the Boutique because tonight, she was testing me ever-loving last nerve! And that is an area that I really do not feel like being pushed in right now," Sydney says as she takes a deep breath and sighs.

"Yeah, sure, no problem," Lucas reassures Sydney. "Hey, by the way, what are your plans for tomorrow evening?"

"I don't know yet. Why, what are you thinking?"

"I'm not sure just yet, but I was wondering if you would like to hang out and do something?" Lucas shyly asks.

"Well, we will be at the Boutique till at least 6 p.m. Emma is gonna want me to eat before I get into anything else. So, we will just have to play it by ear," Sydney states.

"Okay, I guess that will work. Or maybe we can hang out another day. It's no biggie," Lucas states with a little bit of disappointment.

"Oh, okay, I'm sure we can tomorrow, but we shall see how the rest of the day goes," Sydney says as she looks out the window.

"I wanna thank you, Miss Emma, for taking me home. Also, for allowing me to stay the night and hang out with the girls on the camping trip," Lucas kindly thanks Emma.

"No problem, Lucas. You are always welcome at our home. Well, here is your home, Lucas. Please tell your mom we said hello and hope she is well," Emma says as he exits the car.

"Sure thing! I will see y'all tomorrow bright and early!" Lucas states as he gently rolls his eyes.

"Do you need us to pick you up in the morning?" Emma asks.

"I will text Sydney in the a.m. and let her know. I haven't talked with my mom yet to see what her plans are," Lucas informs them.

"Okay, Lucas, sounds good. Now get inside before the skeeters eatcha alive," Emma says, trying to shoo him away.

"Thanks again, Miss Emma. See ya tomorrow morning, Syd," Lucas says as he backs away from the car before turning around and heading inside.

"Okay, young one, do you wanna explain to me what's up?" Emma asks, knowing something is up.

"Well, Em, if I knew what was up, I would be happy to tell you, but all I know is I walked away from Lucas and Sophie and came back to them all but wanting to throw daggers at each other," Sydney says with a shocked look on her face.

"Hmm, well, maybe we can sort this out when we get back to the ranch and talk with Sophie?" Emma hopes.

"Yeah, I sure hope so because I feel like I'm being tested to choose between the two of them for their friendship," Sydney adds.

"I need to stop at the store quickly. Do you want or need anything?" Emma asks.

"I don't think so, Em. Thanks, though," Sydney says, trying to decide if there is anything she may want.

"Okay, well, I will be right back."

"Wait, Em, yes. Can I have some sweet tea?" Sydney quickly adds.

"Yes, certainly!"

"Thanks!"

While Emma goes in the store, Sydney swears she sees Allison turning around the corner about half a block away from the direction of the ranch and turning toward her home. It looks as though Sophie and Eliza are with her. *Nah why would Sophie go home and not stay the night? She said she wanted to stay the night*; Sydney thinks to herself because clearly what she saw was wrong. So, she waits for Emma to come back out so they may leave.

Emma comes out with some milk and eggs and a jug of sweet tea. She hands it over to Sydney as she gets into her car.

"Thanks, Em!"

"No problem, it's fresh too. They just finished brewing it when I went to fill up your jug."

"That's awesome!"

As they near the house, it looks dark. It's not like Sophie to sit in the dark especially when she is slightly afraid of it. Sydney has a sour feeling in the pit of her stomach. As they pull up and park, Parker is walking into the house from the stables. Emma and Sydney get out of the car and follow him inside. Once inside, Sydney looks around and is confused.

"Dad, have you seen Sophie?" Sydney questions.

"No, I'm sorry, Syd. I haven't seen her. I was out with Obee and just making sure the stables are secure before I came in for the night. Didn't you take her home?" Parker asks.

"No, she said she wanted to stay here for the night and decided to stay while Emma and I took Lucas home. I guess she decided to go home. I don't know why. Let me text her and make sure she is ok." Sydney quickly texts Sophie, hoping everything is okay.

Sydney: Hey bestie where did you go? Is everything OK?

"I sent her a text. Hopefully she gets back to me soon. Till then, Dad, I am headed up to my room. Good night, sweet dreams, I love you to the moon and back." Sydney says sweetly.

"Come here, sweetheart!" Parker reaches out to bring her in close for a hug. "I love you too! Get some rest."

As Sydney walks away, he pats her bum.

Sydney heads to her room to wait to hear back from Sophie. After about thirty minutes, she doesn't get a response and starts to worry. She looks at the time and thinks, *It's not too late. I think I will call Allison.* She dials Allison. The phone just rings and rings. Right when she is about to hang up, someone on the other end picks up.

"Hello?" Sydney asks.

"Hello, is this Sydney?" Allison asks.

"Yes, Allison. This is she," Sydney responds.

"Is everything okay?" Allison asks.

"Actually, that's why I am calling. I was wanting to speak with Sophie. I sent her a message. Well, she was here and left, and I was under the impression that she wanted to stay the night. But when I got back home, she was gone. So, I sent her a message and she never replied, and that is so not like her. So, I was calling to check up on her," Sydney thoughtfully replies.

"Well, she is asleep. She went straight to bed as soon as she got home. Can I give her a message in the morning?" Allison offers.

"Ah, nah, I will see her in the morning at the boutique. Thanks, Allison. Good night," Sydney sadly responds.

"Okay, good night, Sydney," Allison says before she ends the call.

Sydney hangs up the phone and gets dressed for bed. She says her prayers and crawls into bed.

CHAPTER 6
No Show

A girl screams, "Please leave me alone!" as she runs through the pitch-black woods. She trips and falls down a hill, rolling and bouncing off other trees.

"I'm gonna find you, and when I do, you are gonna wish I didn't," the man shouts out into the woods. He listens very quietly to see if he can find where she is. Suddenly, she jumps up and takes off running. He hears where she is and charges for her. He's nearing closer to her, and when she is within an arm's reach, he grabs for her hair and pulls her close to him.

"*Agh!* Let me go! Please stop!" she screams as she struggles to get loose from his grip.

"Shut up!" he says to her as he tries to cover her mouth. She bites his hand. He screams out in pain as he gets more furious. He starts to slap her around.

She keeps trying to scream.

"Stop! Agh, someone please help me!" She manages to get free and takes off running away again before she runs into a tree and knocks herself out.

Buzz. Buzz.

"Good morning, Lexington! And what a beautiful morning it is! It's gonna be an amazing 82° out today and not a cloud in the sky!" Sydney hits the snooze.

She opens her eyes with a pounding headache. The sun shining through her bedroom window is so bright it isn't helping matters any with her headache. She struggles to get her nightstand drawer open to take some headache pills.

Meanwhile from downstairs, she hears Emma yells up the stairs, "Good morning, Sydney! Breakfast is ready! Are you up?"

"Ugh, yes, Emma. I am vertical. Give me a few and I will be down," Sydney says as she holds her head.

"Well, hurry please, or your food is gonna get cold." Emma hopes to speed her up.

"Yeah, yeah," Sydney mumbles as she stumbles around for her outfit for the day. She gets dressed and makes her way downstairs. "Wow, Sydney, are you okay? You look rough!" Emma says.

"Yeah, I don't know what's up, but I don't feel so well," Sydney says, holding her head and stomach.

"What about the boutique?" she asks.

"Oh, I am still going in. I just have a pounding migraine. It's just about making me sick to my stomach, though," Sydney says as she holds her head.

"Well, I admire your dedication, but..."

Emma gets interrupted by Sydney. "No buts, I am going in! End of story. I have to run the store, and I have to talk with Sophie," Sydney states with sternness.

"Okay, I was just making sure that you didn't overdo it," Emma says, concerned.

"I will take plenty of water and headache pills. I will be good."

Sydney eats her breakfast and sits there, waiting for Emma to be ready to take her in town. While she waits, she texts Sophie.

Sydney: Hey bestie, do you need a ride?

"Now we wait!"

"We wait? Just what are we waiting for, Sydney?" Emma asks.

"We are waiting for Sophie to respond."

"Well, I'm sure we won't be waiting for too long. She usually gets back to you rather quickly," Emma assures Sydney.

"Yeah, let's hope so. Will we wait to hear from her? Can we just go to the Boutique so I can get it opened?" Sydney asks.

"Yeah, sure. If you want, after I drop you off, would you like me to drive over to her place and see what's up if she isn't at the Boutique?" Emma offers.

"Yeah, sure, I guess so." Sydney has a feeling deep down that Sophie is avoiding her for some reason. But she prays she's wrong.

When they get to the Boutique, they don't see Sophie as they pull in, but they always park in the back, so they move around to the back to park and still no Sophie.

"I will go check on her just as soon as I know you are in and are good to go," Emma offers.

"Okay, thanks, Em!" Sydney appreciates Emma's help.

As Emma drives away, Claire pulls up with Lucas.

"Good morning, Lucas! How are ya?" Sydney says.

"Good! How are you?" he replies.

"I've been better. I woke up with a pounding migraine. I just hope my meds kick in soon!" she says as she wonders how Emma is making out with Sophie.

"So, looks like we are missing someone," he asks, concerned.

"Yeah, Em, went to see if she needed a ride. So, in the meantime, we need to get things taken care off and get ready to open the store. I will work on the registers if you can. Please make sure that everything is straightened up and organized," Sydney orders.

"Sure thing, Syd." Lucas walks around and looks for anything that may be out of place. Then he goes to the back room and gets the dusting wand and dusts the tops of all the shelves then goes to get the window cleaner, and he cleans the doors and windows.

"Wow, you are earning your pay today, Lucas!" Sydney states.

"Well, I figured since Sophie wasn't here yet. I would try to get as much done as possible, so it was a little less to do for when she gets here," Lucas replies as he finishes the last door. "Well, I guess I am glad I did do all that," Lucas says back over his shoulder.

"Oh yeah! Why do you say that?" Sydney wonders.

"Well, maybe Miss Emma can answer that for ya!" he responds.

A few minutes later, Emma enters through the back of the store alone but with her arms full of goodies.

"I'm back, Sydney! I brought donuts and milk," Emma says.
"So, no Sophie?" Sydney says sadly. "And donuts? Nice, I am a little hungry." Sydney rubs her stomach. "Come to the back office quickly, Lucas, and have a donut," Sydney offers.

"Coming, Syd." He quickly grabs the cleaning supplies and heads to the back office. "So, no Sophie?" he shockingly asks.

"Allison said she was still sleeping, and she had not gotten up yet," Emma states with concern.

"Yeah, I don't know what is up with her, but okay, we have to get the store open. Maybe she will show up later. If not, maybe we can stop by later if you don't mind, Em?" Sydney requests.

"Yes, we can," Emma promises. "Would you like to pray for our day before we open Sydney?"

"Yes, ma'am, let's do that," Sydney agrees.

"Sydney, I would like to give it a try if it's okay with you?" Lucas asks.

"Sure, have at it, Lucas."

"Dear Lord,

Please give us an amazing day of sales to boost our donations for the cancer society. Please allow us to meet all the customers' needs. Please watch over Sophie and hope she feels better soon. Many thanks for Miss Emma and the donuts. Lastly but not least, please bless everyone who comes through our doors today!

Amen."

"Thanks, Lucas, that was beautiful!" Sydney states, smiling while thinking about Sophie and wondering what still has her at home and seemingly avoiding her. "Lucas, I will have you on a register today. Emma, can you please help with any customers who may need help finding anything they may need?" Sydney instructs them.

Lucas and Emma agree as Sydney walks to the front door to unlock it and to welcome in the customers who are already standing there waiting to enter.

"Welcome, everyone, to Ivy's Boutique! My name is Sydney. If you need anything, please see myself, Lucas, who is back at the register." Lucas waves. "Or Miss Emma who is over there in the corner." Emma waves.

The days goes by hour by hour, and Sophie doesn't show up. Sydney sends her a text to check up on her.

Sydney: Hey, bestie! Hope you are good! We are missing you here at the boutique. We are super busy today! Ok hope to hear from you soon love you! ❤ ❤

The day flies by, and before Sydney knows it, it's 30 minutes from closing. She makes an announcement to all remaining customers.

"Good evening, everyone. We are 30 minutes from closing, but please do not rush. Please take your time and find all your selections. If you need more time, then our doors remain unlocked. It's okay. We can unlock the doors and let you out whenever you are ready. Thank you all very much!" Sydney walks to the front to see if anyone needs any help as she makes her way to the back of the store.

They get to the end of the day and get the last of the customers rang up and out the door, and still no response from Sophie.

Lucas, Emma, and Sydney straighten up, sweep, and organize the shelves before calling it a night.

"So, Sydney, what would you like to do about Sophie?" Emma asks.

"Well, I am concerned, but I don't know if I should bother her or not. I've messaged her multiple times, and she hasn't responded back to me. So, Lucas, do you need a ride home?" Sydney asks, hoping he does.

"Actually, yes, could you please give me a ride back home? Just to save my mom a trip to town," he asks respectfully.

"Sure, it's not a problem, Lucas," Emma says without even thinking about it.

"Thanks! I will text her and let her know." Lucas goes off to the corner to text his mom.

"Emma, what would you do about Sophie if you were me or in my situation?" Sydney asks looking for advice.

"Well, I would just send her a message every day letting her know that you are worried, thinking about her, and you are here whenever she is ready to talk," Emma tells her.

"Yeah, I have so far basically done just that. Well, how about we all just get outta here and get Lucas home and all of us as well so we can get some rest." Sydney pushes Lucas and Emma outta the store and locks up. They all get in the car and head for Lucas's house.

As they pull in, Sydney starts to say her goodbyes. "Thanks for coming in today, Lucas. We appreciate it. But go get some rest, and we will see you soon."

"Thanks again for bringing me home. Good night, Miss Emma, and Sydney," he says as he walks away backward till they pull out and head down the road then he turns and heads inside.

Emma and Sydney get home. They head inside. They say their good-nights and head to their rooms for bed.

CHAPTER 7

Back To Normal for Now

The girl is running through the woods while something chases her. She is afraid to look over her shoulder to see what it is and how close it is, but she can hear it and it does not sound very friendly. If she had to guess, it sounds like it has gnarly big teeth and big claws. She's trying to find somewhere to hide. She is doubtful that she can even find anywhere to hide. She's growing tired from all the running, but she continues to push on. She prays she comes upon someone or something to help her break free from this massive-sounding beast or thing. With each step it takes, she can hear the branches and dead leaves on the ground being crushed beneath its feet.

"Dear Lord,

Please deliver me from this evil beast, whatever it may be, and save me from being caught within its clutches.
Amen."

She keeps her eyes closed while continuing to run down the path when suddenly, even with her eyes closed, she sees a bright light peering through the dark and dreary forest. She opens her eyes and is amazed at all the beauty surrounding her. It's a small circle of beauty and very bright light. She appears to be safe for now. She hears growling and snorting just beyond the light.

"Go away, beast, I am surrounded by God's love and with him anything is possible!" she shouts out into the darkness.

She hears the beast pacing back and forth, but it is wise enough to stay far enough back that she can't get a good look at it. She wonders what it is. Could it be a vicious bear? Maybe a wolf? Or could it be a coyote? She isn't sure, but whatever it is it sounds utterly demonic.

She begins to pray again.

"Dear Lord,

Thank you for the bright light of love. Now I must get out of these woods. Can you please send help? Somehow please get me rescued from this scary place! I will wait patiently for your response.

Amen."

Suddenly, the circle of light grows more and more dim. The girl screams, "No, no, Lord. Please don't take away the light!" It gets a little brighter. "Thank you!" Then it gets dim again, and she screams out again, "No, no, no! Please no! God, please don't take the light!"

Suddenly, it's completely dark again and very silent. She tries to control her breathing so that she won't be detected. As she quietly tries to look around to see what she can see. She can't see very far in front of her, but suddenly, she smells a strong odor of wet and musty fur when out of nowhere...

"Roar!"

She jumps back and...

Buzz. Buzz.

"Good morning, Lexington! It's a bit rainy out there today."

Sydney hits the snooze and feels her sheets, and they are soaked with sweat. She is breathing heavily, and her heart is racing.

Wow what a dream! Sydney thinks to herself. I don't know what is with all these weird dreams lately, but they are so vivid and wild. I wonder what they mean.

"Syd?" Emma yells up the stairs.

"Yes, Em. I am vertical, and my bum is moving. Be down in a bit," Sydney assures Emma.

"Okay, hurry, or you will be eating a cold breakfast," she yells back up the stairs.

"Yeah, yeah, I know," Sydney mumbles under her breath.

Sydney gathers her clothes for the day and heads to the bathroom to get a shower. She lays her clothes on the bench and proceeds to take off her sweaty, drenched clothes and puts them in the hamper.

She showers and gets dressed for the day. She heads to the kitchen.

As she nears the kitchen, she hears Emma humming.

"Whatcha humming, Em?" Sydney asks.

"It's called '*Just as I Am*.' It's one of my favorite spiritual songs," Emma shares as she notices how Sydney looks for the day. "You look like you had a rough night, young one."

"Yeah, another strange dream. I felt like I ran a marathon by the time I woke up. I'm sorry, but if you have time, could you please wash my sheets? And my sweat-drenched clothes are in the hamper in my bathroom. Thanks. So, I have training with Obee today. I wonder if Sophie is coming over for it. And Lucas too?" Sydney looks down at her phone and starts to text Lucas and Sophie.

Sydney: Hey bestie! I hope you are ok you have me so worried about you. It's been almost two whole days since I have talked to you. I miss you! Please text me and let me know if you will be coming over to do ride practice with me. Ok I♡ve you very much!

Sydney: Hey Lucas! This is one of our first riding practices are you coming over to ride with me?

After Sydney texts Lucas and Sophie, she sits up to the bar and puts her phone down as she thinks about all the strange things happening to and around her lately.

"Emma?" she asks.

"What's up, young one?" Emma asks curiously.

"Do you ever feel like the universe is about to just crash down on your head?" Sydney boldly asks.

"Yes, a time or two. Why, what has you all flustered? Maybe I can help you with it?" Emma gently tries to get straight to the issue at hand.

"Well let's see, it seems to have started a few days ago. I have been having some strange dreams. Some I remember, some I don't. And then on Sunday, Lucas and Sophie were at each other like cats and dogs looking and sounding like they wanted to rip each other apart. And since then, Sophie has not spoken to me," Sydney states, hanging her head about to cry. "I mean I miss my bestie. This is the longest we have ever gone without talking to each other! It's like I'm being pushed or tested to my limits!" Sydney says adamantly, knowing that Sophie would agree if they were talking right now.

"Well, first thing I have to ask is are you eating before you go to bed?" Emma asks, waiting patiently for her reply.

Sydney thinks back and replies, "No, I do not think so or at least as far as I can remember no," Sydney answers.

"Okay, well, maybe you are just stressed. But as far as Lucas and Sophie are concerned, why do you think they were acting like that?" Emma asks, hoping that nothing bad happened while they were camping.

"Well, Emma, I was wondering the same thing. I mean everything was great while we were camping." She happily states.

Emma thinks to herself, *Well, that's a relief.* "Syd, I also wanted to remind you of a great verse for your situation that you are in right now. It is 1 Corinthians 10:13, which basically states that you won't be tested beyond what anyone else would be, God is faithful and won't let you be tested beyond that which you can handle, but when you are tested, God will also provide a way out so that you can endure it. So please just try to remember that."

Just then a message comes in on Sydney's phone, and she looks to see who it is.

"Who is it, Syd?" Emma wonders as she hopes though that it is Sophie.

"It's Lucas. He says he will be over in a little bit. I think I am gonna call Allison," Sydney mentions out loud.

"Oh?" Emma says.

"Yeah, I have to know what's up with Sophie," Sydney says as she takes a deep breath and dials up Allison.

Emma makes like she is leaving the room so she can quietly listen in. She can only hear Sydney's end of the conversation.

"Hello, Allison? Hey, how are you?" "Oh yeah? That's good! Well, yeah, that's why I was calling. Will Sophie be coming over today? We are starting our riding practices today."

"Oh, okay. Cool. Thank you, Allison. Sorry if I disturbed you at all." "Oh, okay. Well, we will see you soon! Thanks!"

"Emma?" Sydney says a little more chipper than she had shown earlier in the morning.

Emma comes around the corner and says, "What's going on, young one?"

"Allison is bringing both Sophie and Eliza over in a few minutes."

"Oh, honey, that's great!" Emma says, smiling with relief.

"Yeah, I know I am getting to the bottom of this today!" Sydney states with determination.

"Just a few words of wisdom," Emma says.

"Sure thing, Em. I'm all ears." Sydney sits attentively listening to Emma.

"Do not use words that can sound like you are being negative, harsh, or accusatory. Be careful how you word what you say to her till you know what's truly going on. She could take offense to it or misunderstand. Just listen and let her speak first," Emma instructs her.

"Oh, for sure. I will do my best to listen and try to understand. Thank you, Em!" Sydney says gratefully.

Sydney gets up to head for the door when she stops and says, "Em, I am headed to look for Obee. I would like to get the horses ready a while for practice."

"Okay, I will go work on your sheets and clothes. Remember, Syd, be patient, listen first, and choose your words wisely," Emma repeats, hoping Sydney listens and remembers what she told her.

"Yes, ma'am, I will! Thanks again, Em, for everything! I know I probably don't tell you enough, but I am truly grateful for all that you do for Dad and me!" Sydney says as she turns to walk out the door.

Emma stands there for a minute and just smiles as a tear forms in her eye. Then she says out loud, "Come on, you ole softy. We got work to get done." She wipes away the tear and heads up to Sydney's room.

Meanwhile, outside, Sydney is walking around looking for Obee.

"Obee!" she yells. "Oh, Obee! Where are you, Obee?" She can't find him, so she walks into the stables and starts to get the horses ready. She takes Loads of Luck, PB Cup, and SOT out of their stalls and hooks them in the aisle of the stable so she can brush them and get them prepped for riding.

After a few minutes, she hears a car pull up. So, she lays down the brush and walks down to the end of the stable to see who has arrived. It's Lucas.

"Hey Lucas!" Sydney says, smiling.

"Hey there, beautiful!" Lucas shyly responds.

"Beautiful? Who are you talking to? Must be SOT!" Sydney says, laughing.

"I mean yeah, sure, but not really, I meant that for you!" he says, hoping he didn't just offend her and completely give himself away.

"Oh well, thanks." She blushes a little as she looks away, playing shy.

"So, no Sophie again today?" Lucas wonders but secretively is hoping she doesn't show.

"Actually, Allison is bringing her and Eliza over in a little bit. So maybe they will be here soon? I really don't know." Sydney guesses while she thinks about the conversation that she and Emma had earlier this morning and decides to see what Lucas may know. "So, I was wondering if I could ask you something?"

"Umm, sure, why not? Fire away," Lucas quickly replies.

"So, I was wondering if you could please shed a little light on what was going on with you and Sophie the other day?" she says, hoping to know something more before Sophie gets there or at least Lucas's side of what happened.

"Well, it was nothing really," Lucas says like it literally was nothing.

"I'm sorry, but how can you say it was nothing!" Sydney says with a raised voice and a bit of attitude.

Then she remembers what Emma said and takes a deep breath and continues. "I'm sorry," Sydney says as she pauses for a minute. "Look, maybe to you it was nothing, but it obviously was something! Because since y'all went off the deep end together, now my bestie won't talk to me!" Sydney sternly states.

"Oh well, I didn't know," he says.

"How could you not know? She didn't come to work yesterday! And she didn't stay the night after y'all blew up on each other. Which I thought I told you but maybe I forgot. So come on before she gets here out with whatever it was that y'all were talking about. Please, Lucas, so I can understand what's going on with my bestie," she demands politely.

"So, I was gonna say something, and I changed my mind. Then we got in a mouth battle about what it was and who was the better friend. And that's it. I'm sorry, Sydney," Lucas states as he throws his hands up in the air and then down abruptly.

"So, what were you gonna say? If you don't mind me asking?" she tries to ask peacefully.

"Well, I was gonna ask to stay the night. But she blew up like it was wrong of me to want to stay. I mean I had just stayed the night before. I honestly didn't think it would be an issue. But according to Sophie, it must have been. Again, I am so sorry," Lucas says, trying not to get angry.

"That's all it was?" she asks, confused.

"Yes, ma'am, cross my heart!" Lucas says honestly.

"Hmm, okay. Well, I will talk with Sophie to see what she tells me. Thank you, Lucas. I promise I will not tell her we talked," Sydney says as she tries to calm down and get Lucas to help finish getting the horses ready.

As they are standing practically next to each other as they brush the horses, they are laughing and carrying on so much that they don't even notice that Sophie has gotten there and has been watching them for a few minutes by now.

Sophie clears her throat as she stands there with her arms crossed and with some major attitude.

Sydney hears Sophie clear her throat. Sydney snaps to her attention. When she sees Sophie, she drops the brush and runs over to Sophie and hugs her then tries to dance around and be silly, but Sophie is just not having it.

"Bestie? What's wrong? Are you mad at me? Are you okay?" Sydney asks, all concerned at why her bestie is acting like this because it seems like something is seriously wrong.

"Well, it just looks like y'all are just having the time of your lives without me!" She says with an envious attitude.

"Well, we are friends, and that's what friends do! I really miss you and I being like that!" Sydney says, hoping that Sophie agrees.

Sophie scoffs and shifts her weight, so she isn't facing directly at the sight of Lucas.

"Bestie, can we have a talk in seclusion together?" Sydney asks, hoping that Sophie agrees.

"Sure, you don't want Lucas there?" She says with even more attitude.

"Lucas, would you please excuse us? We need a little girl time meeting. We will be back in a few," Sydney states as she grabs for Sophie's hand.

"Oh sure, no problem," Lucas says, understanding.

"Now would you please come with me, bestie!" Sydney says as she takes Sophie's hand, and they disappear around the corner of the stable barn. "Now please come on out with whatever is eating you up!"

"I will let you guess in one word!" Sophie says like it's a game they are playing.

Seriously? Sydney thinks to herself. *What are we three again?* "Okay, I will guess one word, and if I don't guess it, you have to spill your guts!" Sydney thinks about the last couple of days and comes up with the conclusion that maybe it's Lucas. "Okay, would it happen to be Lucas?" She asks, hoping it's not.

"Ding ding ding! That wasn't too hard," Sophie says as she acts like a spoiled brat.

"What's wrong with Lucas?" Sydney says, confused.

"What's not wrong with him!" Sophie screams.

"Sophie, Shhh!" Sydney demands as she tries to be calmer as she continues to speak, "Seriously, Sophie, I love you with everything I am, but I do not understand what has been up with you lately."

"Just who does he think he is, thinking that he can just do everything we do together!" Sophie says with resentment.

"Well, first off, he is our new friend. And we need to include him into things we do. Secondly, I think there is a little more to what's eating at you then Lucas. Can you please let me know what happened between you two the other day? What was your reason was for leaving and not staying to talk with me then?" Sydney asks, hoping to get a straight answer from her.

"Ugh!" Sophie says as she makes fists and punches down the air at her sides. She takes a deep breath and then says, "Syd, I am sorry. But you had him stay the night when we camped."

"Yes, okay? And?" Sydney says as she thinks to herself, *this can't seriously be the reason! Is she seriously that jealous?*

"Well, when we got back, he wanted to stay again! And I was like, who does he think he is? Where will he sleep?" Sophie starts to say.

"Wow, Sophie. I am shocked. Excuse me for saying so, but am I detecting a bit of jealousy? Of what? And why? I do not even have a clue. But it sounds like it," Sydney concludes.

"I mean I can see how you could think that. But I don't mean to be. It's just I want you all to me! I love you, Syd!" Sophie says, pouring out her heart.

"And as I do you too! I always have and always will! But having Lucas around is like having Liz around! There's no need to be jealous. We are all just friends. Can't you see that?" Sydney asks, hoping this puts an end to Sophie's jealousy.

"Yes, I know, but I think there's more to Lucas and him wanting to stay that he's not being honest about. Don't you see that, Syd?" Sophie says, hoping Sydney understands what she's getting to without her trying to completely explain it.

"And like I said before, I think you are jumping to conclusions about this, so can we for now just agree to be some kind of normal for now, and I promise I will get you all to myself so we can have what appears to be some much-needed girl time? Please, Sophie? I've missed my bestie!" Sydney gives Sophie a pretend sad face while waiting for a hug.

Sophie puts her arms out to engage in Sydney's hug and says, "Oh, okay, but you promised, so I am holding you to that! So, let's get back to Lucas and the horses so we can whoop his bum in practice!" Sophie says with a little more excitement.

"Now that's my bestie! Welcome back. I've missed you! And yes, yes, yes! Let's go whoop up some Lucas bum!"

CHAPTER 8
First Day of Practice

Lucas is still brushing down the horses as Sophie and Sydney come skipping hand in hand around the corner and into the stables.

"Wow, I see that must have been one heck of an awesome girl time meeting. So, are we all good?" Lucas says, afraid to ask.

"Yep, we are all good, aren't we, Sophie?" Sydney winks at Sophie.

Sophie nods and says, "Yep, all good for now, but don't make me go back to the dark side!" she says as she laughs a vicious laugh.

"So, are they ready for their saddles yet or what, Lucas?" Sydney asks.

"Yes, ma'am, I think they are," Lucas proudly states.

"Okay then, get your saddles ready, and I will try to find Obee again," Sydney says as she starts to run out of the stable and practically right into Obee.

"Whoa, slow down, Syd! Where's the fire?" Obee says.

"Actually, I was on my way to find you so we can get this practice started," Sydney says with enthusiasm.

"Well, I thought I heard someone talking about me because my ears were ringing, and when I got close, I in fact did hear my name, so I am guessing that was good timing on my part?" Obee says cheerfully.

"That sounds exactly right!" Sydney turns to head right back into the barn and eagerly states, "Okay, Obee's here! You guys let's get our saddles on and get this party on the road," Sydney says to stir up some excitement.

"While you guys saddle up, I wanna let you know that we will be going out to the north field to the track over there for practice today. It's one of the wider tracks. So let me get Black Boots saddled up, and I will ride out with y'all," Obee says as he heads for Black Boots.

Obee gets out Black Boots and gives him a quick brushing and grabs his saddle and saddles him up while the kids patiently wait.

"Okay, we are all ready to go. Sydney, can you grab a bottle of water for each of us?" Obee politely asks.

"Sure thing, Obee!" Sydney grabs enough water for each of them and puts it in a small soft cooler bag and throws it up over the horn on her saddle.

"Okay, Syd, you good?" Obee asks.

"Yes, sir, let's ride!" she responds.

"Okay, follow me, kids," Obee says as he leads everyone out of the stables and to the north field.

The north field is up in the northernmost part of the property, not quite all the way to the northern end but it's up there. It takes us about 20 minutes or so to ride up there.

"Okay, we are here, kiddos. So, I just want two of you to go around for like four laps, and then the winner gets to take on the next person for four laps. The best out of five laps gets the inside lane to start when we run triples. So, who wants to go first?" Obee asks.

"Obee, I would like to race Sophie first please," Sydney says, hoping that Sophie would appreciate Sydney, picking her over Lucas first.

"Okay, sure!" Sophie agrees.

"Okay, line up, girls," Obee instructs them.

"You better be ready, bestie! I want you to push the limits with me!" Sydney says to pump Sophie up.

"Oh, I am, and thanks for picking me first," Sophie says with much appreciation. "We can all push each other to our limits." Sophie says as she looks at Sydney and then over to Lucas.

"Sure thing!" Lucas yells back with two thumbs up.

"Like I said, bestie, we are a team, and you are always my first pick. Get ready and just try and keep up," Sydney says, trying to antagonize Sophie.

"It's on like Donkey Kong! I hope to make you eat your words in dust," Sophie says, trying to psych out Sydney.

"Okay, girls. On your mark, get set…," Obee says before he pulls the trigger on the cap gun.

Bang!

Goes the gun, and the girls take off, neck and neck with each other as they push each other around the dirt track.

As Sydney pushes further ahead with SOT, Sophie gets PB Cup to close in the gap. They are rounding around the last corner, and Sydney pulls ahead with SOT just enough to take lap one. They continue to push on. Lucas sits on the side with Loads of Luck and cheers them on.

"Go, girls, go!" Lucas chants.

As they go around and around, they keep within a few feet of each other. Here they come on their last lap. They are both pushing hard, and Obee has his phone ready to get a photo finish. As tight as they are running, it will be needed.

"Whoo-hoo, girls! Way to go!" Lucas yells with excitement. "Obee, who am I up against?" he wonders with anticipation.

"Well, let's look!" Obee says as he checks through his bursts of photos his camera has taken. "Well, it looks like Sydney has it by a nose. So, Lucas, you are up with Syd!" Obee informs Lucas.

"Aye, aye, sir. Let's go, Syd. Don't hold back. I want a tough race," Lucas says, chuckling.

"I have you know I gave Sophie a hard race, so you better be ready!" Sydney says like she's the Queen B.

Lucas heads over beside Sydney, while Sophie goes back with Obee.

"Okay, you two. Are you ready?" Obee says to get their attention.
"You got this, bestie! Give him H-E-double hockey sticks," Sophie yells to Sydney.
Sydney smiles and nods while thinking, *There's my bestie! I'm so glad she's here.*

They both nod, and Obee continues then get set. He raises his arm and pulls the cap gun trigger.

Bang!

They take off with dust flying.

Lucas pulls ahead with Loads of Luck but not for too long before Sydney and SOT pull ahead of them. Sydney gets further ahead, almost like Lucas is giving up, but she keeps pushing on. Then suddenly, when she least expects it, Lucas zips by her and leaves her in the dust.

"Come on, SOT! Are we gonna take that from them? Come on, girl, let's go!" Sydney says to SOT as she kicks her in high gear, and they catch up to Lucas and Loads of Luck.

They have one more lap. Sydney keeps talking to SOT. "Come on, girl, you can do it! Just keep pushing! Come on!"

As they round the last corner, Obee has his phone ready, and it's another close one.

Sophie rushes over to Obee. "Who won, Obee?" she wonders.

Once again, he swipes through his photos and says, "Wow not what I had expected! So are y'all ready?" Obee holds out a little to raise the anticipation.

"Yes, Obee! Come on! Who am I up against?" Sophie says while jumping up and down, trying to reach for Obee's phone to see.

"Yeah, come on, Obee, let us see!" Lucas and Sydney shout.

"Oh, okay, but don't say I didn't warn ya! It's Lucas by half of a nose!" Obee says laughing.

"Dang, that was a great run, Syd!" Lucas says as he raises his arm for a high-five from Sydney.

"Well, I don't think that Sophie will be as forgiving! Let him have it, Sophie!" Sydney says laughing.

"Oh, don't you worry, Syd! He isn't winning this one!" Sophie says with confidence.

"Well, bring it on, Sophie, and show me what you got!" Lucas says, trying to rattle her into messing up. They take their places. Obee says, "Are you ready?"

"Yes!" Lucas and Sophie say in unison.

"Okay, get set," Obee says as he raises his arm and pulls the trigger.

Bang!

They both take off and push hard. They are staying directly beside each other. They get through all their laps, staying almost completely beside each other. Now they are down to the last corner of their last lap. As they cross the makeshift finish line, Obee snaps a burst of pictures.

Sydney thinks she has seen which was first but runs over to Obee to verify.

As Lucas and Sophie make their way over to Sydney and Obee, Sydney asks, "Do you know yet?" then proceeds to whisper in his ear whom she thinks won.

"So?" Sophie says.

Obee shows Sydney, and she just stares at Lucas and Sophie and back down at the pictures. "Nope, you tell 'em, Obee!" Sydney says as she goes and gets on SOT. "I will meet the winner over here at the starting line."

"Okay, are you two ready for the results?" Obee asks.

"Sure!" Lucas says.

Page **82** of **374**

"Yes, please!" Sophie says.

"Okay, I will have to show you the picture, so you believe me," Obee says as he turns his phone for them to see who won.

"Wow! Congrats, Lucas! Well, go give Sydney another run, and hopefully you win this time!" Sophie says as she's glad but also a little sad.

So far, Lucas has two wins and Sydney has one. They are on their fourth race. Lucas and Sydney line up again.

"On your mark, get set," Obee says as he raises his arm, and he pulls the trigger.

Bang!

They take off flying around the track, seemingly pushing harder than their previous race.

As they race around, Sophie notices that Parker is on his way out to the track. Just before Parker makes it out to them, Obee gets another picture-perfect finish.

"Ah, just in time, Parker, to see who won the fourth race," Obee says.

"So how have they been doing, Obee?" Parker says, wondering.

"Well, before this race, Lucas had two wins and Sydney had a win. And now we reveal who won this race! Anyone care to guess who won?" Obee asks.

Lucas pipes up and says, "Sydney! I am pretty sure that Sydney had me on that one."

"Well, that's what the pictures show too!" Obee says in agreement with Parker as they both look at the pictures. "So that's two for Lucas and two for Sydney!"

"Obee, why don't we just let them all race for the last race and head back for some lunch?" Parker suggests.

"Well, it's okay with me. How about you, kiddos?" Obee states.

"Yeah, we are all good with it." They all agree.

"So, since Sophie has not won, she can have the inside lane to start. How's that sound for fairness with everyone?" Obee asks.

They all agree. So, they all take their marks, and Obee leads them off with the last shot for the day.

Bang!

They all take off and race furiously around the track. Lap one down, lap two and three. They are on their last lap coming around the last corner, and Obee has his camera posed and ready to take the last winning picture for the day.

When they slow down and come back around to see who took the win, Obee has his phone held up and says, "Today's winner is none other than...may I have a drumroll please?"

Lucas acts like he's playing the drums while he beat boxes out the sound of playing drums.

"Sophie! Way to go, kiddo! Great job!" Obee congratulates her as they prepare to head back.

"Way to go, bestie!" Sydney says with excitement.

"Sophie, you are a great contender!" Lucas shares honestly.

"Thanks, guys. It is an amazing feeling racing around the track with y'all. I can't wait to do it again!" Sophie shares as she gives a slight giggle.

"Well, I must admit that you ladies definitely brought your game and pushed me to my greatest limits!" Lucas says proudly. "I am thrilled to be a part of this team!"

CHAPTER 9
Let's Get It Straight

As Parker, Obee, Sophie, Lucas, and Sydney start to head back to the stables, Sydney notices her dad grinning ear to ear. So, she rides up beside him and says, "I love you, Dad!"
Parker looks at Sydney and replies, "I love you too, my little filly!"

"So, what has you all lit up, dad?" Sydney wonders.

Parker thinks for a moment, and he gets a bigger grin and says, "I am just so happy that I had gotten the chance to ride out to see all you kids riding. Well, racing around with each other. You guys looked great back there!" Parker said proudly.

"Yeah, we did push each other hard! Like literally, Dad, we were all neck in neck with each other!" Sydney eagerly boasts.

"So, then all your races were that way?" Parker asks.

"Yes, sir! We are gonna be a hard team to beat! Between the three of us, your trophy wall should be shiny this year!" Sydney says with anticipation.

"Well, like Grandad always said, let's not count our chickens before they have hatched. But that sure would be nice! But it's not what I live for! Sydney, I must ask you, are you happy here? On the ranch and racing for me and running your mom's Boutique? Where do you want to be in your future?" Park asks out of curiosity to see where Sydney wants to be.

"Well, Dad, I have to say that I love the ranch, the racing, and running mom's Boutique!" Sydney can see her dad's face change a little when he senses a *but* coming. "But…"

"Ah, there it is! That nasty word *but*!" Parker says chuckling.

"Yes, Dad!" Sydney sadly states. "But you do know my heart lies on the coast where the sand and waves are, and someday, I do intend on moving there and away from all of this! It doesn't mean that I love you any less, but it's my dream, and I have to follow my heart. I will be back to visit often. Especially to see SOT!" Sydney states with all her heart.

"Well, I just want you to be happy. So, if that is what you want, then that's what I have to let you do. I have to let you live your life, and before we know it, I am so sure that you will be living your life just as you dream it," Parker says with a heavy heart. "But also, please don't forget that someday, if ever there comes a day that you need anything, all you have to do is ask! Plus, you know, my little filly, that I am gonna have to come and see you as well!" Parker assures Sydney.

"I know, Dad, and I appreciate all of that! But I pray that God will guide me and be just as much a part of my future as he is now if not a whole lot more! As long as I have God, then I know I can accomplish anything!" Sydney emphasizes.

"I have no doubt about that, my little filly! And I too know that God will guide you every day to the best you can be. He won't give you anything that you can't handle!" Parker states with all the glory of God!

"Yeah, Emma and I had a talk about 1 Corinthians 10:13 and God giving me tests but nothing I can't handle, and if it gets to be too much, he will give me a way out. So yes, amen, Dad! So, what do you think Em will have for lunch today? Because I am starving," Sydney says, rubbing her stomach.

"You know, Syd, I am so sorry. I just hopped on Tall Leaps and headed out here to see if I could get lucky to even catch any riding at all. I didn't get a chance to see Emma before I came out to know what is for lunch," Parker says happily.

"Well then, it shall be a surprise! But I know for sure it will be good!" Sydney states and her and her dad nod in agreement together.

Meanwhile, behind Sydney and Parker, Lucas and Sophie are also chatting together trying to work things out and not be so irritable with each other.

"So, I just wanted to say that I am sorry, Lucas, for acting like I did the other day. It was totally uncalled for and so not like me," Sophie says while trying not to look at Lucas out of fear of embarrassment.

"I accept your apology, Sophie. I can only imagine how you must have felt about me wanting to stay the night again. It's like one day, it's just you and Sydney. And the next, I am here with you both almost every day. I want to say that I am sorry too! I didn't mean to just show up and be a wedge between the two of you," Lucas says, trying to be strong and not weak and look like a little sissy boy. "But I do have to say one thing!"

Sophie looks at Lucas and says, "What would that be?"

"Well, I am so blessed to have two fine young ladies such as y'all in my life. I am also so glad to get the opportunity to even be blessed with your presence every day that you both allow me to. Because since I started hanging out with y'all, I can feel me changing for the better, to be someone better! And I like this new person that I am becoming better than that old sports jock bully of a little boy I once was," Lucas says, pouring out his heart.

"Wow, Lucas, I have to say that I can honestly feel your heart in your words, and I again have to apologize for my rude and selfish behavior. I just felt like since you have been in the picture that I was getting pushed aside," Sophie says with a sigh of relief. "But let me tell you one thing, before I bit off your head and spit it back out atcha. I thought I would just distance myself from you both and give it a few days to see how I felt. And I have to say that when you have such a tight bond with someone and someone else comes along, it's hard to share, but I knew deep down that there was absolutely no way that I was gonna let anyone come between the two of us, not even a boy!" Sophie says, leaving no question as to how hurt yet determined she was for her relationship with Sydney to remain strong.

"Well, I am sorry. I never meant to be hurtful to either of you. I am just glad that we are talking again and that you and I have time to air out our issues so we can all get back to being good friends again," Lucas says with a smile on his face and a special little twinkle in his eye that catches Sophie's attention.

"Well, Lucas, since we are being honest and airing out our differences, I have something that I would like to ask but feel as I should just leave it alone, but at the same time, I am Sydney's friend and I just have to know," Sophie says as she looks for the words she wants to say.

"Well, spit it out already. Quit leaving me guessing what you are trying to say," Lucas says, trying to hurry her along so he can figure out what it is she is wanting to ask.

"So, I get this feeling when I am around you that has me a little uneasy. And I think that's why I had such an issue with what you said the other day," Sophie says, trying to open up to Lucas.

"What did I say? And what kind of feeling?" Lucas wonders.

"Well, it's not that feeling," Sophie says, looking at Lucas like *Yeah, I got your number, boy!* "I'm not interested in boys and what they have to offer. I promised myself I was gonna get an education, a job, and a beautiful place of my own before I even have a chance of being mentally violated or any other type of violation from the opposite sex. Besides, I think it would be amazing to save myself for that one true love of mine whom, when the time is right, God will put right in front of me, and I want him to know that I have waited till I was united with him to share what God has given me to offer him." Sophie looks as if she is way off in outer space somewhere.

"Wow, okay, earth to Sophie," Lucas says, snapping his fingers at Sophie, trying to regain her attention. "Hey, Sophie! Enough with the riddles just ask your question already." Lucas chuckles. "I mean, I am glad you feel that way, but I would like to get this resolved sometime this hour. You know, before we get back and we can't talk because of people being around."

"Oh yeah, sorry!" Sophie says with a bit of attitude. "Okay sorry for the 'tude, but I was just worried about you taking my best forever life friend away from me!"

"Wait? What?" Lucas says, confused.

"Well, I'm sorry you wanted to spend the night again. What was I supposed to think?" Sophie quietly shouts out to Lucas.

Lucas pulls on the reins to get Loads of Luck to slow down and says, "What does me wanting to spend another night here have anything to do with taking away your best friend?" Lucas asks, trying to figure out where in the world Sophie would have gotten that impression.

"Well, isn't it what you wanted? Please tell me you don't want my friend, and I will be forever sorry for jumping to conclusions!" Sophie says, very sure she knows the answer.

"I want your friend? Wow, I know I do not know you very well, but I get this feeling that even for you, this is a stretch," Lucas says while looking at Sophie and seeing something that he had not seen before from her. "Wait, are you serious? You are! You thought I was trying to take Syd away from you. All I wanted to do was spend the night even if on the couch so that no one had to make a special trip to take me home. And you think I wanted your friend? I am so blown away right now." Lucas feels a little upset that Sophie would just jump to conclusions like that.

"Well, see, you didn't deny it," she lashes back.

"Deny what?" Lucas says, confused.

"That you want my friend. Don't play coy with me, Lucas. I've seen all the signs that you want my friend. And I'm sorry I won't let her get hurt, so you have to get through me before you can have her," Sophie says sternly.

"*Whoa!* Whoa, slow down there, little lady! Nobody wants your friend. And just what signs am I giving that make you even think that!?" Lucas says with some noticeable irritation.

"Come on, Lucas. I am a girl, and I have boy radar! You asking Sydney to the dance! You suddenly wanting to ride horses, and you want to spend the night suddenly. You are always wanting to talk with her alone, and not to mention I've seen how you

Page **91** of 374

look at her!" Sophie confesses. "So come on out with it before I blow your cover right here and right now!"

"Wow, when Syd said that you were crazy, I didn't think she meant mentally crazy!"

"What? Take that back! Syd never said I was crazy!" Sophie says, feeling hurt. "Did she? Does my best friend think I'm crazy?" Sophie hangs her head and starts wondering why her best friend of her whole life would even say such a thing.

"Sophie, I'm sorry I didn't mean that. She never said you were crazy, but you were bashing me saying all these things. Did you forget I took you to the dance too? And as for the horses, I do have a fond love for horses. Before my dad passed away, we used to go to the track and watch them race, and we've been trail riding a few times. The camping thing Syd asked me to come and do that with y'all. And I do not know what look you are talking about, but I will say this and please listen carefully to what I am about to say because I do not want any jealousy issues!" Lucas says with strong emphasis on jealousy issues. "I will say that she has caught my eye, and I think she is a pretty girl, and that's about it! But I think that you are pretty too! So now can we just get over this already?" Lucas hopes that Sophie can get over all this nonsense.

Sophie thinks about what Lucas has just stated and is speechless. Sophie thinks to herself and decides to let it go for now. "Okay, if you say so, but I got my eyes on you, Lucas Devinshire!" Sophie assures Lucas.

"Okay, if you say so," Lucas says as he laughs and puts out his hand. "Friends?"

Sophie hesitates then shakes Lucas's hand and says, "Sure. Friends."

CHAPTER 10
Trip of A Lifetime?

After the long ride back, everything has been worked out for now with Lucas and Sophie, and Parker has a better understanding of what Sydney wants to do with her future. It's now time for lunch.

"Okay, everyone, so we can all get in to eat at the same time, let's each clean up and care for the horse we rode," Parker suggests.

"On it!" Lucas states.

"Sure thing, Parker!" Sophie says.

"I don't know about the rest of you, but I am starving! I hope Em made something yummy!" Sydney says as she unsaddles SOT.

"Syd, you know Em always has amazing food. What's wrong with you, girl?" Obee says, shocked like it's a known thing in this family.

"I know, Obee! It's just that when I am super hungry, my brain gets clouded, and I can't think straight when I am this hungry!

I'm almost hangry!" Sydney says as she tries to hurry everyone along. "Come on, guys, let's get moving! Before I have to start eating the horses' grain because it smells so good." Sydney gives each of the horses a scoop of the molasses grain. As she does, she smells it. She gets even more hungry.

"Okay, kiddos, looks good. Let's go get some eats before Syd eats the horse's grain!" Obee says, laughing.

They all head to the house, and Sydney is first in line. Parker shouts up through all of them and says before they get inside, "Please wash up, everyone. Then we can eat."

"Ugh! Dad, I may die till I can get to eat!" Sydney jokes.

"Sydney, just wash up please!" Parker asks.

"Okay, but I'm headed to the kitchen to wash up!" Sydney promises.

"I don't care where you do it. Just do it!" Parker states.

As Sydney opens the door, she smells lunch! And it smells amazing. "Oh, Em, lunch smells awesome!" Sydney says to Emma as she comes into the kitchen.

"Well, I hope so. I made one of your favorites," Emma states.

"Mmm, I see that, Em! Yummy tacos and caramel apple empanadas. Oh my, you have outdone yourself, Em!" Sydney says with excitement.

"Yes, I made you all the choices: chicken, beef, and steak," Emma says as she sets the table with all the toppings, food, plates, and utensils. "Here we have tomatoes, lettuce, a couple of different kinds of cheeses, salsa, sour cream, guacamole, soft and hard shells, refried beans, rice. Here's tea, milk, lemonade for all your drink choices. We also have bottled water. So, grab a plate, and let's do our prayer so we can eat," Emma says, laughing to try to hurry everyone to sit so Sydney won't die from starvation.

"Who's saying a prayer?" Parker asks while everyone gets seated.

"I will, Dad!" Sydney waits for everyone to get seated.

"Dear God,

Thank you for an amazing day and for this amazing food that has been cooked by the amazing Emma! Please bless her as well because without her, where would we be? Please take care of her so she can take care of us.

Amen"

"Oh, Sydney, that was so sweet. Thank you," Emma says sincerely. "But I just do it because I love you all, and it makes me feel good."

"You're welcome, Em! Okay, peeps, let's eat!" Sydney says as she goes for the soft shells and starts piling on the goodies.

"Don't stuff yourself, Sydney. We have empanadas," Emma warns Sydney.

"Yeah, I know, and I'm all good," Sydney responds.

"So how did it go out there today, kids?" Emma asks.

"We did great! It was so tight and close for each race!" Lucas states.

"Yeah, and we each won at least one race," Sophie chimes in.

"We are a real powerhouse team!" Sydney adds.

"Well, all I can say is that I am so proud of my powerhouse team! I am so thankful for each of you! I can't wait to see how we clean up this upcoming season," Parker says proudly.

"It should prove to be interesting," Sydney says, smiling at Lucas and then Sophie.

"Well, I still think we should have at least two practice days a week," Parker suggests.

"Yeah, we should be able to do that," Sydney confirms. "Wow, what a busy summer with our practices and working at the Boutique. Hey, Dad, I did have a question for you at some point," Sydney informs Parker.

"Well, ask away, my little filly," Parker says welcoming her question.

"I would, but this requires your approval first, then I can let it be known amongst the others," Sydney says respectfully.

"Oh, okay, I gotcha. How about after dinner?" Parker asks.

"Yep, that will be great!" Sydney says.

"Wow, Miss Emma, your food is awesome! These are the best tacos I have ever had!" Lucas says with a mouthful of tacos.

"Lucas? I thought you had more manners than that!" Sophie says while looking at him and being grossed out.

"Em, do we have any vanilla ice cream to eat with our apple empanadas?" Sydney asks.

"I believe so. Let me look, though." Emma gets up and checks the freezer. "Yes, ma'am, we do."

"Awesome. I would love some with my empanadas, please, Em," Sydney asks.

"Sure, would anyone else like some?" Emma asks.

"Yes, please!" Lucas says.

"Me too, Em!" Sophie adds.

Parker and Obee also nod in agreement that they want some too.

Emma plates up and hands everyone an empanada and ice cream.

Everyone finishes up and parts ways. Obee goes outside, Parker goes to the living room, the girls help Emma clean up, while Lucas stands off to the side and watches while he texts his mom.

Lucas: Mom are you busy?

Lucas waits for a few minutes before his mom responds.

Claire: Just cleaning up around the house. Why what's up?

Lucas: I was just wondering if you have time and would want to come get me, or do you want me to see if I can get a ride?

Claire: Actually, I have to go out anyway so I can pick you up. That's just fine.

Lucas: Ok see ya when you get here. Love you mom.

Claire: Ok love you too!

By now, the kitchen is cleaned up, and Emma sits back down at the table to take a breather for a few minutes.

"Okay, excuse me, everyone. I must go speak with my dad," Sydney states as she leaves the kitchen headed for the living room.

"Hey there, my little filly. So, what was it that you wanted to talk to me about?" Parker asks.

"Well, I was wondering if Obee or you would mind being a chaperon for Lucas, Sophie, and I to get away to the beach sometime before the summer is over and we have to go back to school? Or later this fall?" Sydney asks, being very hopeful that he will say yes!

Well, Syd, we would have to check with Obee, but I think we can talk about possibly getting something set up," Parker says with positivity.

"Awesome. Thanks, Dad!" Sydney is absolutely ecstatic. She runs into the kitchen and begins to talk to Lucas and Sophie.

"What made you so chipper suddenly?" Sophie asks.

"Well, I spoke with my dad about that question I had for him," Sydney starts.

"Well, it must have been some question," Lucas says as he is curious as to what she even asked her dad.

"Well, it is, but I can't tell y'all just yet! But what I can say is I hope it works out because I am so excited for this to happen!" Sydney says while acting like she had way too much sugar and is bouncing off the walls.

"Ah, uh ok! I know that excitement all too well! So, I won't spoil it, but I think I know what the subject of the matter is," Sophie says, so sure of herself.

"Maybe you do and maybe you don't, bestie! But I hope that y'all share the excitement I have when you know what I have planned or rather what I am trying to get planned for all of us!" Sydney states, trying to contain her excitement.

"How long do we have to wait before we can know what these supposed plans are?" Lucas asks eagerly, hoping to know.

"That depends on me!" Parker says while coming out of the living room and half-scaring Sophie to death.

"Parker, you about gave me a heart attack!" Sophie screams as she puts her hand across her chest and breathes heavily.

"I'm sorry, Sophie, I didn't mean to startle you," Parker apologizes to Sophie. "I have to see if and when I can make it happen. But I will do my best to make it happen!"

Beep. Beep.

They hear from outside.

"Someone must be here," Parker says as he walks to the door to look. "Ah yes, Lucas, your mother is here."

"Okay, let me get my things. Can you please let her know I'll be just a minute?" Lucas asks.

Parker opens the door and steps outside with his index finger up. Claire nods back.

Once Lucas has his things, he goes up to Sophie and hugs her and says, "Thanks for a good time and great race. I hope to see you very soon!"

Lucas walks over to Sydney, hugs her, and says, "Thanks for including me in the camping. I had a blast. I can't wait for the next excursion. We shall see who has the most wins next time."

"Bet! And I will let you know when I am thinking about camping again. Be safe, see you soon," Sydney says as Lucas walks out the door.

Lucas stops and puts his hand out to shake Parker's hand and says, "Thanks for everything. It means a lot!"

Lucas turns to wave goodbye to everyone and sees Emma. "Ah, Miss Emma, thanks for the amazing food! Can't wait to have more of your cooking."

"Oh, thank you, sweet child." Emma waves and smiles as Lucas turns to leave.

Parker follows him to Claire's car. Claire puts down her window. "Hey there, Parker. How are ya?" Claire asks.

"Not bad. How about yourself?" Parker asks.

"I am good. How's my little pita? He's not giving you too much trouble, is he?" Claire says with a chuckle.

"Actually, he's been totally great! He gave the girls a run for their money at practice today. I was impressed!" Parker says with excitement.

"Well, that's good to hear. That he's behaving." Claire turns to look at Lucas and smiles at him. She returns her look to Parker. "Well, we must be going. I have some errands to run on the way home. Thanks again, Parker, for everything!" Claire gratefully replies. She gets turned around and heads out the lane.

CHAPTER 11
Worth the Wait

Now that lunch is over and Lucas has gone home, Sydney and Sophie are trying to figure out what they want to get into.

"Syd?" Sophie asks.

"Yeah, bestie. What's up?" Sydney replies.

"Can we go to your room and just talk for a bit? There is something that I would like to discuss with you," Sophie says.

"What could you want to discuss with me?" Sydney wonders.

"Well, it's something that happened this weekend, and I want you to hear it from me first," Sophie says sadly.

"Sure, let's go." Sydney agrees with Sophie as she shouts out to Emma, "Emma, we are headed to my room."

"Okay, young one."

Sydney and Sophie head upstairs to Sydney's room. Once they are in, Sophie closes the door behind them.

"Wow, this must be top secret," Sydney says, wondering what she has to talk about.

"No, not really. I just want it to be just us and here goes. So, Lucas and I had a big blowup. No, a huge blowup!"

"Sophie when?" Sydney asks. "Well, it couldn't have been too big because I didn't even know," Sydney says, confused.

"Well, it wasn't just once but twice," Sophie says, hanging her head.

"Twice?" Sydney says with a shocked look on her face.

"Yeah, but for now, Lucas and I are okay," Sophie says, worried about what Sydney thinks.

"Well, I can't say I'm surprised!" Sydney says unfazed at Sophie's actions.

"Wait, *what*? You are not surprised?" Sophie says with some attitude.

"Well, yes, I am a bit surprised, but I did notice the other day that y'all seemed to be in a heated conversation. But I just thought nothing of it. So no, really, I am not," Sydney regrettably states.

"Well, that's fair. So today we had a blowup. So, I confronted him about you." Sophie springs in Sydney with a *"Please forgive me"* expression.

"About me? Sophie, I said that there was nothing there. So why would you even bring it up?" Sydney says, a little irritated.

"Well, Syd, because I care about you, and I know he's up to something. And I wanted it stopped, or at the very least I want him to know he doesn't even have a chance with you," Sophie states like she's protecting Sydney.

"Okay, so how did that work out for ya? Did you get the answers or responses you were looking for, Sophie?" Sydney asks.

"Well, no, not really. He played it off. He had a good excuse for each thing I questioned him about," Sophie says like she has everything all wrapped up in a nice and neat package.

"Wait, Sophie, how many things did you question Lucas on, and what were they?" Sydney asks, confused.

"Well, I mentioned the dance..." Sophie starts to say when Sydney interrupts her.

"Come on, Sophie. We both went with him. That was not a fair question," Sydney says, standing up for Lucas. "What else?"

"Well, I mentioned about him wanting to spend the night after we camped," Sophie says.

"Sophie, what does that matter?" Sydney irritably responds.

"Well, I know now. Supposedly nothing," Sophie admits with a slight attitude.

"Wait! What? What is supposedly nothing?" Sydney asks, confused.

"Well, he said it was because he wanted to save someone a trip of having to take him home. He said he could have just slept on the couch, and of course, my stupid head just went right into him thinking he was gonna sleep in your room with us," Sophie snaps back.

"Wow, Sophie, what is up with you? You are never like this! If I had known he wanted to stay, I would have let him, and I would have made up the couch for him. This isn't your home, and it's not really in your place to make judgment calls for me like that," Sydney scolds Sophie.

"Yes, I know that now," Sophie says as she hangs her head. "Look, Sydney, I am sorry about my behavior. And that was what set me off and started the whole conversation that backfired. I was just trying to apologize for my rudeness and my bad behavior the other day. And one thing led to another, and next thing we knew, it had snowballed into another huge blowup," Sophie reports honestly.

"And why did I not see or hear this? When did it happen?" Sydney asks out of curiosity.

"Well, it was when we were headed back from the track. You were up ahead talking with your dad, and Lucas and I were lagging back, airing things out," Sophie says.

"Obviously. So, what else did y'all talk about? Anything that I should be aware of?" Sydney asks like she's afraid to ask.

"Well, that was mostly it," Sophie responds.

"Mostly it? Do I even wanna know?" Sydney says, rolling her eyes and shaking her head.

"Well, there was one thing that I wanted to ask you. First, he said you said it, then he said he made it up," Sophie hesitates to say.

"What's that, Sophie?" Sydney says as she shows noticeable irritation while shaking her head.

"He said you called me crazy!" Sophie quickly states and cowers away like Sydney may hit her.

"Really, he said that?" Sydney asks.

"Yes, he did!" Sophie swears.

"Wow, okay. Well, no, I have never said that. But if you keep acting like this, I may have no choice but to call you crazy."

Sydney pauses for a moment then gently punches Sophie on the shoulder and starts laughing.

Sophie grabs a pillow from Sydney's bed and whacks Sydney with it as she starts laughing hysterically.

"Oh, so it's a fight you want?" Sydney says as she grabs another pillow and returns fire with it.

After a few minutes of Sydney and Sophie beating each other with the pillows, Sydney says, "Okay, let's stop before we get pillow stuffings everywhere!"

They both lay down the pillows, and Sydney asks, "Do you feel better, Sophie?"

"Yeah. I'm sorry, Syd, for my behavior lately. I don't know what is up with me. And I do not want to lose you as my bestie. You are the only bestie I have known my whole life! I would be lost without my bestie!" Sophie tries to reassure Sydney.

"I agree, Sophie!"

"Hey, Syd?"

"Yeah, what's up?"

"Can we agree to never let a boy come between us?" Sophie asks.

"I mean sure, but why ask that?" Sydney wonders.

"Just trust me. I know we have never had an issue like that, but we are getting older, and boys are gonna wanna start dating us, and I want you to know that you will always be first in my mind! Any boy is gonna have to work hard to get me away from you!" Sophie promises.

"Aww, Sophie, I love you! And yes! Let's make a pact that it will always be us first!" Sydney says in agreement with Sophie as they give each other a huge hug. "Okay, bestie. I think it's getting close to dinner. Let's go see what Em has cooking," Sydney suggests.

"Oh, that sounds amazing! Let's go," Sophie says as she jumps up off the bed and grabs Sydney's arm and pulls her along as she runs down the stairs to the kitchen.

"Oh, girls, slow down!" Emma says when she hears the girls stomping down the stairs and as the girls quickly round the corner into the kitchen.

"Sorry, Em. We are starving and wanted to come see what you were making for dinner!" Sydney says as she rubs her stomach.

"Agreed!" Sophie mocks Sydney, rubbing her stomach too!

"Well, it is gonna be just a little while longer. I just put it in the oven to finish. Can you guess what it is, Sydney?" Emma asks.

"Well, I can tell you that it smells amazing, Em!" Sophie quickly blurts out.

"Yes, Sophie, for sure, and if I had to guess, I would have to say it's one of my favorites," Sydney starts.

"Yes, Sydney, but which one?" Emma questions her.

"Well, judging from the mess, I would say 5 meats, 5 cheese Stromboli! Oh, please tell me that I am right?" Sydney stresses.

"Bingo, Sydney! You are very good." Emma chuckles.

"Well, it is one of my favorites!" Sydney happily adds.

"So how long, Em, till we can have some of this amazing food?" Sophie asks as she looks like she is about to start drooling.

"It should be about 30 minutes. Do you think you can wait that long, ladies?" Emma asks, hoping that they don't wither away in a few minutes.

"Maybe we can have a snack till then?" Sophie asks.

"Ah *no*!" Sydney quickly replies. "If you have a snack, you will ruin dinner! For sure you do not want to do that!" Sydney reassures her.

"Ah, bestie, I don't know. I will try my best to wait though," Sophie says as she gets hungrier by the minute.

Sydney goes to the fridge, gets a bottle of water, and hands it to Sophie. "Here, bestie. This will help and won't affect your appetite for dinner."

"Thanks, bestie. I will take your word for it," Sophie says as she opens the water and takes a sip. As quickly as she takes a sip, she reports, "Thanks, bestie. I think it helped that quickly. That is amazing." Sophie takes another sip and another.

Sydney smiles as she walks over to the oven and peeks in. "Mmm! Smells amazing, Em! Do you smell it, bestie?" Sydney asks as she licks her lips.

"Oh, I do!" Sophie quickly responds.

"Looks close to being done, Em," Sydney teases.

"Okay, Syd! Please shut the oven so it can finish, or it will never get done and it will just take longer. And I don't think Sophie will last having to wait any longer," Emma jokes as she whips a towel at Sydney's bum.

"Ouch! Sorry, Em, I'm closing it!" Sydney says as she closes the oven door and takes of running around to the end of the table.

"What are ya running for, young one? You know that I can't chase ya." Emma chuckles.

"I know. I'm just playing. Sophie let's set the table while we wait," Sydney suggests.

"Yes, there you go. That will help pass the time and keep your mind off being hungry for just a few more minutes," Emma tells them.

"Sure thing, Miss Em," Sophie chimes in.

"Sophie, you get the silverware, and I will get the plates," Sydney conveys to Sophie.

"That's a big ten-four, bestie!" Sophie exclaims, hoping that the food will be done by the time they are.

"Let's set for five. Em, did Liz go home?" Sydney wonders as she looks around realizing that she doesn't recall seeing her in quite some time.

"Oh yes! I thought y'all knew since you didn't ask. She wanted to go home to be with her mother. So, I called to confirm that Allison was gonna be home, and I took her," Emma tells them as she feels bad for not telling them.

"Oh, it's all good, Em. We are just sorry that we didn't notice till now," Sydney sadly replies.

"Yeah, there's been so much going on, and I can't believe that I, her sister of all people, who should have noticed, didn't. Am I really that bad of a sister?" Sophie says, hanging her head in disbelief.

"It's just like you said with everything that has been going on, we all just got wrapped up in the moment, and it just completely got by us. That does not make you a bad sister," Sydney says as she rethinks everything that has been going on and thinks to herself, *Wow, yeah. That is so true. It's not Sophie's fault she didn't notice because to be honest, I never noticed either.* Sydney gives a very subtle nod in agreement with herself and Sophie.

"I mean I guess so, but still, I should have picked up on that a little sooner," Sophie says, struggling with the idea that she didn't notice, and she should have.

"It's okay. Let's not add more stress to all the stress that we already have been dealing with," Sydney says, smiling.

As they set the table and talk between themselves, they don't even notice that Emma has already taken the Stromboli out of the oven and sat it on the stove top.

"Mmm, dinner suddenly smells absolutely amazing," Sophie shares as she takes in a deep breath.

"Ah, Sophie," Sydney says, trying to get her attention.

"Yeah, Syd?"

"Look behind you!" Sydney quickly instructs.

"Well, that would explain why I was able to smell it so much more." Sophie laughs as she slowly walks closer to the stove and takes another deep breath. "Now don't you whip me, Miss Em, I am just getting close enough to get a bigger, better nose full of all that amazing goodness," Sophie says, moving ever so slowly as she takes another deep breath and watches Emma to make sure she doesn't try to towel-whip her this time.

"Silly young one. I won't towel-whip ya," Em laughs. "But how's about someone gets some glasses from the cupboard and drinks from the fridge while I cut this to serve?"

"I'll get the cups," Sophie yells.

"Then I will get the drinks," Sydney adds as they scatter quickly and carefully to get the items needed and get seated at the table. Sydney looks at Sophie and jokingly states, "Well, we know one thing that never gets by you!"

Sophie looks at Sydney, puzzled, and asks, "Oh yeah, what's that, Syd?"

"Food! You just have a nose for food." Sydney chuckles.

"Maybe food should be my sister then because I can keep a better eye on that than her," Sophie sadly states.

"I'm sorry, Sophie. That was meant to be a joke. I didn't mean to poke fun and make you feel guilty," Sydney replies, not understanding why Sophie is taking this so hard.

"I'm sorry, Syd. I know that you were joking, but deep down, it doesn't excuse my lack for attention to my sister. I'm supposed to oversee her especially when we are away from home." Sophie feels horrible as she hangs her head yet again still in disbelief with herself.

"Well, if I must say so myself, it's not entirely your fault, Sophie, dear. I was the one who was taking care of her while y'all were out at the track. I should have said something myself to you. But I didn't know that she had not texted you and left, you know. Not that it was her responsibility or anything like that. I guess I just let it slip my mind as well, just assuming or maybe taking for granted that she would have done that. So, it's not like you are the only one to blame here, Sophie," Emma thoughtfully states.

"Really, Em, no one is to blame, but what we can do from here on out is when one knows something like this, let's try to do better and let others involved know. I'm not saying that we are all perfect and gonna remember, but let's try. Even if some of us forgetful people." Sydney scans the room, looking at each of them and smiling. "And by some, I mean all of us. Have to make a note somehow like on paper or a text to ourselves. Cool?" Sydney asks.

"Now that I can agree with Syd, I love you, bestie!" Sophie says, reaching for Sydney, looking for a hug.

"Come here," Sydney states, reaching back.

"Yes, what a great idea, Sydney. Okay, now I do not know where the boys are, but what do y'all say about us eating a while?" Emma wonders.

"Well, let's see. If we can rally up the boys before we dig in, just to be fair, at least that way we can say we tried, right?" Sophie says, excusing herself from the table to go shout out for Obee and Parker.

"Okay, bestie, but hurry!" Sydney exclaims.

As Sophie gets up and walks around the corner, Sydney can hear her open the door to step out and shout out to the boys as she looks at Emma with a worried look.

"What's with the look, young one? Is everything okay?" Emma asks, concerned.

"Remind me later, and I will chat with you, Em. I don't want to have this conversation right now." Sydney tries to shut Emma down as fast as she asked her what was wrong. As she hears Sophie on her way back as she shuts the front door. "So, any luck, bestie? Did you even see them out there anywhere?" Sydney sure hopes so.

"Yes, I got Parker's attention. He waved and gestured one sec as he went to get Obee. So even as hangry as I am, I think out of respect, we should wait," Sophie requests.

"Well, if Sophie can be patient enough to wait then I have to say that I agree. Plus, dad would really appreciate the gesture." Sydney proudly states.

"We shall wait," Emma states.

As they sit there to wait, Emma observes Sophie acting more different than normal. She wonders what's up with her and suspects that this is why Sydney wants to talk with her. She would love for her to spend the night again but figures she will wait to say anything to see what gets said at the dinner table. Maybe she can get a few minutes with her to see if she is okay and possibly needing someone to talk to. As Emma thinks about Sophie, she is suddenly distracted when she hears the front door as Parker and Obee come in for dinner.

"Hurry and wash up, boys. There are famished young ladies in here who are a bit tired of waiting to eat this wonderful meal," Emma quickly tells them.

"We're on it, Em, and little ladies," Obee respectfully replies.

"If they are that hungry, Em, I wouldn't be objected to someone saying prayers a while. But just this time," Parker suggests so they can eat sooner because he is starving too.

"Ladies, which of you would like the honor?" Emma asks. "I will, Em." Sydney quickly jumps at the chance.

"Dear Lord,

Please bless this family and all who grace us with their presence today, tomorrow, and in the days to come. Please help us to remember not to forget important things that need to be said or done for ourselves and others. Also please continue to keep my family and friends in perfect health so we may have the pleasure of their love with us daily.

Amen"

"Beautifully said, sweetheart," Parker says as he enters the kitchen and kisses Sydney on the head. "Emma, dinner smells amazing as always." Parker professes as he sits, and they all take a serving and dig in.

"So has anyone else heard the weather report for the next couple of days?" Obee wonders.

"No, but please tell us what you heard, Obee," Parker insists, knowing that Obee doesn't usually say anything unless he has a concern.

"Well, it's supposed to be extra hot and steamy. Apparently, there's an early heatwave headed our way. And you know what heat waves and hot and steamy bring us, boss," Obee reports with hesitation and caution.

"Thanks, Obee. I guess we should be on extra high alert then. Let's make sure that all gates and fences are sturdy and secure," Parker instructs.

"Well, hopefully it doesn't rain on my birthday! I was thinking about asking to have some friends over to have a small party outside," Sydney says, doubtful that it may even happen now.

Sophie starts to feel more anxious than normal and decides to change the subject. "Miss Emma, this tastes as amazing as it smells. I think I may have a new favorite now," Sophie states as she smiles.

"Well, I am flattered that you love it. It's been a favorite of Sydney's for years and Ivy's too," Emma says proudly.

"It was definitely worth waiting for! You just have to give me the recipe to make it. Hopefully it's not too hard," Sophie exclaims.

"I can do that, and no, it's super easy just like lasagna but it's a boli and the cheese is your noodles. I will write it down for ya after dinner," Emma assures her as she whispers across the table, "but don't let me forget." Emma winks at her.

After dinner, Parker, and Obee head out to start checking fences and gates, while the girls clean up the dinner mess.

"Well, I guess I best get going home soon," Sophie says so as not to overstay her welcome.

"You really wanna go home already, bestie?" Sydney asks, not wanting her to leave, but she knows it will give her time to talk with Emma about her.

"Yes, I am sure. Besides, we have to open the boutique tomorrow, don't we?" Sophie again says, trying to change the subject.

"Oh, man. I guess you are right, and if you were to stay, I am positive that we probably wouldn't sleep. We would probably sit up all night just CC-ing!" Sydney says, trying to be clever.

"CC-ing?" Emma asks curiously.

"Yeah, chatting and chilling!" Sydney says, laughing.

"Makes sense. So what time were you thinking about heading out, Sophie?" asks Emma.

"Honestly, the sooner, the better. Not that I don't want to be here but just so I have some time to shower and wind down at home so I can sleep," Sophie quickly rattles off.

"Okay, well, let's go now so we can get back and relax a bit too," Emma declares.

"Miss Emma?" Sophie calmly says.

"Yes, Sophie," Emma quickly responds.

"The recipe?" Sophie slightly pauses, waiting for Emma's response.

"Ah yes, let me just make a note, and I will sit down, and do it when we come back, so it will be here for you when you come over next, or better yet, I will bring it with me tomorrow. How does that sound?" Emma offers.

"Perfect! Okay, I just have to grab my things, and I will be ready," Sophie says as she takes off upstairs. Just as quickly as she made her way up the stairs, she is coming back down, and she is ready to go.

They all make their way out to the car and head to Sophie's home. It's a quiet ride there. As they pull in, Emma says, "Here you be, young one. We shall see you tomorrow. Do you need a ride in the morning?"

"Thanks. I have to ask my mom what her plans are, but I will let you know. Love ya, bestie." Sophie hops out of the car and starts to head for the front door.

Sydney quickly says out the window after Sophie, "Love you too, bestie! See ya tomorrow." Sophie darts into her house like she didn't even hear a word she said.

"What was that just now? Correct me if I am wrong, but it seems like she is avoiding you, Syd," Emma says, concerned.

"Nope, you aren't wrong. I noticed that too! That's what I wanted to talk with you about. It's her behavior lately," Sydney says as Emma backs out the driveway, and they head home.

CHAPTER 12
Storm Out of Nowhere

As Emma and Sydney make their way home, it starts to get darker, not because of the time of day but because there seems to be a storm rolling in. As they ride back with the windows open, Sydney can hear off in the distance a slight rumble of thunder.

"Wow, that was quick," Sydney observes.

"What's that, Syd?" Emma asks.

"Obee said we may be in for some storms. I wasn't expecting them this early."

"Well, even though it is beautiful here now, if what we are supposed to get is hotter by just enough, the two atmospheres combining can make storms too!" Emma says, knowing from experience how the storms seem to be.

"I pray that it doesn't get too bad before Dad and Obee have time to check all the fences and gates." Just as Sydney finishes her comment, a bright streak of lightning cracks across the sky. "Wow! Em, that was super bright!" Sydney exclaims.

"That is for sure. Hopefully it doesn't get into full-on storm mode till after we get home." Emma prays,

"Lord,

I am sorry I am praying with my eyes wide open, but I must see to drive. I ask that you make this storm hold off for a while yet so we may get home safely, and Parker and Obee can get out of the field before it hits.

Amen"

"Emma, I am sure that Dad and Obee are seeing this too, but I will text them to make sure." As quickly as Sydney finishes her statement, lightning flashes, and cracks across the sky again as another streak goes from the clouds to the ground.

Sydney: Dad, are you and Obee, okay? Are you seeing this storm headed in?

"I messaged Dad. I will give him a few to respond," Sydney says as she gets more scared and practically jumps outta her seat as more lightning flashes and cracks across the sky.

"Someone's a little edgy, aren't they?" Emma picks with Sydney to try to loosen her up a bit.

"Yeah, I guess so. I never did really like storms. It becomes more apparent to me with everyone we have," Sydney says as she seems like she is miles away.

"Good thing is that we are almost home then," Emma says as she gets interrupted by Sydney's phone ringing.

"Hello?" Sydney says, answering her phone.

"Yes, we are good. We are almost home," Sydney tells the person on the phone.

"Yep, okay. Love you too, Dad! See you very soon!" Sydney says as she hangs up the phone.

"Ah, so it was Parker?" Emma guesses.

"Yep! He said that he and Obee are headed to the house. The wind seems to be picking up in the back field where they were." Sydney passes along what Parker had said as Emma tries to remain strong, but Sydney can sense her fear.

Sydney reaches over to hold Emma's hand to not only comfort Emma but herself as they pull into the lane and head toward the house. Emma parks as close as she can to the house.

"Quickly, let's get inside before the storm hits," Emma calmly tries to instruct Sydney.

They no more than get inside when the skies just open up and start dropping buckets of rain. Sydney looks out the door in hopes that she can see her dad and Obee.

"Syd, please come away from the door. Come sit in the living room with me. I have some drinks and snacks. Maybe we can play a game of cards, or something till this storm lets up," Emma suggests.

"In a minute, Em. I am watching for Dad and Obee. I want to make sure that they are okay," Sydney says just as the sky lights up, and she can see Parker and Obee in the stable waiting to make a dart for the house. Sydney starts screaming, "Emma, I see them, I see them!"

Emma quickly makes her way to the door where Sydney is. "Calm down, Syd. Just be ready to open the door when they come running," Emma advises Sydney.

By now, the rain is almost coming down as if it is sideways. "Emma, look at that rain when it lights up out there. It's like it's sideways. Is it really that windy out, Em?" Sydney says, worrying about how her dad and Obee will get inside safely.

"Usually, it's because of high wind. Do you see it dancing across the driveway in, like, sheets?" Emma asks Sydney.

Sydney waits for the next batch of lightning so she too can see the rain dancing on the driveway. Suddenly, the sky lights up, and they hear a loud crack and a pop, and the lights go out. It startles Sydney, and she screams out of reaction, as Emma jumps and holds tight onto Sydney.

"Oh look, Syd!" Emma quickly points out as the sky lights up again. "Quick, get the door for your dad and Obee while I go and try to find some towels here in this darkness, as they are headed for the house," Emma states as she carefully heads for the bathroom.

"I'm on it!" Sydney says as she opens the door up and quickly cheers on her dad and Obee to hurry up.

Parker and Obee come running as fast as they can splashing in the huge water puddles, as they head toward the house in the direction of Sydney's pleas to hurry. By the time they hit the steps, there's another bright flash of lightning and loud crack of thunder! The force of the thunder almost seemingly shoves Parker and Obee into the open door where Sydney was standing while directing them into the house.

"Quick, shut the door and get back Sydney," Parker insists.

"Here, you boys are drenched," Emma says, handing them towels. "Quickly, dry off, and let's get you into some dry clothes before you catch pneumonia."

"We are lucky that we didn't drown on the way in here. This is the heaviest rainstorm we have had in quite a while!" Parker declares.

"I think the water on the driveway had to be at least six inches deep," Obee adds.

"I was just telling Syd that we should all come into the living room and have a snack and play a game of cards or something to that nature. But now I have to dig out some candles so we can even see. Give me a minute I will be right back." Emma pauses for a moment then turns to Parker. "Also, could someone please go make sure everything is okay with the electrical box? There was a crack and pop just as the lights went out that didn't sound very good."

"Sure, Emma. Do you have a flashlight?" Parker asks.

"Yes, out here in the kitchen by the candles. I will get it for you," Emma offers.

"I will come with Emma," Parker says as he accompanies her to the kitchen.

"Are you good, Syd? I would like to go help Parker," Obee says, checking with Sydney to see if she needs anything.

I'm good. Go ahead, Obee," Sydney says.

As Obee heads for the kitchen, he yells ahead, "Get me one too please!" Obee disappears into the darkness on his way to the kitchen. Sydney decides to check up on Sophie and her family.

Sydney: Hey bestie! How is everything over at your place? Is it storming there yet?

While Sydney waits, she hears Emma, Obee, and her dad coming from the kitchen.

"I will go light some candles, and Sydney and I will wait for you and Obee in the living room," Emma assures Parker.

"All right. Just go and sit tight. We will be back shortly. Syd, please go in the room with Emma?" Parker asks Sydney.

"I will, Dad," Sydney states.

"Now please, I want to make sure that you are safe," Parker instructs her.

"Okay, I am going jeez," Sydney says as she heads for the living room. "Dad acts like I am like three or something. I am inside I'm safe." Sydney whines.

"Young one, he just worries for you. And with this weather, he is just stressed, so please just overlook his attitude and bossiness right now. Come on, let's have a snack and get a card game together for when they return," Emma politely suggests.

"Oh, okay." Sydney reluctantly sits by the coffee table to pick a game to play.

"So, let's see. We have Go Fish, Uno, Old Maid, or we can play with a regular deck of cards. What's it gonna be?" Emma wonders. "How about Uno?" Sydney states as she gets a message.

Lucas: Hey how are you? I was wondering if you had a few minutes to talk.

Sydney: Not right now Lucas I am sorry.

Lucas: Oh, ok no problem may be later?

Sydney: No, it's just, well aren't you under a massive storm right now?

Page **121** of **374**

Lucas: No but I can hear a bunch thunder. So, ok I didn't realize I will let ya go.

Sydney: Ok cool cause I have to try to save my battery because we lost power here ttys.

Lucas: Cool no problem ttys2.

"Someone seems like they wanna chat," Emma points out.

"Yeah, it was Lucas. But I explained that we were under this storm and that we lost power, so he let me go. I wish I could get a response from Sophie. I wonder if it's storming there?" Sydney wonders.

"I'm sure it is," Emma says.

"I honestly don't know because it's not at Lucas's house," Sydney tells Emma.

"Oh, really? Huh, guess he's lucky then," Emma tries to assure Sydney.

Just then, Sydney gets another message.

Sophie: Hey sorry I was in the shower. What's up?

Sydney: I was just checking in to see if y'all were under the storm right now?

Sophie: It's just rainy here at the moment.

Sydney: Ok well you all are ok then so I will let you go gotta save my battery our power is out.

Sophie: Ok yes, we are good. Hope you get your power back soon.

Sydney: Love ya bestie cya 2moro

Sophie: Ok love you too bye

Sydney waits for a moment to see if Sophie responds any further since she didn't make mention of seeing her tomorrow. She waits and waits. *Well, I guess she will be in tomorrow,* Sydney thinks to herself.

Emma sees the expression on Sydney's face and asks, "Is everything good?"

"I sure hope so," Sydney quietly responds.

Just then, Parker and Obee come into the living room. "Well, ladies, I am sorry to say it must be something out at the pole or transformer somewhere because we couldn't find anything here," Parker informs them. "So, what game will we be playing?"

"Sydney picked Uno," Emma tells the boys.

"Ah, one of Ivy's favorites. Okay, well, get prepared for a butt-whooping, ladies." Parker antagonizes.

"You're on, Dad!" Sydney says, taking the offer. "What are the stakes?"

"Oh, you wanna make bets?" Parker suggests.

"A fair game with a small wager is always fun!" Sydney playfully suggests.

"Okay, let's say winner gets outta chores for a day. Loser has to do winners chores?" Parker says, laying out the rules of winner and loser.

"Seems fair. I'm game," Sydney adds.

"What about Emma and I?" Obee asks.

"Depends do you want to be part of the wager?" Parker asks.

"To be fair, we should if we are playing," Emma adds.

"I is game if you is, Emma," Obee states.

"Okay! I'm in. Let's see where this goes." Emma chuckles.

Parker shuffles the cards and deals them out to everyone. Before he is ready to stop dealing, he asks for everyone to count their cards to make sure they each have seven. They all nod that they do, so he places the rest of the cards face down and then flips the top one over to make a discard pile.

"Since I dealt, the person to my left gets to make the first move, so that would be you, Emma. Go ahead. It's game on!" Parker says like a game show announcer.

They are playing a hard game throwing out a lot of draw fours, skips, reverses, which seems to stretch on forever. Then suddenly...

"Uno!" Emma yells out.

"Someone has to lay a draw four or skip down for her," Parker quickly shouts.

Sydney and Obee get into a reverse war to try to lessen the number of cards that they are holding before Emma can drop her last card, and one of them ends up having to do her chores.

Finally, it gets reversed to Sydney, and she lays a skip card, which luckily skips Emma and goes to Parker. Which now puts Sydney and Parker in a skip war. Parker skips Obee, and Sydney skips Emma. Parker uses his last skip, and now, the ball is in Sydney's court.

She has three cards left, none of which is a skip or extra draw card. She has to think very carefully which card to lay that isn't the same as Emma's number because those odds are a lot higher than color. She has a one-in-four chance of laying the color that Emma has as her last card but a 1 in 10 that it's the same number. As she closes her eyes to let fate pick her card, she hears.

Emma humming.

"Tick, tick, tick. Time is ticking away. Sydney, you have to lay a card," Emma says as she hopes she lays one that puts her out.

"Yeah, yeah, I know! I am letting fate pick for me!" Sydney exclaims.

"Syd, the kid! Pick wisely," Obee says as the anticipation rises.

"Okay, it's fate making the call. As I lay a blue four!" Sydney says as she lays the card down blindly so she can't see what Emma lays till she hears Obee and her dad's reactions.

"Amen!" Emma states as she lays her last card, a yellow four!

"What! No! It can't be!" Parker exclaims wildly.

Obee claps and screams, "Whoo-hoo!"

Sydney opens her eyes to see that Emma has laid her last card as she looks around the table to see who has the most cards out of her and the guys. By the looks of it, her dad has the most.

"So, let's count and see who has the most for their total," Sydney requests.

As she quickly gets her total, she shouts out, "I have 5 from a 0 and a 5 card. Obee, what do you have?" Sydney asks.

"Well, Syd, I have a 3 and a 7, which makes 10 for me. Guess that just leaves Parker. What's ya got, boss?" Obee asks, hoping Parker has a bigger total.

"I hope you all like takeout, and you can be glad we only said for one day's worth of chores. So, my numbers are 2, 4, 6, and 8,

Page **125** of **374**

which comes to 20," Parker says as he then decides to ask the group, "Just how soon do I have to start these daily chores?"

"Good question, Parker. I think we should let that up to the winner. Dontcha think, Syd?" Obee asks.

"I think it's fair," Sydney responds.

Parker then looks at Emma with a "be easy" look to give him a light duty day. Not that any day is a light duty day for Emma. "Well, Em, what's the day that you would like for me to do your chores for you?" Parker kindly asks.

"I was thinking how about tomorrow? Mondays are my least busy days," Emma says, taking it easy on him since he too has many busy, chore-filled days.

"I will take it. Since I have an extra-long day before me tomorrow, I guess I better hit the sack so I can get plenty of rest. Good night, everyone," Parker says as he slips away to his room to sleep.

"Obee, since it's still storming out, why don't you just sleep here in the house for the night?" Emma offers.

"I think I will take you up on the offer. Thank you, Emma." Obee fixes a spot on the couch as Sydney gets up to head to her room too.

"Good night, Obee and Em," Sydney says as she yawns.

"Good night, Syd the kid!" Obee replies.

"Good night, young one," Emma says as she heads off into the dark.

"Obee, would you mind if I slept down here with you on the other couch?" Sydney asks, worried about being three floors up in a storm all by herself.

"Sure, have sweet dreams, kiddo," Obee says as he rolls over and is almost instantly asleep.

CHAPTER 13
Storms Persist

Even sleeping downstairs in a more secluded room, Sydney lies there throughout the night, tossing and turning as the lightning flashes, and seemingly lights up the whole entire room, and not long after the lightning, the thunder cracks and spooks her almost right out of her skin. She lies there trying so hard to get some sleep. While thinking about everything that has happened over the past few days.

She continues lying there, catching short bursts of Obee's snores in between the rolls and cracks of thunder. Suddenly...

Her heart is racing, and she is having trouble breathing almost like she's out of breath. Very close nearby, she hears heavy breathing and starts to feel warm air blowing on her from somewhere. *Wait, no, that's not just air. It's...no, it can't be! Or is it?* she thinks to herself.

Out of nowhere, she hears the breathing turn more into a slight growl. *What is this? Where am I?* she continues to think to herself.

Then she decides to quietly call out to Obee.

"Obee?" She pauses for a moment then says, "Obee, wake up!"

She feels around, looking for the flashlight. She can't seem to find it. *It was right here on the table*; she thinks to herself. *Wait!* She continues to reach and feel around. *Where's the table?* she wonders to herself. *Wait. Where's the couch?*

"Obee! Where are you, please? I need you!" she screams as she decides the best option is to run. Just run for her life and pray to God she can find Obee.

"Obee, where are you!" She lets out a bloodcurdling scream. Next thing she trips and feels as though she is falling and falling. With a thud, she hits the ground or what surface she falls on to and has the wind knocked out of her.

She lies there for a moment, trying to remember how to breathe without all this pain. She starts gasping for air when she feels like everything is trembling and shaking. She hears a faint voice over her heart racing and her gasps for air.

"Sydney, wake up!"

She tries to scream out, but she can't get sound to come out. It's like she lost her voice when she had the wind knocked out of her. The shaking continues as she hears a voice again.

"Syd! Syd the kid! Come on, come back to me! It's Obee!" he screams.

Obee, she thinks to herself, *it's Obee!*

Again, she tries to call out. Nothing! *Come on, you can do it. You are strong. Just scream with all you got!* she thinks to herself.

Determined to get help and let Obee know she's wherever she is, she tries one more time to scream "Obee!" Just as she does, Obee shakes her, and she wakes up!

"Obee! Wait, where am I?" Sydney asks, puzzled.

"You are right here where you were. You are...well, now you are on the floor," Obee pauses for a moment so as not to seem like he is laughing at her but chuckling because she ended up on the floor kicking and wailing like she was drowning or something.

"But you were up there on the couch. You must have fallen off in your sleep. Somehow the coffee table got way other there. Not sure if you kicked it there or if when you fell off the couch it flew over there." Obee very colorfully describes his version of how it happened.

"Well, that explains a little of what I experienced in my dream." Sydney starts to say when Obee interrupts her.

"What do you mean by that, Syd?" He patiently awaits her response.

"I felt like I fell," Sydney says as she looks from the couch to the floor, "but for what seemed like a much longer fall than the couch to the floor." Sydney recalls this from her dream.

"That must have been some dream. I tried and tried to wake you. I was starting to get worried," Obee professes to her.

"Wait, Obee, what time is it? Is it still storming?" Sydney wonders.

"The storm seems to have let up a little for now, but I don't think it's nearly over just yet. And as for a time, it's like 6:30 a.m." Obee smiles.

"Wow, where did the night go? My dream only seemed like a few minutes long, and it's been hours since I last looked at the time," Sydney painfully recalls.

"Well, what time do you need to be at the Boutique?" Obee asks.

"Not till 9:00 a.m. Why do you ask?" she wonders.

"Maybe you can get a little more sleep?" Obee just kinda throws it out there.

"I could, but I don't know if I can even get back to sleep. I must be up soon anyways. Maybe I will go out and see how the horses are doing after all the noise last night," Sydney states as she gets up and goes to walk away.

"Do you want me to come with Syd?" Obee quickly asks.

"If you want to," Sydney replies.

Obee jumps off the couch and runs after Sydney. As he catches up with her, they put on some boots and go walking outside. There are leaves and flower petals all over the place. As they near the barn, they notice small branches scattered about as well.

"That must have been some storm last night, Obee. Just look at all this debris everywhere," Sydney says in astonishment. "I can't wrap my head around the true strength of wind and rain, two of the most destructive weather forces out there." "Agreed, Syd!" Obee states.

They reach the barn, and everything seems to be okay.

"Help me, Obee. Let's feed them since we are out here. This way, we are kinda giving Dad a hand," Sydney suggests.

"Yeah, his hands are gonna be full today with having to do all Emma's stuff and his." Obee chuckles.

"Hey there, SOT. How are you, sweetheart? I hope you weren't scared last night," Sydney says as she pets and rubs SOT's neck and forehead. "You are such a good girl. I pray these storms stop and don't get too bad today and in the upcoming days. Okay, I have to get going. I will see you later. Love you, SOT!" Sydney says as she moves over to PB Cup.

"Hey there, Cups! How are ya?" Sydney gives a little loving to PB Cup and moves on down the line till she has shared a little love with each horse.

"Okay, Obee, they are fed. Everything seems to be okay, so I need to head in to get ready. Have a great day and be safe. I will get with you when I get back," Sydney says as she walks away toward the house.

"Okay, have a great day at the Boutique! See ya later. Tell everyone I said hello," Obee expresses to her.

"Got it, Obee. Consider it done!" Sydney says as she rounds the corner of the barn and disappears.

Sydney quickly heads into the house and is about to go up to her room when she hears Emma shout.

"Sydney, is that you?" Emma requests.

"Yes, Em. I am headed to get ready," Sydney quickly states as she takes off up the stairs in a hurry.

She gets to the top of the stairs at the second floor when Emma shouts out again, "Sydney?"

Sydney stops and scoffs, "Yes, Em, what's up?"

"Nothing. I am sorry. I will get with you when you are done," Emma apologizes.

Sydney continues up the stairs to her room as she mumbles under her breath, "Ugh, why is it when I am in a hurry, I keep finding so many hurdles to get over?"

She quickly gathers her things for the day, and she gets a shower. A few minutes later, she returns downstairs.

"I am ready, Em!" Sydney calls out. "I'm gonna see if Sophie needs a ride."

Sydney: Hey bestie! Good morning! Do you need a ride this morning?

"Emma, do we have any English muffins?" Sydney asks. "Em?" "What's all the ruckus out here?" Parker asks as he comes out to get started for the day.

"I was wondering if we had any English muffins. But Em must be showering because she has yet to answer me," Sydney says as though she is irritated but understanding.

"Well, I have breakfast this morning, so I can get you whatever you like. So, what will it be?" Parker asks as he heads into the kitchen and puts on Emma's apron.

"I said I wanted an English muffin," Sydney snaps back.

"Down killer! I heard you but wanted to make sure that there wasn't something else you would have rather preferred. Why so snappy today?" Parker asks, knowing that this isn't normal for her.

"Sorry, Dad. It's just I haven't been sleeping well, and last night was no different," Sydney states as she yawns.

"Well, last night was understandable. I mean it was storming pretty bad out," Parker adds.

Sydney just looks at him with a glare. "Really? No, the storm had nothing to do with it. I just think I'm overly stressed or something. Though I do not feel stressed. I am irritated, and I don't know why," Sydney scoffs. "Or maybe it's because I can't sleep, and I want an English muffin!" She raises her voice in a demanding way.

"Did I hear someone wanting an English muffin?" Emma says a little too cheerfully as she makes her way into the kitchen.

"It's about time!" Sydney demands.

"Ouch! Someone must have gotten up on the wrong side of the bed this morning," Emma sternly comments.

"Sorry, Em, I didn't sleep well last night, and I just want an English muffin," Sydney says, trying to be less demanding.

"Again, child? Well, the storm..." Emma starts to say when Parker quickly interrupts her.

"Ah no, that's not it, she said," intervenes Parker.

"Well, it was..." Emma tries continuing when Parker interrupts her yet again.

"Yes, Emma. We know it was bad, but she has already stated that the storm had nothing to do with it. So, do we have English muffins? So, I can get this beautiful young lady of mine her breakfast that she would like to have," Parker asks to try to make Sydney happy if even for a few minutes while she eats it.

"Yes, they are in the bottom shelf in the fridge. She likes strawberry jam too!" Emma adds, trying to be helpful.

"Sorry, guys. I didn't mean or want to snap. But I just feel ugh!" Sydney starts to say as she slumps down on a chair to wait for the muffin. "Yes, Dad, please, strawberry jam. Thanks!"

"One English muffin with strawberry jam coming right up." Parker quickly zips around the kitchen making her muffin. "Toasted I assume?" he politely asks.

"You would assume correct," Sydney responds.

"Okay, one strawberry toasted muffin coming up in five, four, three, two, and one!" Parker says as he finishes it and sets it down in front of Sydney.

"Would you like a drink, madam?" Parker asks as if he is a waiter.

"Just milk please," Sydney says a little nicer.

"Ah, right away, as you wish." Parker quickly gets her a glass of cold milk. "Your delicious tall glass bone juice."

"Thanks, Dad," Sydney says laughing.

"Food heals the beast, and the young lady emerges from within," Parker jokes.

Just then, Emma sits down.

"And for you, senior madam?" Parker continues to pretend to be a silly waiter.

"Actually, I think I will have what she is having please," Emma tells him while trying not to laugh.

"Okay, one strawberry toasted muffin with a tall glass of cold bone juice. Coming right up," Parker states.

As he gets the muffins, drops them into the toaster, gets a plate and a glass, and sits them on the counter just as the toaster pops, and he grabs the muffins throws them in the air and catches them on the plate. He butters the muffins then applies the jam. He lays them on the plate with a few sliced strawberries. Then he grabs the plated muffins and glass of milk then quickly turns to Emma.

"Your order, ma'am. Enjoy, madam," Parker says as he takes a bow.

"I shall, sir. It looks amazing!" Emma says as she takes a bite.

"You are hired, good sir!"

Parker says, puzzled, "Hired?"

"Yes! You make breakfast for me and my young lady every day!" Emma repeats.

Parker tries changing the subject by saying, "Don't you ladies gotta be somewhere soon?"

Emma looks at her watch and shrieks, "Oh, my young one, we have gotta get this show on the road."

Emma gets up from the table and grabs her purse and fishes out her keys. "Good, sir, we must be going. Please keep in touch today, and as you for, little lady, we must get the pedal to the metal."

"I will text Sophie and make sure that she and Eliza have a ride," Sydney offers.

As they head out the door, Emma says, "Good thinking."

    Sydney: Do you ladies need a ride this morning?

Just about the time they reach the car, Parker is making his way out the front door. "Please be safe, ladies. I look forward to spending some time with you ladies when you get home."

"You too, Dad!" Sydney says as she climbs in the car.

"Later, Parker." Emma quickly says as she too climbs in the car, and they drive off.

Sydney watches her dad walk toward the barn and disappear as they get further out the lane. When she can no longer see the barn, she says to Emma, "Do you think that Dad and Obee got around to all the fences?"

"I sure hope so," says Emma.

"Yeah, me too!" Sydney says, hoping that if they didn't, that they don't have much more to do. "Look at that sky, Em. Looks bad!" There is a hint of fear in her voice.

"Everything will be just fine, Syd," Emma reassures her.

"I sure hope so," Sydney says with a ton of doubt.

        Sophie: We are running behind we will just meet you there.

"Well, that's a relief!" Sydney says with a deep breath.

"What's that, Syd? Was that Sophie just now?" Emma asks.

"Yep, sure was. She said her mom is dropping them off because they're running behind too!" Sydney says while she gets her key ready to open the shop. As they pull up to the shop, they can see Lucas is already there waiting for them.

He waves as he sees them pull up.

"Seriously, I am gonna have to get you a key if you keep beating me here." Sydney chuckles.

"Works for me. I would be happy to get here early and get things ready for the day," Lucas admits.

"Careful. I may hold you to that," Sydney promises.

As they walk into the shop together, Sydney asks, "So, Lucas, how was the storm at your place last night?"

"We just had a little light rain. Nutting too messy. How about you and out your way?" He asks Sydney.

"Other than the power we lost, I guess it wasn't too bad. We had a bunch of lightning and thunder."

"Well, they say we are in for some more bad storms today as well. I just hope it doesn't get bad. They say it's supposed to be worse than yesterday," Lucas reports sadly.

"Well, I sure hope Dad and Obee can get through all the fences to make sure that they are strong and sturdy," Sydney says hopefully.

"I am sure they will have a challenge ahead of them, but your dad and Obee are a great team together especially when there is an urgent situation such as this," Emma reassures the kids.

"I know, but I am just worried about the horses, and if it's bad enough, I am worried that they could get hurt or how bad could they get hurt? If they get out, where would they go? If they got too far away, would they know how to get back? Would they even come back?" Sydney questions as she seems to be more anxious with each question.

Emma notices her anxiety level rising and tries to calm her down. "Sydney, breathe, young one, before you pass out!" Emma states as she puts her hands on Sydney's shoulders. "Just breathe. Please, you are getting Lucas and I worked up now. How about we just keep our minds on the Boutique for now and pray that everything is safe and holds up well throughout the storm? Okay, can we do this?" Emma asks Sydney.

"Yes! I-I mean we can do this! We got this! Let's rock this joint with God's love and peace and hope it pours out the doors and goes home with everyone today! Let's get it spread across town!" Sydney cheers on.

"I'm all for it! One for all and all for the love of God!" Lucas blurts out.

Emma and Sydney both simultaneously respond with "Amen!" as they all laugh.

They each quickly move about the store, getting last little things tidied up and ready to open. As Sydney opens the blinds, she sees Allison pull up with Sophie and Eliza.

"Sophie and Eliza are here!" she shouts from the front of the Boutique.

"I will go let them in," Lucas says as he quickly runs to the back door.

Eliza comes running in all happy and hyper. Sophie comes in with Lucas as Allison follows them in.

"Hello, good morning, everyone!" Allison says, trying make eye contact with Sydney, and Lucas as she waves and looks for Emma.

Emma comes out of the back office when she hears Allison and says, "Hello, y'all! How is everyone?"

Sophie pipes up first. "Good, I guess."

"You guess? Oh well, okay. By the end of the day, we will see how you are feeling. It's early, and that can often make us feel not so eh. But we are boosting God's love here today in hopes of keeping the nasty storm clouds far away. Or at least not as bad."

"I'll second that one, Emma. Last night was bad enough," Allison tells them.

"Yeah, we didn't even have electricity for most of the night," Sydney adds.

"Wow, really, Syd? I betcha were really scared, huh?" Eliza asks.

"No, we played cards and sat by candlelight till we went to bed," Sydney tells Eliza.

"Well, the reason I came in today was because I have a showing. Actually, two showings later, and I do not think I will be able to pick up the girls when y'all are done here," Allison starts to say.

Emma quickly stops her by holding up her hand and then a finger. "No worries. I will see that they get home." Then she turns to Sophie and Eliza and asks, "Do you girls have a key in case your dad isn't home?"

"I have mine!" Eliza quickly shows it to Emma. "Mine is a necklace so I don't lose it," Eliza proudly states.

"Okay, that's all I need to know." Emma turns to Allison and says, "Definitely not a problem. We can get them there. Good luck with your showings. I hope you get two awesome offers."

"That definitely would be a gift from God!" Allison says as she waves for the girls to come over to her.

They move closer to Allison, and she hugs the girls and tells them she loves them.

"Bye, Mommy!" Eliza says as she takes off running for the kids' corner.

"Okay, before we open the doors, let's do a quick prayer. I just feel as though today we need it more than ever. Who would like to pray for us today?" Emma asks.

"I would love to, Emma!" Lucas says volunteering to pray for the day. "Can I have us all hold hands?" Lucas reaches out to hold Sydney and Sophie's hands. Once everyone is holding hands, Lucas starts the prayer:

"Dear Lord,

Please bless everyone who enters the Boutique today, the Ashcraft's, the Aboott's, the Devinshire's, and everyone in this town. Please be easy with these storms. We know that we need rain, but we don't need the fancy sparks show that comes with it. Please also keep the horses at Sydney's ranch safe. Do not let no harm come to them. Thank you.

Amen

P.S. Lord,

Please bless the Boutique with awesome sales today so we may continue to send funds to cancer research and make a cure to stomp it out for good!

Amen"

"Wow, Lucas, what a beautiful prayer! Okay, let's roll out the carpet and welcome everyone in," Emma says in a sweet but very chipper tone.

As the day goes by, the weather seems to be holding off. Sales are great! Everyone seems to be very happy. Even Sophie seems to have come around a bit.

"Well, today is absolutely spectacular!" Emma states as she comes out to walk around the floor for a bit.

"I know, right!" Sydney cheerfully adds. "Everything is just perfect!" Sydney says grinning ear to ear.

"Just remember that if you are having a good day or having a bad day, tomorrow is another day! It's a chance to start over and have new adventures." Emma quotes one of Grandad Jack Jones's sayings.

"So true, Miss Emma!" Lucas chimes in, smiling.

Now do you ever just wonder if God likes playing pranks just as much as we do? Well, if he does, he has perfect timing. Sydney no more than mentions how great the day is when out of nowhere, the sky just opens up and it begins pouring cats and dogs. Lucas runs to the window as Sophie and Sydney follow.

"Wow, so much for the perfect day!" Sydney not-so-happily states.

"See, it changed already, so counting your chickens before they hatch is also another great saying that Granddad Jack Jones liked to use."

Crack! Boom!

"Yes, I hope that was a strike!" Eliza screams with excitement as she looks as though she is grabbing something invisible and pulling it in towards her.

Sophie notices everyone with odd looks on their faces.

Sophie chuckles and whispers, "Mom told her that when she hears the thunder, it's just God bowling so that she doesn't get scared."

"Well, that's awesome. Because a child being afraid of thunder is not good," Emma says.

"Yeah, it beats her screaming from fear, but her excitement thinking about God up there bowling can get pretty loud sometimes too!" Sophie explains.

"Hey, whatever works," Sydney says.

"You used to be a screamer, Sydney!" Emma states, laughing.

"Sorry, Em!" Sydney apologizes.

"None needed. Thank God it wasn't long till you outgrew that!" Emma states like she's relieved.

Suddenly there's another bright flash of light and then the thunder almost directly after.

"Wow, that was close," Lucas says as he starts to get worried about how bad it's gonna get.

"Maybe we should close the blinds?" Sydney suggests.

"Sure, we can do that," Emma agrees.

Then the boutique phone starts ringing. Sydney looks at Emma, and Emma is looking at her.

"I will get it," Emma says quickly.

"Hello?" Emma answers. "Hello?"

"Ah, yes, Parker, how is everything?" Emma wonders.

Sydney tries to listen in to Emma's conversations with what appears to be her dad. She motions for Sophie and Lucas to be quiet for a moment.

"Oh my. Well, what would you like me to do, Parker?" Emma asks.

"Yes. Oh, okay, yes, I can do that. Consider it done," Emma assures Parker.

"Well, so far, everything is good here, but it just started..." Emma gets interrupted by thunder cracking, and the line goes dead. "Parker? Can you hear me? Parker?" Emma takes the phone from her ear and sees that the call is no longer active.

Sydney sees the look on Emma's face and gets concerned that something is very wrong. Sydney walks closer to Emma and asks,

"Em, is everything okay? That was Dad, right?"

"Yes, sweetheart, it was your dad." Emma hesitates to say more.

"But...?" Sydney says like she knows that Emma isn't telling her everything.

"Your dad says everything is okay, and he has everything under control. He said he will talk with us more when we get home," Emma says, trying to remain calm so as not to get Sydney all worried.

"Emma, come on. What is going on? I have a bad feeling in my gut that there's more you know and aren't telling me," Sydney says, trying to get Emma to spill on what's up.

"Sydney, please let's just get through this last hour, and we can go home so your dad can speak to you. He asked me to not say any more. So please respect his wishes," Emma states, trying not to be too nasty.

"Syd let's just get done what we can here. I'm sure it's not all that bad or your dad would have talked to you personally," Sophie adds.

Lucas has his suspicions about what is up, but knowing how Sydney gets so anxious over things, he decides it just best to leave well enough alone and wait till they get back to the ranch.

But he chimes in too and states, "Syd, let's do like Sophie said and get cleaned up here so we can be closer to getting out when we lock up." Lucas hoped it helps a little bit.

"If you want, I will ask my mom if we can just come to your house and stay the night?" Sophie asks Sydney.

"Really? Oh, Sophie, that would be awesome! I love you, bestie. Oh, wait a minute." Sydney looks at Emma and hesitates for a moment then asks, "Em, can the girls come along and spend the night?"

Emma thinks for a moment and decides what is best for this situation and says, "You know what, if Allison agrees, I say sure thing! But Sophie needs to double-check with her mom."

"I'm on it, Miss Emma! Thank you so much. I pray Mom says yes!" Sophie quickly texts her mom. While she waits for her response, she straightens up the boutique.

"Syd." Lucas quietly waves Sydney over to him.

"Hey, what's up? Why are you whispering?" Sydney wonders.

"Listen, I'm in the same boat as you, and if it's not too much of a bother, I was wondering if I could possibly stay the night as well, but I don't want to cause ripples again with Sophie. I have a bad feeling too, and just in case, whatever it is, I want to be there with and for you. So can we somehow see if I can stay too?" Lucas prays she can make it happen.
"Okay, give me a minute. Let me see what I can do. Till I come back, can you help Sophie straighten up?" Sydney says as she walks away and pulls Emma into the back room.

Lucas watches as she walks away and then starts to straighten up.

Meanwhile in the back office

"Sydney, is everything okay?" Emma is concerned with Sydney's sudden attempt at being so secret.

"Yes, well, I hope so." Sydney cautiously begins with her question. "So how would you feel about us having another sleepover guest tonight?"

"Oh well, I guess just who might this other guest be?" Emma wonders but has her sneaky suspicions as to who Sydney is referring to.

Sydney looks around the corner in the way of Lucas and looks at Emma and back to Lucas.

"Lucas?" Emma quickly questions.

Sydney nods.

Emma thinks for a moment and says, "Sure, I think it would be for the best. Just please have him ask his mother. Why so secretive though, Sydney?" Emma asks, confused.

"Lucas and I didn't want to stir the pot with Sophie. It's what's started this whole mess with her last time she went silent and wanted no parts of us or anyone for that matter," Sydney reminds Emma.

"Gotcha. Well, I will make like I asked him to. Can you send him back here after you go back out?" Emma asks.

"Sure thing. I will get him now! Thanks, Em!" Sydney says as she walks out the door, trying not to let on that she knows anything.

She walks over to Lucas and lets him know that Emma would like to speak with him in the back room. As she winks so that Sophie can't see, Lucas nods and heads back. Sydney walks over to Sophie. "So did your mom get back to you yet, bestie?" Sydney asks.

"Yes, she said that was fine and to be careful. She said that the roads are awful. There's trees and branches down everywhere. What do you think is happening at your place?" Sophie asks, concerned.

"I don't know, but I have a feeling it's not good. I keep praying I'm wrong. But now hearing what your mom said has me even more concerned," Sydney says as she gets an uneasy feeling.

"I'm sure that everything is okay. We are just getting over worried. Do you think Em will let us leave a little early?" Sophie says, hoping she says yes.

"Well, as bad as it is storming, I think I can talk her into it. Let me go ask. I'll be right back." Sydney heads to the back room.

"Em, I don't mean to pry, but since it's so bad and no one is obviously out in this mess, do you think we could shut down early, please?" Sydney asks with desperation.

"Can you please give me five minutes and I will come out and let you know?" Emma politely asks.

"Oh, okay, sure! Come on, Lucas. Let's clean up in hopes of getting outta here early," Sydney says as she takes Lucas's arm and guides him out with her.

"So?" Sophie asks, hopeful that Emma said yes.

"She will come out in five minutes and let us know." Sydney relays what Emma said.

They all straighten up, fill up stock, clean counter and doors, and sweep till Emma comes out to deliver the news.

How's everything looking out here, young ones?" Emma looks around and is pleased when suddenly it happens.

Crack! Boom! Pop!

Complete silence, and it's a bit darker now.

God, are you giving me a sign that it's time to close up and go home? Sydney wonders to herself.

"Well, looks like you got my answer. Apparently, God wants us to close up and go home," Emma says happily. "So, let's clean up and get home. Sophie, did your mom get back to you?"

"She sure did, and she said it's okay. And to be careful because the roads are horrible there's trees and branches down everywhere," Sophie cautions Emma.

"Lucas, did you make your call or message?" Emma asks.

"Yes, ma'am, and we are all clear to proceed," he assures Emma.

They all gather together to make last finishing touches on the Boutique that they can with no power till next time. They leave a note on the door stating, "Closed early due to no electricity" and hung it on the door. Then they all head to the back door and quickly all head to the car as Sydney locks up and joins them in the car.

Emma starts the car, and they start to head home.

CHAPTER 14

The Aftermath

As they make their way out of town it's pouring so hard Emma can barely see to drive. There's leaves, branches, and trash cans knocked over with trash just thrown about everywhere.

Lucas sat up front with Emma. He's keeping an eye out for things that he may see on the road to warn Emma ahead of time. In between the heavy-soaked windshield and the wipers swooshing by as fast as they can go, Lucas thinks he see something up ahead.

"Be careful, Emma! There appears to be something up ahead. I can't make it out, but it looks like a trash can in the middle of the road. Do you see it?" Lucas warns her, hoping too that she sees it.

Emma slows down, hoping to see it better and miss it. "Yes, since I slowed down some, I see something. Hopefully nothing comes the other way till I can get around it."

Everyone is looking and watching for other vehicles to come from other directions. It is a trash can. Emma drives around it and continues. There are cars off the side of the road. They pass one house where a tree came down on the people's home. The power seems to be out everywhere. It's not typically dark this time of day, but it's getting darker by the minute, and without streetlights, it makes it so dreary and ominous out. Up ahead, Lucas spots something else.

"Emma, stop!" Lucas shouts.

Emma locks up the breaks, and they start to fishtail. Eliza holds onto Sophie as she tries to remain strong and not cry, but she is getting more scared, and Sophie can feel her trembling. Suddenly, the car comes to a stop. There is a tree down across the road.

"Well, looks like we have to find a way around because this way is closed," Emma tells them.

"I seen a road just back to the right, that maybe we can try," Sydney shares.

Emma gets turned around and slowly makes her way to the other road. "This one, Sydney?" Emma asks as she comes upon a road ahead.

"Yeah, this road will take us a bit out of the way but hopefully it's open," Sydney says, and she silently talks to God to get them home safely.

As they make their way down this road, they see fence posts and pieces everywhere along with tree branches and other kinds of debris of all sizes. Then they see a truck into a fence, and suddenly, up behind them, they are startled by sirens. Emma tries to move over, but they are headed for the truck into the fence.

"Wow, that scared me!" Emma states.

"Yeah, what was with that? It's not like we needed to get out of the way. Why did they have to run their sirens like that?" Sydney asks, strangely confused.

"Well, at least whoever is in that truck has some help, I hated to drive by and not help them. But I wouldn't know how to help them, anyway, that's not my expertise," Emma says, relieved.

They continue on, and the storm just isn't letting up. The sky lights up almost as bright as day when the lightning strikes across the sky. It's the lightning that comes straight down that is wild; it makes the whole ground shake. The destruction they see almost looks as though there may have been a tornado or at the very least some super strong straight-line winds. The farther they drive, the more Sydney worries about what she will find when she gets home. She starts getting overwhelmed and breathing heavier the more she thinks about it. She can feel her heart racing. Sophie has taken notice of Sydney's ever-building agitation.

"Syd, are you okay, bestie?" Sophie says, concerned about her showing signs of being distressed.

Emma looks in the rearview mirror to see what Sophie sees. Sydney just sits there as she gets progressively more labored breathing with each breath and a dead stare into nowhere.

Sophie snaps her fingers to try to get her to snap out of it to no avail; she just sits there.

Sophie whispers up to Emma, "Em, is this normal for her?"
"No, but we are almost home. She's probably worried about what Parker called for. And seeing all this devastation out here probably has her more worried. I think she will be okay. It shouldn't be too much longer." Emma hopes as she tries to keep calm and keep her eyes on the road, so she doesn't work everyone else up more than what they already are.

Just when they think things couldn't get any worse, Lucas yells, "Look out, Em!" Just as he screams, she sees it too, a huge bull right in the middle of the road. Emma is able to come to a stop, and she blows her horn to try to scare the bull off the road.

"Come on, big guy, get off the road before you get hit," Emma says to the bull.

Lucas starts to laugh as he says, "Really, do you think the bull can hear you, Em? Let alone understand you." He smirks.

"I wonder where he even came from," Sophie says. "Syd, look there, a bull on the road!"

And like that, Sydney starts a full-on panic mode. "SOT! Oh, Emma, we have to get home, I have to check on SOT! Oh, and PB Cup and Black Boots and Loads of Luck! And all the others!" Sydney very loudly exclaims.

Well, apparently, the bull heard her shriek, and he took off back to the side of the road.

"Good job, Syd!" Lucas says, thanking her for her help.

"Huh, what did I do? Are we almost home?" Sydney wonders as she is clearly confused about where she is.

"We should be home soon. Just stay calm and breathe. I don't need you getting so worked up that you get sick, young one," Emma pleads with Sydney.

"I just hope that the horses are all okay!" Sydney states as she begins fidgeting with her fingers and hands.

Sophie puts her hand on Sydney's shoulder and gently rubs it.

Sydney put her hand on top of Sophie's and says, "Thanks, bestie."

"Are you gonna be, okay?" Sophie wonders.

"I am just worried about SOT and the other horses. I pray everything is okay," Sydney replies to Sophie as she redirects her attention to Emma. "Are we almost home now?"

"As a matter of fact, I can see the driveway up ahead," Emma assures Sydney.

"That's awesome! I'm excited to check on the horses," Sydney says, relieved that they are finally almost home.

As they go into the drive, Emma stops the car and turns to look at the kids. "So, when we get back to the house, Parker may need our help, but I am not for certain just yet since our call got cut short, but let's go see how things are and go from there," Emma says as she turns to start driving when Sydney questions her.

"Umm, just what is going on, Em? We are almost home. Can't you just tell me? Well, us now that we are this close. Come on," Sydney says trying to persuade Emma.

"Okay. Yes, you are right. We are this close, so you will find out soon enough." Emma hopes she isn't jumping the gun by telling them before Parker has a chance to speak with them.

"Emma?" Sydney responds with a bit of anger.

"Okay, Sydney, calm down. He called to tell me that some of the horses had gotten out." Emma gets cut off by Sydney.

She is hearing about all she can manage at the moment.

"Seriously, Em? And you didn't think this was important enough to tell us or me for that matter?" She says with more anger now than just a moment ago.

"Syd, this is what I and your dad were afraid of, you just flying off the handle, when really at the time, there wasn't much you could do anyways," Emma says as she gets interrupted by a car door slamming. "Was that Sydney?" Emma asks Sophie. "Yes, ma'am!" Sophie replies.

"She isn't thinking with her right mind. Do you see her anywhere?" Emma asks.

"No, I don't," Sophie states.

"Is that her up there running, Em?" Lucas points out.

And just before Emma can answer, the sky lights up again and Sydney drops to the ground as Emma pulls up beside her. She opens her car door up and yells, "Sydney, get your tiny bum in this car right this minute!" Emma demands.

Sydney gets up and climbs in the car on Sophie's side since she has her door open ready for Sydney to jump in.

"Young lady, what in the world are you thinking? That was either the craziest or dumbest thing you have ever done! I do not want to ever see you pull another stunt like that again! You could have been struck by lightning!" Emma severely scolds Sydney.

"But, Em, I need to help find SOT!" Sydney strikes back.

"I understand, but that was reckless behavior right there just now! What good are you to SOT dead?" Emma says as she remains quiet till they get to the house.

As they pile up, Parker is at the edge of the barn waiting for them. When Emma parks, she tells all the kids to stay put till she comes to get them. Then she gets out and goes over to Parker. The kids stay in the car and watch as Emma talks with Parker. Emma waves the kids to come over to her and Parker.

"Sydney, I need your help, but only if you do as I say. I do not need any reckless acts going on. So, if you can do as I say, then you may come along," Parker sternly states directly up front.

"Okay, Dad. I will do what you say. Now won't you please tell us what is going on here?" Sydney asks as she is becoming very irritated.

"Yes, some of the horses got out. Obee and I were able to get a few of them back in. Now, Syd and Lucas, we have yet to find SOT and Loads of Luck. Tall Leaps is out there somewhere too. We found PB Cup, but we need help bringing her in. So, what I need from y'all is to ride in the back of the truck, which will mean that you will be getting drenched, and when we find them, I need you to hook a lead rope to their halter so we can lead them back. Now I know we will be okay with all of them that are out there yet except for Loads of Luck. Only because we don't know all his tendencies just yet. But I think if we can get the others he will come willingly. So, who's game?" Parker asks as he looks around for Sydney. "Where did Syd go?"

"I'm already in the truck." Sydney says eagerly, waiting for everyone else.

Sophie and Lucas join her.

"I'm headed to the house. Please be careful. I will make some soup and sandwiches till y'all get back." Emma waves at them as she heads to the house.

Parker gets in and picks Obee up at the other end of the barn, where he stands holding extra leads.

They head out into the pasture to get PB Cup since they know where she is first and bring her back to the barn. Then they head off, looking for the last three. They drive all over and nothing. Sydney taps on the glass to get her dad's attention. He stops the truck.

Sydney hangs out over the side of the truck and says, "Dad, did you try back at the Survival cabin?"

Parker shakes his head no and gives her the thumbs up. They head off toward the survival cabin. When they get closer, Sydney can see Loads of Luck rearing up and acting very spooked. SOT is there too. She is pacing back and forth, trying to get away from him like she wants absolutely nothing to do with him. Parker doesn't want to spook the horses even more, so he stops and waits to see if they come to them.

Sydney calls out for SOT. "SOT here, girl. Wanna go back to the barn? I have a carrot!" Sydney says, waving her hand around like she had one in her hand. After a few minutes, she starts to head Sydney's direction. "Good girl. Come on. Over here!" She is almost close enough for Sydney to reach her when the sky lights up again. Easy girl, whoa. Come here." Sophie reaches out quickly and snags her halter and hooks her. "I got SOT! She is hooked!" Sydney ties her lead off onto one of the truck D-ring anchors, so if she gets spooked, she won't get rope burn on her hands.

Lucas gets out of the bed of the truck and calmly walks over to Loads of Luck and tries to hook him. Loads of Luck rears up and just about hits Lucas on his way back down. But Lucas tries not to show fear. He calmly and gently talks to Loads of Luck, and he calms down just enough, so Lucas can grab him and hook him. Lucas carefully guides him over to the truck. He hands Sydney the lead to tie him off. As Lucas climbs into the bed of the truck, Parker gets out of the truck quickly to talk to them.

"Great job, you two! Now we just need to find Tall Leaps. Let's see if we can find her. Any ideas where she might be? Since you pinpointed these two pretty well," Parker says pleasantly.

"Well, if I had to guess, I would say out by the track we were at last with her. You know the one you rode her out to?" Sydney suggests.

"Obee? Hey, didn't you already check out by the north track?" Parker asks.

"Oh no. I didn't get that far," Obee states.

"Well, it's worth a try. Sit down, everyone, and let's see what we can find." Parker gets in, and he drives off.

The sky lights up again, and it cracks and rumbles when Lucas thinks he hears something "Syd, listen. Do you hear that?" Lucas says, trying to pinpoint where it is coming from.

"Hear what, Lucas?" Sydney tries to listen, but all she hears is rain, thunder, and wind.

"I think I hear it. It sounds like a horse whinnying," Sophie says.

Sophie taps on the window to get Parker's attention to stop.

Parker stops and gets out, "What's up?" He asks frantically.

"Listen, there's a horse nearby. We just get determine how close or where," Lucas states, concerned it may be hurt and can't get to them.

"I think I hear it. Lucas, can you come look with me? Obee, can you come out with us and look for this horse we hear?" Parker requests.

Obee gets out of the truck and goes with them to look. They all spread out to look and listen, hoping that they spot it soon. Lucas heads back toward the cabin. The sounds seem to be getting louder, so he yells out for Parker and Obee. They hear Lucas and head in his direction.

"What do you hear, Lucas?" Obee asks.

"Listen back there. It sounds like it's back there. Do we have a flashlight?" Lucas wonders.

"Lucas, you stay here. Obee let's go around back and see if we can shoo her out to Lucas. Be ready, she could come a running out fast!" Parker says, unaware of her actions in her current given state.

As Parker and Obee split up and go around back while Lucas waits, hoping she is somewhat calm and will come to him. Lucas hears Parker and Obee calling out for Tall Leaps as he hears rustling coming from behind the cabin. Suddenly, he sees a beautiful horse, which he believes is Tall Leaps.

"She's out, she's out!" Lucas yells back to them in hopes that they can hear him. "Come here, Tall Leaps. Come on, girl," Lucas says calmly as Tall Leaps walk over to him cautiously.

He keeps calm, and she continues to slowly walk closer and closer as he very softly speaks to her. "Come here, girl. Yes, that's a good girl. Oh, you are so beautiful. Just a few more steps. Come on, you can do it. Let's get you back to the barn, beautiful."

As Lucas coaxes her closer, Parker and Obee have come around the side of the cabin and are absolutely impressed with how well Lucas has managed to get her so close to him. They watch as Lucas reaches calmly and ever so slowly for her halter. He gets it and hooks the lead rope on as he starts to pet and rub her neck.

Lucas notices Parker and Obee and waves it's all good. That he has her. He points toward the truck as he walks her over so they can tie off her lead rope and get the horses back to the barn.

As Parker gets closer, he comments on Lucas's bad-ass skills. "I am super impressed, young man! You have found your gift in life! I am so glad to have you on my team," Parker states as he reaches for Lucas's hand to shake it.

Lucas reaches out, and as he shakes his hand, he says, "Thanks, but I am sure that y'all would love to get warm and dry? So, let's save the appreciation for when we get these beauties back to the barn and secured and we are dry in the house."

"Amen, Lucas! We agree. Come on, Obee. Let's get in the truck and get back," Parker says as he and Obee get in the truck, and Parker starts to drive back ever so slowly, hoping that the horses follow right along. As the kids hold onto the ends of the leads so that they don't slip through the hooks on the edge of truck.

CHAPTER 15
Heart to Heart

Parker manages to get the horses back safely with the help of the kids and Obee. Everyone goes into the barn and helps to make sure that the barn is secure that the horses can't get out again.

"So, I am wondering out of pure curiosity, how do you think that they got out Parker?" Lucas asks.

"Well, that too has me completely puzzled Lucas. But we can go take a look. It just so happens that I had just bought security cameras and put them around the farm," Parker states. "So, with that, we will know exactly what happened just as soon as we go inside." He smiles and double-checks all the stall doors.

"That awesome, Dad, but why did you buy security cameras?" Sydney asks as if it was odd.

"It was something your mother and I had discussed, but I just never got around to it. So now I finally got around to it, and boy, am I glad that I did because now we will know exactly how or why they got out," Parker says as he looks around at everyone.

Obee has a look on his face that you can almost tell exactly what he is thinking. Like, *Oh crap. I hope I didn't leave any doors not secure.* But Obee is really good at making sure that the horses are secure every night because he knows just how important they are to the ranch, Parker, and of course, Sydney. As Parker and Obee finish making sure everything is secure before we go in, Lucas, Sophie, and Sydney start to head for the house.

"Hey, where's everybody going?" Parker asks.

They all stop, and Sydney turns and speaks up. "I'm sorry, but aren't we done, Dad? We were just headed in a while." Sydney replies like it's no big deal.

"Well, technically, yes, but it's storming out there. I don't want you just taking off in this stuff," Parker says, concerned.

"Seriously, Dad?" Sydney scoffs.

"Yes, seriously! This is no joke! These storms are bad!" Parker sternly says to them.

"Dad, we just rode around in the bed of your truck in the middle of a pasture! Like come on, you are being ridiculous! We are headed in to get outta these wet clothes. We shall see you inside," Sydney says. As she turns to walk away, she adds, "Are you guys coming?"

With that, Lucas and Sophie follow her.

"Some days, Obee, that girl just gets under my skin. These teen years without her mother is gonna break me," Parker says, shocked at her behavior.

"It's okay. It's just a phase. She still loves you. And not to side with her, but she did have a very valid point, though. Dontcha think?" Obee says, trying to make Parker see.

"Yeah, I guess you are right. It's just some days, it's hard to see her growing up, man. It wasn't supposed to be just me taking care of her and raising her. Oh, how I miss her mother so bad," Parker says as he hangs his head.

"If you don't mind me saying so, you are never alone raising or caring for her. Emma and I have your back always! We know running this ranch is no small feat, so we do everything in our power to help wherever we can, especially when it comes to that young lady. I think, and please forgive if I am overstepping my boundaries, but I really think you should maybe try to find some lady friends to hang out with to let loose and who knows maybe even date and move on," Obee says, hoping he can let Parker know he's not alone.

"Thanks, Obee. I do know that y'all do a lot for me, and I found out today just how much else Emma does when I decided to take that bet and got stuck doing all her chores. And I know she took it easy on me, so I praise her even more! That woman is amazing! Okay, well, I think we are as secure as we can be. How about we go in and check the cameras to see what we can see and get outta these wet clothes before we get sick and add even more work to that poor woman's list of to do's," Parker says as the walks out of the barn with Obee.

"Definitely sounds like a plan. So, you wanna play a game again tonight?" Obee asks as he chuckles.

"No, absolutely not!" Parker laughs. "I have played enough games for one year. Are you gonna stay in the main house again tonight?"

"Sure, you don't have to ask me twice," Obee quickly replies before Parker changes his mind.

As they walk in the door, Emma shouts out to them, "Come on in the kitchen, boys. I have coffee and hot chocolate or, if you prefer, some homemade loaded chicken rice soup with grilled cheese."

"Obee?" Parker asks.

"When have you known me to turn down food, boss! Come on, let's go get some grub!" Obee says as he heads to the kitchen.

"Eh, eh, wait one minute, Obee!" Emma scolds.

"Yes, Emma. I am going to wash up," Obee says as he turns right around and heads for the bathroom just down the hall.

"Thank you, Obee! Parker? Don't tell me that you think you are getting any food without washing up," Emma says, stopping him in his tracks.

"I love you, Emma!" Parker says as he heads to wash his hands too.

"I know, Parker. I love you too! Ah, there you are, all cleaned up, Obee. So, what will you have?" Emma asks, ready to get him what he wants.

"I would love some of your soup and two sammiches please, and how about a coffee?" Obee says, dying to eat and get warmed up.

"Here you are, sir, a hot bowl of soup, two sammiches, and a coffee," Emma says smiling as she hands over his food. "Parker, what would you like?"

"Actually, Emma, I will have what Obee is having, please," Parker says, smiling at Emma and rubbing his hands together while waiting for some delicious grub.

"Okay, here you are, sir, big, piping hot bowl of soup, two sammiches, and a coffee." She smiles back and asks,

"Okay, last call on food. Does anybody want anything else? If not, I am cleaning up and the kitchen is closed."

"I would love a grilled cheese please," Sydney asks.

"Me too," Lucas adds.

"I am stuffed. May I please go to the living room?" Sophie asks.

"Yes, Sophie. You may be excused. Eliza, honey, are you done? And here are your sammiches, Sydney and Lucas," Emma says smiling.

"I would just like more hot chocolate please," Eliza asks, "but just a little please."

"Okay, a little hot chocolate for the little lady." Emma pours Eliza about a half a cup and starts to clean up.

"May we be excused, Em?" Sydney asks for her and Lucas.

"Yes, go have some fun," Emma tells them.

"When we are done here, Emma, would you like to come to my office with me? We are gonna pull up videos from the barn to see how the horses got out," Parker asks.

"Sure, that will probably be an interesting view. Just give me a few more minutes," Emma pleads.

"It's no rush. Whenever you are ready, we will go," Parker responds.

"Five more minutes is all I need," Emma says.

"Oh, okay. Well, I will go get my program loaded and get everything set up. Just come in when you are finished Emma." Parker excuses himself from the table and heads to the living room. "Hey, anybody in here, wanna see how the horses got out? Come to my office in about five minutes," He chuckles.

"Okay," the kids all say simultaneously.

While Parker goes to load up the program and get things ready, the kids continue to play their game.

"This is a pretty cool game, Syd," Lucas tells her.

"It was one of my mother's favorites. So, is this like the first time you have ever played it?" Sydney asks him.

"Actually, yes. My family was never about card games or board games," Lucas shyly shares.

"It's okay. There's no reason to be embarrassed by it. I think we may have an extra one that we use when we used to have big parties. But since we don't do that anymore, I will see if you would be able to have it. If you would like?" Sydney kindly says.

"That would be cool," Lucas says with excitement.

"Umm, I think it's time for us to go to your dad's office," Sophie says, trying to get Lucas and Sydney to follow her. "Eliza, do you wanna come too?"

"Sure!" Eliza says as she jumps up to her feet.

They all gather together and wait for Sydney to lead them to Parker's office.

"Okay, right this way," Sydney says, leading them to up to the second floor.

As they walk into Parker's office, they are shocked at all his cool technology. Lucas seems to be most intrigued.

"Wow, what a setup, Parker! This is a beaut!" Lucas is impressed with the big screen set up.

"Yeah, when I decided to go with the security system, I thought, why not have a big screen so I can see the screens better as individuals or a group?" Parker brags to them, especially Lucas, about his system.

"I am here. You can start, Parker," Emma says, a little out of breath.

"Take a breath, Emma. We can wait for a minute or so," Parker insists.

"Okay, so let me load the cameras." As Parker loads the cameras, Lucas notices something odd in the one frame.

"Parker, what's with the frame down in the left corner?" Lucas asks.

"What in the world? Now, Obee, we both double-checked those doors! How is that one hanging open?" Parker says, confused.

"I will go close it again, boss," Obee gladly offers.

"Do you have your phone, Obee?" Parker asks him, still puzzled as to how that happened.

"Yes, sir, I do," Obee says, pointing to it in his shirt pocket.

"Okay, we are gonna see why while you go and close it, and if we need you for anything, I will call you," Parker assures him.

"Okay, boss. I will return soon!" Obee says as he heads downstairs.

Everyone else has their eyes peeled to the monitor. Parker rewinds the video to see what's going on and who's playing such a nasty trick. As they watch, they can see Loads of Luck open the door!

"Wait, did I really just watch my horse open the door?" Lucas says, shocked.

"Horses have been known to unlock certain latches, so we have to find a way to keep him in his stall," Parker says, laughing.

"I am so sorry, everyone. I didn't realize that my horse was a Houdini of sorts," Lucas states still shocked that Loads of Luck is so mischievous.

"It's not your fault. We didn't know. Horses are amazing creatures and are very, very smart!" Parker says, not surprised in the least.

"Wait, so you are saying that Loads of Luck left all the other horses out too?" Lucas asks, scared to know.

"Good question. Let's look and see." Parker rewinds the video more. After a few minutes, Parker says, "Lucas, it appears so! Look here!" Parker says as he sees and can't believe it himself.

"What the...wow, this or that is absolutely the craziest thing that I have ever witnessed," Lucas states in disbelief. "I wonder why he did that?"

"There's no way of knowing for sure, what his past family had trained him to do, or he may have learned from them. But what I do know is that we must keep an eye out to lock up better because if he can, maybe the others could too!" Parker reassures them.

"That's for sure!" Lucas agrees.

"Okay, well, now we have that mystery solved. I am headed out to help Obee secure the barn up better. What's up with all of you young ones? Are you staying the night?" Parker asks.

"Yes, Dad, they are. Come on, guys. Let's go finish our game so we can hit the sack soon. I don't know about y'all, but I am beat!" Sydney says as she starts yawning.

"Sounds good to me, Syd," Lucas says as he leaves the room to head downstairs.

"I'm right behind you, Lucas," Sophie blurts out. Eliza gets in line behind Sophie.

"All righty then, I am the caboose," Sydney says, laughing.

"I'm so glad to see them all happy again," Emma tells Parker.

"Yes, I feel the same way. Okay, I will be back in a bit. I must go help Obee." Parker shuts down his computer and heads out to help Obee.

Meanwhile, downstairs, Lucas, Sophie, and Sydney finish up their game of Uno, while Eliza is drawing at the coffee table. Everyone is having such a good time that they almost forget about the storms until...

Crack!

Lightning lights up the room, and the thunder rolls across the sky, gently shaking the ground.

"Wow, that scared me a bit only because I wasn't expecting it, though," Sophie says.

"Sure, did me too! I wonder how much longer we are in for these storms?" Sydney asks.

"The last I heard was anytime this week. But you know Mother Nature, she makes her own rules," Lucas jokes.

"So, when it storms like this, I sleep down here because it's loud and quite scary sleeping in my room during storms like this. That means I will be sleeping in here with y'all tonight!" Sydney says with excitement.

"Oh, cool, so it will be like our camp out minus the campfire. And now we have Eliza too!" Lucas says ecstatically.

"Exactly! How's that sound to you, Eliza?" Sydney happily asks her.

"Yippee, Skippy nut butter!" Eliza shrieks.

"Awesome, yes, but not so loud. The adults will be sleeping soon, so we are using our quiet indoor voice," Sophie instructs Eliza.

"When we are done with our game, I will go and get pillows and blankets for everyone," Sydney informs them.

They each take a few more turns, and the game is complete. As promised, Sydney leaves the room to go get blankets and pillows for everyone. She's not gone long before she returns. She walks in on Lucas and Sophie sitting over in the corner very close like they are trying to devise some great plan that they don't want anyone to hear what they are saying.

"I'm back. Did anyone miss me?" Sydney says to try to get Lucas and Sophie's attention.

"I did!" Eliza says, trying to be extra quiet, which is hard for her since she is so hyper and excited all the time.

"Look what I got for you, Eliza!" Sydney whispers as she hands her a princess pillow and blanket.

"Oh, wow! Thank you, Syd!" Eliza takes the pillow and blanket and goes and lies on the floor under the coffee table.

"Be careful you don't hit your head, Eliza," Sydney warns her.

"There's a bunch of room under here, Syd! You should come under too!" Eliza tells her.

"There may be enough for you, but honey, there's no way I can't fit under there too! But I can lay beside you out from under the table if you would like?" Sydney offers.

"Yes please!" Eliza quickly responds.

"Give me a few minutes, and I will lay down with you. Okay, I promise," Sydney whispers to her.

Sydney walks over to Lucas and Sophie. "Here are blankets and pillows for you. You may lay anywhere you would like. I am lying next to Eliza because she asked me to. So good night, y'all," Sydney says as she hands them their sleeping supplies and turns to go lie next to Eliza.

"Where would you like to sleep, Sophie?" Lucas gives her first choice.

"I'll sleep on that couch over there," Sophie says, pointing to the one over closer to Sydney and Eliza.

"Got it. I guess I will sleep here by the fireplace. I will pretend there's a fire in it," Lucas says smiling. As he lies down, Lucas tries making eye contact with Sophie. When she finally sees him trying to get her attention, he motions to her that he needs to talk with her some more after Sydney and Eliza fall asleep. She nods and closes her eyes like she's sleeping.

Some time has passed, and it's very quiet in the room. Lucas opens his one eye and tries to look around; everyone seems to be asleep. So, he quietly gets up and goes to get Sophie. She opens her eyes, and he motions for her to follow him. He has her follow him to the kitchen.

"Thanks. I figured it would be easier to talk out here because we are further away," Lucas whispers.

"What's up?" Sophie wonders what's with all this secrecy.

"Well, I have been wanting to have a chat with you for a little while now, and this ended up working out great," he replies.

Sophie, in her mind, thinks she knows what the conversation is about but decides to hear Lucas out just to make sure. "I'm listening."

"So, I don't know where to start or how to." Lucas pauses for a moment as he thinks about how he wants to word his thoughts. "Sorry, I didn't think this all through very well. It was kinda last minute for me to be asked to stay. But okay, I will just come out with it! How does Sydney feel about me? Do you know?" Lucas says, fumbling his way through it.

"To be honest, I don't think she has any feelings for you or any boy for that matter," Sophie states to the best of her knowledge. "Why?"

"I want to say that I think about you both a lot! Especially since that date with you two beautiful ladies for the dance. You were both absolutely stunning! But you both have a very special place in my heart." He notices Sophie getting a little flustered. "You, okay?"

"I am good. It's just very hot in here. I need a drink." Sophie gets up from the table to get herself a bottle of water from the fridge. Before she sits back down, she dampens a paper towel and dabs her face. Then she sits back down to finish hearing what Lucas has to say.

"Are you feeling better?" he asks with concern.

"A little, thanks," Sophie replies.

"Okay, so back to me. Yes, umm, well, I think now I am not for sure like one hundred percent or anything, so please do not say anything to Syd, but I think that I may be developing feelings for her," he says, relieved he made it through the hard part.

"Oh! Umm, okay, not what I was expecting," Sophie tells Lucas but deep down knowing that all this time she was right! She tried telling Syd and she refused to listen!

"Well, I kinda wanna feel out the summer with you two and make sure before I ask her. I just wondered if she ever said anything to you about me?" Lucas asks.

"Well, first off, we are best friends, and we won't tell secrets about each other to anyone else, especially a boy. I think you are on a good path, though, but I want to tell you this for sure, we will not allow you or any other boy to come between us. We made that pact with each other, and we will stand by it," Sophie reassures Lucas.

"I completely understand where you are coming from, but I also wanted to let you know that I heard a little rumor. Now till school starts up, I cannot verify the info I have, but I will definitely look into it if you would like me to," Lucas offers.

"Really? And just what does this little rumor entail?" Sophie asks out of pure curiosity.

"Well, someone apparently has a tiny thing for you. But like I said, I will not reveal my source nor the person with said feelings. We will say till school starts and I can verify it there again, that's only if you want me to," he states with satisfaction that he has her hooked.

"I will think about it. Can I have a tiny little hint?" She cautiously asks for fear of actually knowing.

"All I will say is that you already know this person. That's all I will say. No more questions, just an answer to whether you want me to investigate it?" Lucas waits for her response.

Sophie thinks about it and responds, "I am not sure. I am going to need more time to think about it. That's a lot to lay on a lady in such short notice."

"Well, it's good we still have most of the summer for you to think about it," Lucas says smart-like. "I figured if everything works out, you and I will be going on a double date for homecoming. What do you think about that?" Lucas seems like he's trying way too hard.

"First off, famous last words from Sydney's grandad: Don't count your chickens before they hatch. And you are starting to sound a bit like jock Lucas. Tone down the cockiness. It'll get you nowhere especially with Syd and definitely not with me," Sophie says, putting Lucas back in line to keep him straight.

"Okay, it was just a comment," Lucas starts to say when he sees Sophie with that look of her wanting to lay him out. He changes his tone. "I'm sorry. It is how I envision it if everything works out and…" Lucas gets interrupted by Sophie.

"Yes, it's how it should work out. If it's meant to be that way, then it shall be that way!" Sophie says with an "end of story" look about her.

Lucas just sits there looking at her and wondering if he should try to continue or just let it go. "Exactly how I see it, Sophie. Thanks for taking time to come out here and chat with me. What do ya say we get some sleep?"

"I say I thought you would never ask!" Sophie says as she jumps up from the table and quietly tiptoes back into the living room. She winks at Lucas, turns away, and closes her eyes to sleep.

Lucas picks up on her wink and thinks to himself, *nah, it couldn't be*, as he lies down and goes to sleep.

CHAPTER 16
If You Only Knew

"Dad, where's SOT? She's not in her stall! I thought you fixed the latches so she couldn't get out!" Sydney screams at Parker.

"I just came from the barn no more than 20 minutes ago and she was in her stall! So, I don't know how or where she would have gone!" Parker declares.

"We gotta find her!" Sydney says as she runs out of the house in a panic.

Parker runs after her. "Syd, wait! We can go look together!"

Lucas comes running from out of the stables. "I looked everywhere. I can't find her."

"It was probably your stupid horse again! You better hope she's okay!" Sydney screams in Lucas's face as she runs off in desperation looking for SOT.

Suddenly, Sydney comes upon a barbed-wire fence. She thinks to herself, *when did Dad put this up? We've never had barbed-*

wire fences on account of the horses getting out and getting caught in them.

She hears a horse whinnying like it's hurt.

"SOT? Is that you girl?" Sydney says as she tries to see in the dark with only her phone light.

Then she sees something up ahead. She takes off running for what seems like forever till she gets to the object. It's SOT.

"Oh, SOT, I'm so sorry. I will be right back. Let me get some help!" Sydney takes off running and screaming for her dad and Obee or anyone who can hear her. "*Help, please help! Its SOT! She needs help!*"

She sees headlights of what she believes is her dad's truck. She starts jumping up and down, waving her arms around so that hopefully she can be seen. As it gets closer, it's moving rather quickly and headed right for her. She starts screaming out in hopes that they hear her in case they don't see her. "Hey! I'm right here! Do you see me? Hey! Dad? Obee?"

Right when she thinks that it's gonna hit her, she jumps outta the way, and the driver locks up the brakes as it comes to a complete stop. Sydney gets up and runs to the door. No one is getting out, so she opens the door. There is no one in there.

Sydney thinks to herself, *What? How can that be? Where is everyone?*

Suddenly, there's a loud gunshot!

"SOT! NO!" Sophie takes off running back toward SOT. When she gets closer, she sees SOT on the ground and her dad standing over her.

"*No! What did you do? I hate you!*" Sydney screams.

"Wake up, Sydney!" Lucas shakes Sydney, trying to wake her.

"Lucas, be careful. I heard you are not to wake a sleeping person!" Sophie says, concerned that Sydney could be disoriented and punch him by accident.

"It's a chance that I am willing to take," Lucas assures Sophie.

As he continues to try to wake Sydney, he takes heed of Sophie's words and is prepared to move quickly should she decide to wake swinging hands and fists.

Then as quickly as Sydney started screaming, she takes a deep breath, wakes up, and screams at the top of her lungs when she sees Lucas up in her face.

"*Get* off me! What are you doing?" Sydney screams.

Lucas falls back to get back away from Sydney as Emma and Parker come running into the living room.

"What's going on in here? Syd, are you okay?" Parker asks, hoping that Lucas wasn't trying to come on to his daughter.

"It's nothing, Parker. Syd was screaming in her sleep, and Lucas was trying to wake her." Sophie steps up and tells Parker before Lucas has a chance.

"Yes, sir, that's correct. Sorry, I didn't mean to make her scream more," Lucas adds. "I'm not sure what she was dreaming about, but she was screaming, '*No, what did you do? I hate you.*' So, whatever it was, it must have been bad," Lucas says as he replays her screaming in his mind as he tells Parker what he heard.

"Syd, care to elaborate what you were dreaming about?" Parker asks, concerned about what she was dreaming about.

Sydney starts bawling her eyes out.

"Syd, honey, you have to talk to me." Parker tries again to get her to talk.

Sobbing, Sydney tries to explain her dream. "I'm sorry, Dad. But please do not ever put up barbed-wire fences!" Sydney pleads.

"Sweetheart, you know I will never put up barbed-wire fences. It's not safe for the horses. Does that have anything to do with your dream?" he asks, confused.

Sydney continues sobbing as she tells more about her dream. "Yes, dad, and SOT got out and was somehow badly tangled in it. And when I went looking for help, your truck came flying through the pasture right at me, and when I went to open the door, no one was inside. I heard a gunshot ring through the air," Sydney says as she pauses and begins sobbing even more now.

"It's okay, Syd. Take your time," Sophie says, trying to calm her down.

"Sweetheart?" Parker wraps his arms around Sydney. "I love you, sweetheart! You are and always will be my little filly," Parker says, full of heart.

"But you shot SOT! I hate you!" Sydney screams as she pushes her dad away and runs out of the room, sobbing.

"I'll go after her," Sophie quickly offers.

Sophie goes out after Sydney just as she exits the living room. She hears a door slam upstairs. So, Sophie heads upstairs to Sydney's room.

When she reaches Sydney's room, she gently knocks on the door. "Syd, can I please come in?" Sophie waits for a response. She can hear Sydney inside sobbing and bawling her eyes out. "Syd, please?" Sophie asks, knowing that she just needs someone to talk to and she should not sit in her room alone. Sophie knocks again but a little harder this time.

"Go away!" Sydney yells from behind the door.

"Syd, it's me. May I please come in?" Sophie asks again.

"Leave me alone!" Sydney screams back at her.

"Syd, I am your best friend, and you should know by now that I am not going away that easy. Come on, it's just me. Can I please just come in with you?" Sophie asks one last time.

"Please just go and leave me alone!" Sydney shouts out. "I don't wanna talk!"

"Okay, we don't have to talk, but I am not going away either. So please either let me in or I will force my way in. I just don't want you to be alone," Sophie says right before she decides she's going in one way or another. "Oh, you wanna do this the hard way? Fine. Don't say that I didn't warn you. I am coming in!"

Just as Sophie gets ready to go in Sydney's room, Sydney opens the door. Sophie goes in and closes it behind her. Sydney walks over to her window seat and sits down. Sophie walks over to Sydney's bed and takes a seat.
Sophie realizes that Sydney really doesn't want to talk, but that doesn't mean that she can't talk while Sydney listens. So, she starts and hopes that Sydney at least listens.

"You don't have to say anything if you don't want to, but I would like to say that I am sorry that you had such a bad dream. But that's all it was, a bad dream. I know that I do not know the whole dream, but from the little bit I heard, you and I both know that it will never happen because like your dad said, he would never use barbed wire. It's very bad to use for horses. So, you don't have to ever worry about that. You also know that your dad loves you very much, so I'm not exactly sure why you said what you said to your dad just before you ran out of the living room. But I am certain that you really did not mean that you hate your dad. Did I also hear that he shot SOT?" Sophie says, waiting to see if Sydney will open up.

After a few minutes, Sophie hears Sydney clear her throat and quietly starts to speak. "I did say that, and you are right. I don't hate my dad. But when I said that I had just been woken up and was still very full of rage," Sydney says as she turns and faces Sophie. "Have you ever had a dream that seemed so real that when you wake up, you feel just as you did in the dream?"

"I mean I guess so. But I haven't really had any dreams that were very emotional to know for sure," Sophie says, trying to think of a time when she had an emotional type of dream.

"Well, this dream had my emotions pushed to the max. From anger, disbelief, rage, heartbreak, and yes of course, hatred. It's just taken me a bit to calm down and realize it really was just a dream, and you are right, dad would never use barbed-wire fences. So that alone should have been a sign that it was just a horrible nightmare. But I honestly can't believe how real it felt!" Sydney states, relieved that it was just that, a horrible nightmare!

"I am so glad you are talking about it, and I bet you feel better too!" Sophie says to her.

"Actually, yes, I do, and I should probably go apologize to my dad," Sydney says with sincerity.

"Well, yes, but since we are here together alone, I want to make sure that I do some apologizing myself," Sophie starts to say.

"You apologize? For what? What did you do this time, Sophie?" Sydney asks, afraid of what she will hear coming out of Sophie's mouth next.

"Yes, I want to apologize for everything that I messed up or did wrong lately. And no, I didn't do anything else wrong since the day at the track that you already know about. We have a new school year starting in a few weeks, and I want us to be as strong as ever in our friendship," Sophie says as she keeps that tiny little secret of Lucas's tucked down deep. She doesn't want to have tell Sydney, *'I told you so.'*

"Yes, for sure! I agree we need to be stronger than ever in our friendship. A new year means chances for new friends, and I do not want anyone to come between us and what we have!" Sydney exclaims in excitement.

"Oh, bestie, if you only knew," Sophie says, trying not to slip up.

"If I only knew what?" Sydney asks, curiously confused.

"Oh, it's nutting, and if I told you, I may have to kill ya! And I don't wanna lose my bestie! Just kidding about killing you not being your bestie. Let's go tell your dad you are sorry for earlier," Sophie sincerely jokes.

"Some days I just don't get you, bestie!" Sydney laughs it all off as she gets up and hugs Sophie.

"I love you, bestie!" Sophie says.

"I love you more, bestie!" Sydney responds. "Come on. I really need to apologize to my dad."

They head downstairs and look for Parker. As they get to the bottom of the steps, they hear voices coming from the kitchen. Sounds like a very heated discussion. Sydney stops in her tracks and grabs Sophie by the arm and puts her finger up to her lips and very quietly shushes Sophie. They sneak over near to the entrance of the kitchen and listen to see what's got those in the kitchen so roweled up.

As they listen, they hear Emma, Parker, Greyson, and Allison all talking about Ivy's hit-and-run. Sydney looks at Sophie with a confused look, both of them not understanding why they are even talking about that anymore.

"Well, when is the hearing?" Greyson asks.

"The letter states it's this Friday. See here on the court documents," Parker says as he shows the letter to Allison and Greyson.

"Well, they don't give you much notice, do they?" Greyson scoffs.

"Honey, it's okay. Given the circumstances, I am certain that your boss will let you off," Allison tries to reassure Greyson.

"I just pray I get a subpoena, so I have to be there. That way, work can't give me any issues and I can be there not only as a witness but as the friend that Parker needs," Greyson says as his temper gets shorter and hotter by the minute.

"Chances are you will get one. I figure you both should since you were both there the night of, and because Greyson was with me not only when we found the car but when Dylan confessed. They are gonna want all our testimonies from every aspect," Parker assures them.

"I'm most worried about Syd and her relationship with Lucas," Emma says, concerned about the impact that it could have.

"Look, right now, I do not feel as though she even needs to know anything about this. As far as I am concerned, the less she knows, the better!" Parker says very adamantly.

Sydney has heard all she wants to hear. So, she motions to Sophie to follow her lead. The girls go running into the kitchen as Sydney asks, "The less who knows, the better? And what don't you want them to know?" Sydney quizzes Parker while quickly adding, "Oh, hey, Allison and Greyson, I didn't know that you were going to be here! Aww, man, do Sophie and Eliza have to go home now?" Sydney tries to act normal and not let on that she knows anything of their conversation right before she came through the door.

"Mom! Dad!" Sophie says excitedly as she runs to hug them. "I did miss you, but I am not really ready to leave just yet!"

"Oh, we just came to see Parker. You can stay longer as long as it's okay with Emma and Parker!" Allison quickly says with no hesitation.

"It's okay with us. Right, Emma?" Parker says, trying to avoid Sydney's questions.

Emma nods and replies, "Yes, absolutely!"

"So, who don't you want knowing what?" Sydney asks again while trying to test them to see if they will be honest.

"We are just talking work things, honey. No need to worry yourself with any of that," Parker says then quickly tries to change the subject. "So, you seem to be feeling better, my little filly!"

"Oh, okay. Well, yes, and I really wanted to tell you that I am so sorry for saying that I hated you earlier. I was still feeling like I was still dreaming but had just woken up, so the shock didn't have a chance to wear off by the time you had come in," Sydney wholeheartedly apologizes.

"Wow, it must have been some morning here this morning!" Allison shockingly states.

"Oh, was it ever!" Sophie exaggerates.

"It wasn't all that bad," Sydney says as if it was nothing.

"That's a matter of opinion, bestie!" Sophie says as she walks away as if that was the end of that conversation.

"What happened if you don't mind me asking?" Allison wonders.

"I just had a horrible nightmare and would rather not think about it because it was truly just terrible," Sydney says, trying not to think about the nightmare.

"Well, while I am here and I have you ladies all present, I wanted to see if y'all would like to take day before school starts and go shopping?" Allison asks while eagerly waiting for responses.

"Mom, you know I am all for it!" Sophie says happily.

"You mean like you and Mom used to do?" Sydney asks, hoping so.

"Yes, ma'am, complete with lunch too!" Allison adds to sweeten the deal.

"Count me in!" Sydney says before she even thinks to ask if it was even okay. "I'm sorry, dad, Em? May I go too?" Sydney says putting herself back in check before her dad does.

"If I may interrupt? I am also asking you to come with us, Emma!" Allison says, making sure Emma knows she is included.

"Really? Allison, I have enough clothes," Emma starts to say when she gets interrupted.

"I'm sorry, don't mean to interrupt again, but don't you start teaching that new class this year?" Allison asks, making sure that Emma's situation with the school and her new job has not changed.

"Well, yes, but..." Emma starts to speak, and once again, she gets interrupted.

"Okay then, wouldn't you like a few new to you outfits for the new year?" Allison asks, knowing that she is pretty sure that Emma will agree.

"Yes, I suppose that would be nice," Emma finally gets to say. "So yes, Sydney and I will join you."

Greyson sits there, barely being able to contain himself.

"What so funny, Greyson?" Allison asks, confused.

"Dear, you are just so funny." Greyson laughs.

"Really? I'm sure you would love to tell me how funny I am," Allison states like she sees nothing that funny about herself as she looks over herself, thinking that something is out of place.

"No, dear, it's just you kept saying that you were sorry for interrupting, but you kept interrupting her. I'm sorry, I do not mean to pick on ya. Please don't take offense at my crude humor!" Greyson says as he chuckles a little more.

"Well, I was truly sorry but also super excited to do this with the girls and Emma. It's been a while since we really have had a chance to just spend the day just being girls! I also realize that we have a few weeks to plan this, but we all know how time gets away with us. So, I just wanted y'all to be aware so we can plan a date soon," Allison apologizes. "Maybe one or both of you guys can take Lucas since he doesn't have his dad around anymore?"

"Actually, she has a great point, Greyson. I think we both should take Lucas out. We can do some guy stuff, shop and lunch or dinner?" Parker agrees to Allison's great idea as he tries to get Greyson to join them.

"If we make it for a weekend, I think I would be game for a guys' day out," Greyson says, seeming happy about the guys' day.

"This has been very entertaining and awesome! But I must get back to my friends in the living room. You coming, Sophie?" Sydney asks her bestie.

"Sure, I think I have had enough of adult interaction for one day," Sophie jokes. "Just kidding, mom and dad. I love you!"

"Sydney, can you please ask Lucas to come out here for a minute?" Parker asks.

"Sure, Dad. I'll send him right in," Sydney says as she heads for the living room.

As Sydney and Sophie enter the living room, Lucas sees them and smiles.

"That's a little creepy," Sydney states.

"What is?" Lucas replies to Sydney.

"The way you smiled as we walked in the room like a creeper." Sydney laughs. "By the way, you are temporarily needed in the kitchen, Lucas."

"Oh, okay. Thanks. I will be back," Lucas says as he goes to see what's up.

"Can you believe that they basically fibbed to us about what they were talking about?" Sydney says, confused about why they did that.

"Yeah, I think I understand why, but it's not his nor your fault, so why does it matter?" Sophie wonders.

"Who knows, but it'll be our secret, bestie," Sydney whispers so that Eliza doesn't hear.

"What secret? Can you tell me?" Eliza hears and asks.

"Nah, there's no secret, sissy," Sophie says, trying to throw her off track.

"That's not what I heard," Eliza says, being slick.

"If you only knew what you think you heard." Sophie chuckles. "But seriously it was nothing, Liz."

Lucas returns only to catch the tail end of that conversation and asks, "What was nothing?"

"Nothing'!" Sophie laughs.

"Really?" Lucas asks, puzzled.

"Yep, nothing was nothing!" Sydney responds.

CHAPTER 17

The Big Secret

Parker comes into the living room and just stands there for a moment not saying a word but just like staring like he's in deep thought.

Sophie whispers to Sydney, "Uh, what's up with your dad?"

"I don't know, but it's very creepy what he is or is not doing there right now," Sydney eerily states. "Dad, you, okay?"

"Oh, sorry, guys. I was just thinking about trying to get in some training today. It looks as though the rain is letting up finally, and what better time than now to train," Parker states without hesitation.

"I'm sorry I don't know much about horses and racing, but it's wet and muddy. And you think this is a better time than ever to train?" Sophie says, being very confused.

"Yes, little lady, it is. It is great to be trained in controlling a horse in any weather condition or on any surface substance. It gives you the leg up," Parker informs Sophie.

"Oh, well, bring on the mud! Let's test our perseverance and push it to the limit!" Sophie cheers on.

"Okay, I will meet y'all out in the stables in fifteen minutes. Get dressed for mud because I am certain we will find some." Parker chuckles as he walks out of the living room. "See you kids in just fifteen minutes," Parker yells back from the hallway as he walks away to his room.

Sydney yells back, "Yes, dad, we know." Then she whispers so her dad can't hear, "That part he said about being trained in any weather or on any surface I think is just something we do."

"Well, it definitely seems like a good strategy," Lucas adds.

"Okay, we need to get changed and get out to the stables before dad comes looking for us," Sydney says to get them to get moving. "Do y'all have something to change into that doesn't matter?" Sydney knows that they are not just gonna come back a little muddy, but they will look like little mud babies.

"I do, and I am on it right now!" Sophie sates as she runs upstairs to quickly change.

"What you see is what you get with me," Lucas sadly shares.

"Okay, follow me. I have something that you may try to use." Sydney waves for Lucas to follow her. She takes him to the hall closet. "Now it's nothing much, but it will definitely keep you cleaner than without it. Here ya go. Put it on." Sydney hands him an old pair of Obee's denim overalls and an old sweatshirt. "I'm gonna go change really quick, be right back," she says as she takes off upstairs and just about runs Sophie over at the very top of the stairs. "Sorry, bestie. Be right down."

"Okay, Syd!" Sophie says in passing as she hurries downstairs.

When Sophie gets to the bottom of the stairs, she can't help but bust up laughing at Lucas. "I'm sorry, but what are you wearing?" she stresses in between her laughs.

"What? You don't like my styling new digs?" Lucas says as he shows off his new temporary style.

"You look like some hillbilly!" Sophie says while she continues laughing.

Just then, Sydney comes flying down the stairs and walks right in on Sophie laughing at Lucas. "Wow, what did I miss?"

"Sydney, you didn't miss it!" Sophie says as she gasps for air. "It's still here! Look at Lucas!"

"What's wrong with Lucas?" Sydney wonders.

"Well, just look at him!" Sophie just cannot control herself.

"Yeah, I see him. And to me, he looks more prepared than we are!" Sydney smiles. "Just you wait till we get back and see who's laughing then!" Sydney says as she winks at Lucas.

It was like someone had hit Sophie and knocked her out cold. There was instant silence. Lucas and Sydney just turned to see what happened to Sophie. And when they turned around and looked at her, it was as if you told her the worst news ever. They couldn't tell if she was upset or about to cry.

"Sophie? Are you okay?" Lucas asks.

"Yeah, I think we best be going before Parker comes looking for us," Sophie says, not so happy.

Sydney thinks about her comment and replies to Sophie, "I'm sorry, bestie. I was just kidding. But yes, let's go before my dad comes in. Are we all ready to test each other's limits?"

"I say bring it on and push me today like no other!" Lucas says as he smiles at the girls and heads to the door.

"Let's go, bestie." Sydney watches Lucas walk out the door. "Let's give Lucas a run for his money! Show him who he's up against. Yeah?" Sydney says, trying to get Sophie to cheer up and agree.

"Oh, okay, let's go whip some Lucas bum, bestie!" Sophie says in agreement with Sydney but still not letting her off on her previous muddy comment.

They both head out to the stables. Just as they get out the door and down to the bottom of the stairs, Parker comes out around the corner of the stables.

"There you girls are! Come on, we are burning daylight." Parker pushes then to hurry up.

The girls take off for the stables as if Parker was in a game of chase with them. As they go running around the corner of the stable, they all but run into the rear ends of Loads of Luck and PB Cup. They both stop dead in their tracks, look at each other then back towards Lucas, and they both burst laughing so hard.

"I am so glad to see that you two are having such a great time," Lucas says, shaking his head at their craziness, "but laugh it up, ladies, because you will be eating my mud very soon!" Lucas winks and pretends to do a double draw and then blows off his imaginary guns.

Sophie hands Lucas enough 'tude laid out on a tray with all the fixings for and Sydney as she says, "Whatever, Eastwood!" Then she rolls her eyes.

"Sophie, be nice. Save it for the track!" Sydney says sarcastically.

"Wow, listen to the roasting going on in here. I hope y'all bring all this energy to the track today! I wanna see you push the envelope and test each other's abilities to the max! Are we ready?" Parker says, pumping them up like a drill sergeant.

So, Sydney, Sophie, and Lucas return the act and respond in unison with, "Yes, sir!"

"Let's mount up and get to the starting point," instructs Parker.

Everyone mounts up and walks their horse out from the stable. Obee is at the fence waiting to open the gate and let them out. He has his ride waiting on the other side so he can mount up and ride out with them. It doesn't take them long to get out to the track they will be riding on. There are posts with neon flags on them to outline the track.

"Okay, here are the rules for today. You are gonna ride for distance endurance. As you can see, there are stakes or poles in the ground with little neon flags on them outlining the track. It's basically about half a mile out, then pick one of the three barrels and return. Now so we don't have anyone running into each other, whoever is on the right will take the barrel to the right. So, you will continue past the barrel then go right to come around it and continue back to here. Whoever is on the left will go to the barrel on the left, and the center person has their own choice. Please be careful to not run anyone over. Understand, everyone?" Parker asks after he gives them instructions.

"Yes, sir!" Lucas says with respect.

"Got it!" Sophie screams.

"Let's ride!" Sydney states.

"Okay, Obee will go out about halfway to be able to see all the way up to both ends of the track," Parker starts to say as Obee rides out to the midway point.

"Take your places, on your mark, get set," Parker says as he watches for Obee to signal that he's ready. Parker raises his arm with the cap gun in hand and shoots it.

Bang!

They take off with mud flying and raining down on Parker and Tall Leaps. He sits there so pleased with how well they are pushing each other up the track. They have reached Obee as he waves to let Parker know. Obee continues to watch them fling mud up as they pass by him. As they push closer to reaching the barrels, Obee gets ready to signal when each one rounds their barrel. Parker watches as Obee starts waving his arms around like a crazy fool who's lost his mind. Parker's anticipation of who will win this race has his heart racing harder than ever before. He feels kinda weird like something isn't quite right, but that quickly slips his mind as he sees Obee waving his arms again to signal that they have made the halfway point.

Parker quickly gets out of the way so he can get out his phone and snap some pictures to see who will be blessed with a win. As they grow ever closer, Parker pulls up his phone and gets ready to snap pictures. Parker snaps away as they zoom past him once again with mud a-flying everywhere.

After they cross the finish line, they circle back around to see who won.

"So out with it," Sydney demands.

"Well, it looked very close. Y'all did a great ride! But the camera does not lie! The winner for this race is..." Parker looks at Lucas and says, "Drumroll please, Lucas!"

Lucas smiles, nods, and begins his drumroll.

"This first time around, the winner is..." Parker holds out in making the excitement grow "S-S-S!" he starts.

Lucas stops drum-rolling for a second to say, "Congrats, ladies, it is obviously one of you two!" Lucas says then he continues to drum-roll.

"Okay, I have left you waiting long enough. The winner this round is Sophie!" Parker exclaims.

"Way to go! To my favorite bestie ever!" Sydney praises her.

"What? Wait! Seriously? Oh, dang! How cool! Wait, Parker, what do you mean by this round?" Sophie asks.

"Well, I was thinking that we would do at least two more rounds if y'all don't mind before it gets dark?" Parker informs them.

"Ah, sure, dad. I guess so," Sydney says, uncertain if it will be good or not.

"What's wrong Syd you afraid you won't win those either?" Lucas picks.

"Nah, not an issue," Sydney assures Lucas.

"Is everything okay, Syd?" Parker asks, concerned because it's not like Sydney to be hesitant about riding.

"Well, I don't know. It's just…" Sydney pauses for a moment then continues, "I guess I'm just over thinking things."

"Oh, okay. Well, we will do just one then, okay, guys?" Parker says, changing his mind.

"Whatever floats your boat! Man," Lucas adds.

"Okay, guys, excuse me, kiddos! Line up for our last race today. I wanna see a three-way tie! So, give it everything you got. Push, push, push! On your mark, get set…" Parker raises his arm.

Bang!

Once again, they tear off with mud flying! Parker watches as they pull away and race down the track away from him. Obee waves at the halfway point, again as they round the barrels, and again as they make it back to Obee! Parker gets ready to snap away at the finish line as he waves for Obee to make his way to the finish line, just as they blow past Parker and complete the second round. They circle back around. Lucas is already drumming away.

"Thanks, Lucas! This time our winner is... I believe I need the opinion of my partner. Obee, am I really seeing what I think I am seeing?" Parker asks in shock.

Obee whispers to Parker, they both nod in agreement, and then Obee says out loud for all to hear, "Yes, boss, I believe we have a tie!"

"Well, don't keep us waiting! Who tied whom?" Sydney asks, eager with excitement.

"Okay, this is very hard to say, but our tie is between Lucas," Parker states as Lucas nods, "and Sophie!" Parker finishes sadly, while Sophie smiles the biggest grin, they have ever seen on her.

"Congrats you guys," Sydney says as she kinda sounds a bit let down.

"It's okay, Syd. It was just for fun," Sophie says, trying to cheer her up.

"It's okay. I can't win everything. How fair would that be? I need to learn to lose occasionally," Sydney says, swallowing her jealousy and trying to keep up a happy façade.

"Okay, we will do this again sometime soon. Great job, kiddos! If we hurry, we should be able to get back just before dusk," Parker says.

Sydney gets this crazy idea that she wants to race everyone back so she can regain her winning status. So, she just takes off running as fast as SOT will go with mud flying and leaving everyone in the rear.

"Does anyone get the distinct notion that Syd wants to race?" Lucas asks.

"That's how I would see it," Sophie rebuts.

"Well, are you two gonna just let her win?" Parker antagonizes them.

"No, sir!" Lucas states as he takes off after Sydney with Sophie close behind.

"Come on, Obee. Let's join them!" Parker says as he kicks Tall Leaps and starts gaining on the kids.

"Right behind ya, boss!" Obee chuckles.

They are all in a race back to the stables. This time, Sydney wins. As she starts to take the glory, they quickly shoot her down and put her back in check.

"Whoo-hoo, I won!" Sydney states.

"Only because it wasn't a fair race. You had a huge head start. So, you may have won," Lucas starts to say.

Sophie finishes, "But it wasn't fair!"

"Oh, well. Doesn't matter anyways. I am super exhausted, and hungry," Sydney says, trying to change the subject.

"Me too!" Sophie says.

"Count me in on that one!" Lucas adds.

"As soon as all horses are put in their stalls and fed, then we can go in to clean up and eat," Parker sternly suggests.

Once all the horses are stalled, fed, and watered, they all head inside.

"Everyone, wash up before you even think about heading to the kitchen, please," Parker insists.

"I'm headed upstairs to change quickly and wash up, dad. Be right back," Sydney states.

"Right behind ya, bestie!" Sophie chimes in.

"Whatever!" Sydney says with some 'tude.

"Syd, are you okay?" Sophie asks.

"Yeah, sorry. I'm just tired and hungry," Sydney responds.

"Okay. I feel ya there. I am pushing hangry stage!" Sophie quickly informs Sydney.

The girls finish up and head back downstairs and to the kitchen just in time to catch the dinner prayer.

"Hurry up, sissy. I am gonna do the prayer!" Eliza softly shouts. "Sorry!" Sophie says as they quickly take their seats.

"Dear Jesus,

Thank you for this awesome meal made by Miss Emma! Please Bless her and everyone at this table, my mommy and daddy, and Lucas's mommy. Thank you for letting the rain stop too!

Amen."

"Very good, Liza," Emma says.

Everyone eats up, and Emma thinks about the kids needing to go home.

"So do I need to drop everyone off at home?" Emma asks.

"I can take them, Emma," Obee offers. "If that's okay with everyone?"

They all nod, and when they are finished, they gather their things and say their goodbyes, and Obee takes them all home.

"I'm really surprised, Syd. Normally, you ride along," Emma says, worried that something is up again. "Is everything okay?"

"Yeah, I'm just super tired. But I did want to chat with you before I went to bed," Sydney says as she yawns.

"Looks like we better hurry with your chat then before you fall asleep on me." Emma chuckles.

"Can you go with me to my room so we can speak in private?" Sydney asks, knowing this late at night that Parker will be too tired to care or even come up to her room.

"Sure thing. Let me just wash my hands quickly. Go ahead on up. I will be right behind you," Emma assures Sydney.

Sydney gets up from the table and heads to her room. She slips into her pj's and under her sheet till Emma gets there.

Emma comes in and asks, "Would you like me to shut the door?"

"Actually, yes please," Sydney replies.

Emma shuts the door and makes her way over to the chair beside Sydney's bed.

"So, what's up, young one?" Emma asks curiously.

"So, I have something I need you to be honest with me about. So earlier today, I overheard dad talking about Dylan's court case," Sydney starts.

"Oh, okay. I see. Yes, what do you want to know, dear?" Emma offers, knowing there's no use in her lying. She's mature enough to handle more than her dad gives her credit for.

"Well, obviously dad doesn't know about me knowing mostly everything, well enough that I know he lied to me today! Please tell me what's so hush hush that I can't know about Dylan's case?" Sydney wonders.

"Okay, I would like to first state that it's not entirely as it seems. Your dad did not want you knowing mainly because of your relationship with Lucas. He didn't want to interfere with putting a wedge between the two of you," Emma relays to Sydney.

"Relationship? What relationship? We are just friends!" Sydney freaks out, wondering why everyone seems to think that there is always some kind of relationship between her and Lucas.

"Well, your friendship is what we are obviously talking about because we know that you aren't dating or anything or as far as we know you aren't." Emma pokes to see if their friend status has changed.

"Absolutely not! We are still just friends, and it is all we will ever be!" Sydney says, stomping that out at the source. "So seriously it's because we are friends?"

"Yes."

"Okay, that's the craziest thing I have ever heard but okay." Sydney decides to just let it go.

"So, since I now know you know and you now know what you know, let's vow to keep this just between us, okay?" Emma asks, hoping and knowing Sydney should agree.

"I'm zipping my lips and throwing away the key!" Sydney says as she portrays zipping up her lips and throwing away the key in silence.

Emma kisses Sydney's forehead and pulls her cover up over her and turns out the light and heads to her room!

"Good night, Em! I love you!"

"Good night, Sydney. I love you too!"

CHAPTER 18
You Got Served

Sydney wakes feeling refreshed and like she had the best night of sleep in a long time. No dreams or interruptions, just peaceful sleep. As Sydney gets herself ready for the day, she thinks about everything that has happened in the recent days and decides that she is going to ask to spend the day at Sophie's just relaxing and hanging out in a different environment. When she is finished, she takes one last look in the mirror before heading downstairs.

As she goes down the stairs, she seems to have a little more pep in her step. She can't believe how well she slept last night. She says out loud to herself, "I really must figure out what allowed me to sleep so well so I can continue sleeping' that well!"

Emma hears Sydney taking to herself when she walks into the kitchen. "What was that Syd?" she asks.

"Oh, I was just talking to myself," Sydney says.

"Oh, pardon me. I didn't mean to eavesdrop, but did I hear something about sleeping?" Emma wonders.

"Well, since you asked, yes, I was just saying to myself that I must figure out what was different from last night compared to previous nights. I didn't have any nightmares or any dreams for that matter. I feel like I slept very well. I woke feeling refreshed and ready to get away," Sydney informs Emma.

"*Get* away? Where to?" Emma asks curiously.

"Well, nowhere in particular, but I was wondering if I could go to Sophie's house today for a change of scenery. And possibly stay the night?" Sydney asks, hoping she says yes.

"I don't see why not. But if you haven't already, you need to make sure it's okay with them that you come over, please," Emma kindly asks.

"Sure, I will do just that!" Sydney assures her.

Sydney sits down to have her breakfast while she messages the Abbotts.

Sydney: Bestie you up yet?

While she waits for Sophie's response, she finishes up her breakfast and excuses herself from the table.

"Em, I am going to pack a few things while I wait for Sophie to respond," Sydney says as she walks to the bottom of the stairs and heads to her room. On her way to her room, Sophie replies.

Sophie: Yes, I am what's up?

Sydney: Awesome cool! Would you mind some company?

Sophie: Sure, let me just ask my parents if it's okay.

Sydney: Sure, hope it is.

She just feels as though she needs to get away. Hopefully too so Lucas won't be able to come by and bother her.

Sophie: Yes, you can come over! Do you want us to come get you?

Sydney: Nah I will have Emma drop me off I think I heard her mention something about getting groceries so she will already be going out.

Sophie: Ok just let me know okay.

Sydney: Ok will do.

Sydney finishes packing a small bag then heads downstairs to find Emma.

"Emma?" Sydney yells out.

"Yes, dear?" Sydney faintly hears.

"Sophie said it's okay that I stay. Can you please take me over?" Sydney asks.

"Yes, I can. Can you please just give me a few minutes?" Sydney faintly hears again.

"Okay, I am going out to the stables. I will be out there when you are ready," Sydney says excitedly.

As she nears the barn, she overhears Obee and her dad talking about a special gift for Emma.

"Oh, I know what she would love!" Sydney quickly throws out there.

"Shhh. First off, my little filly. Keep it down! This is supposed to be a secret. Secondly, please tell us your idea!" Parker pleads.

"How about a day spa experience? You know what I mean? With a massage, hot tub, mud masks, the works! What lady could resist that?" Sydney pleasantly reports to her dad.

"Sydney, have I ever told you just how much I truly love you?" Parker gratefully asks.

"Well, I know, but you haven't told me yet today!" she cleverly states.

"Well, I do very much! Obee, can you stop by and get her a gift card. Here's one hundred and fifty dollars towards it," Parker says as he hands the cash to Obee.

"Yes, sir. I am on it right now. So, I don't forget." Obee takes the money and goes and gets in his truck and heads for the spa.

"Just so you know, dad, I am headed to Sophie's just as Em comes outside," Sydney says, trying to play off that she's bored at their house. "But for right now, though, I came out to see the world's most beautiful lady horse that I know!" Sydney walks up to SOT and rubs her neck.

SOT throws her head up almost as though she doesn't know Sydney. "Would you like a carrot, girl?" SOT throws her head up and down like she is nodding. Sydney walks away to the mini fridge and pulls out a carrot from the bag of carrots. She walks over to SOT, and SOT rips the carrot from her hand.

"Dang, girl. Next time, please take it a little easier," Sydney says, shocked at her behavior.

SOT walks to the back corner as far away from the other stalls as she can get. Sydney tries to call out to SOT to get her to come to Sydney and no luck. SOT just will not budge.

"Maybe it's just my imagination, or maybe it's just from all the recent storms, but SOT is acting very strange, dad! Don't you agree?" Sydney asks, searching for answers.

"I really don't know. I haven't noticed anything. But I will keep a closer eye out while you are gone," Parker offers.

"Okay, dad, thanks. I think I heard Emma calling my name," Sydney says as she walks to the end of the stables to look. "Yep, that's her! See you later, dad. I love you!" Sydney says as she runs over to Emma's car.

"I love you too, my little filly!" Parker shouts out after Sydney.

Sydney jumps in the car, and off they go.

"We sure will miss you when you are gone, young one. Do you know how long you are gonna be staying with Sophie?" Emma wonders.

"Probably just the day and night I should be home tomorrow sometime," Sydney shares.

"Do you think that you would like us to come getcha?" Emma asks as quickly as she adds, "I don't need to know now. Just think about it."

"You know I will let you know in plenty of time, Emma. Everything will be good. I will miss you guys too!" Sydney reassures Emma, knowing that it may help calm her nervousness about Sydney leaving again.

Sydney looks out the window deep in a trance as she thinks about how life has been with her leaving for the day or even the night since her mom was so violently taken from them. It's like they are afraid to let Sydney out of their sight for fear of something bad happening to her. But she can't stay cooped up there in that big house forever.

"Well, here you are, Syd. Have a great time. I promise not to worry too much," Emma says as she fights back the tears.

Sydney is so spaced out she doesn't even realize that they are there already at Sophie's. "Oh, yes. I know, Em, you are just a phone call away. I love you. Thanks again for the ride."

"No problem. Please tell Allison, Sophie, and everyone I said hello!" Emma relays to Sydney.

"Okay, Em. I love you!" Sydney says as she crawls out of the car and waves to Emma as she walks to the house and rings the doorbell.

Emma waits to make sure that Sydney gets in just fine before she backs up to leave. As she backs up and checks the street for cars, she notices a sheriff car pulling up to the curb in front of the Abbotts' house. She checks again for cars and carefully backs out and drives past him as she heads in town. She watches in her rearview mirror to see where he goes till, she can't see him no longer.

Back at the Abbott house

Sydney, Eliza, and Sophie are all in the living room getting ready to watch move when there's a knock at the door.

"I'll get it, Mom!" Eliza yells across the house.

"I'll go with her, Mom!" Sophie shouts as she gets up and follows Eliza to the door.

As the open it, they see a sheriff standing there.

"Hello, may we help you?" Eliza kindly asks.

"Yes, little lady. I am Sheriff Hutchins. Is your mommy and daddy home?" he asks.

"Just a minute." Eliza slams the door shut and runs yelling for Allison. "Mommy, Mommy, there's a sheriff at the door wanting to speak to you and daddy!"

Allison comes upstairs from the basement as she says, "Slow down, child. Go watch your movie. Thanks, girls. Why did you shut the door on him?" Allison says as she goes to open the door. "Hello. Sorry they shut the door on you."

"Oh, it's no harm done, ma'am," Sheriff Hutchins replies.

"What can we do for you?" Allison asks as she stands in the doorway.

As Sheriff Hutchins gets ready to speak, he starts to try to look past her like he's looking for someone or something else. "Ah yes, you are?" He asks.

"I am Allison Abbott. What's this about?" Allison asks, feeling a little on edge about how he's acting.

"Ah, yes. Exactly who I need to see!" He says as he opens a folder and pulls out an envelope with her name on it. You've been served."

"What's this for?" She asks, confused at first.

"It states everything you need to know with the letter contained inside the envelope. Ma'am is Mr. Abbott home?" he asks, still trying to look past her like she's trying to hide something.

"He should be back in a few minutes. Can I help you?" Allison asks confused but thinking it's probably the same thing for Greyson.

"No thanks, ma'am. I need to speak to him directly please," Sheriff Hutchins replies.

"Well, would you like to come inside and wait for him?" Allison offers.

"Thanks. I think I will." He accepts her offer to come in.

There's a desk close by the door that has a chair. Allison pulls it out for him and says, "Here's a place. You may sit if you so wish."

"Thanks, ma'am," he says as he takes a seat and looks around the room.

The girls just sit there with their movie paused as they stare at him from over the top of the back of the couch.

He notices them staring, and he nods at them. They quickly duck down so he can't see them, and then slowly they reemerge back up to the top just enough so that they can see him with just their tops of their heads down to their eyes sticking out.

Allison notices and says to them, "Girls! Stop staring!"

"Oh, it's okay, ma'am. I rather enjoy their little hide-and-seek playing. I miss having little ones around," he says, remembering back to when his son was just five.

"Oh, I'm sorry. I didn't know that you had any children, Sheriff," Allison apologizes.

"Well, it was just before we, my wife and I, moved here. He would have been thirteen this year." Colton thinks back to that devastating day as tears start to form in his eyes.

"I am so sorry. Do you mind me asking what happened?" Allison asks, feeling sorry for him.

He clears his throat and continues, "Ah, we were visiting family back from where we came from, and there was this small party with a couple children and their parents. The parents were inside just chatting and having some cocktails. The kids were all out at the pool. And, well, looking back, I...umm, well, let's just say everyone that was there that day no longer drinks because we all feel like it's everyone's fault especially my wife's and mine." Colton pauses as he wipes tears from his face.

"I am so sorry, Colton! I didn't know. I get what you are saying. You don't have to say any more." Allison apologizes for even bringing it up.

"It's okay. They had a pool alarm, but with people in and out of it all day, they just turned it off. I guess that the kids decided to take off and go out to their treehouse and didn't realize that he had stayed behind till it was too late." Colton sobs in agony like he was right back at that house, and it was happening to him all over again. "The sad thing is it doesn't matter how high your fence is or whether your pool sensor is on. No amount of security works unless you are paying attention when it's not being used."

Eliza goes over to Allison and whispers to her, "Mommy, why is the sheriff crying?"

Allison starts crying too as she tries to make Eliza understand. "Baby, his little boy went to heaven to live with the angels eight years ago," Allison whispers back.

Eliza runs over to Colton and gives him a strong hug and doesn't seem to want to let go. Colton is confused as to how to handle what to do next. He looks over to Allison for support and checks that it's okay. As Colton looks down at her, he remembers his little boy hugging him like that. He would always pick him up and sit him on his lap to hug him and kiss his little head. He picks up Eliza and sits her on his lap and hugs her as he cries so hard.

Then Eliza looks up at him and says with the saddest eyes and biggest heart, "I'm so sorry that your little boy is with the angels above. I am sure he watches you every day." She says it so sweetly that Colton has a major breakdown.

"I am the one who is sorry. I am such a wuss," he says as he kisses Eliza on her head and puts her back down on the floor. "Thank you, little one."

"I'm Eliza. What was your little boy's name, sir?" Eliza asks.

"His name was Brian Charles Hutchins. My wife and I named him after our dads, who both passed away before we got together. But we thought it would be nice to remember them by our firstborn son to share their first names," Colton shares as he remembers his dad.

With his response, Eliza is satisfied, so she walks away just as Greyson comes through the front door. As he does, he starts talking to Allison before he completely gets inside and sees the sheriff. "Honey, did you know there's a sheriff's car sitting out...side." Greyson stops talking as he gets inside and realizes that she knows because he is sitting in their house.

Colton quickly jumps up and wipes his face when sees Greyson come through the door. "I am Sheriff Hutchins," he starts when Greyson interrupts him.

"Yeah, I know who you are, but the real question is, why are you here?" Greyson can tell that something is not quite right, so he continues, "What did I walk in on? Someone care to tell me?"

Eliza stands up on the couch and says, "He was telling us a story about his little boy who is up in heaven with the angels, daddy." Then Eliza sits back down.

Greyson feels like a complete jerk. He then says, "Please forgive me. I didn't know that you even had a child."

"So, it would seem. But it's okay. I would not expect you to know. When we moved here eight years ago, it was to try to start over and not to forget about our son but to have a fresh start without people staring and whispering about us everywhere we went. So, we vowed to keep his memory alive in a special room we have set up for him, but we kept it secret from the community for fear of what people would think."

"Again, I'm so sorry for your loss, Colton. It must be so hard for you and your wife," Greyson sadly says as he hangs his head and thinks about what life would be like without one of his girls around.

"Some days such as today, it is very hard. It still seems like yesterday some days. But we are just living life one day at a time," Colton says, still sobbing a little. "God tested us that day, so we all vowed no more drinking because even social drinking can be a hazard. We have the proof in a memory in a room at home."

"So not to change the subject, but what really brings you out to our home?" Greyson wonders.

"Ah, yes. Well, that, sir, is all here in this letter. I'm sorry to have to do this, but this is to you." Colton takes out his folder, opens it, and hands him an envelope with his name on it and hands it to him. "You have been served."

"I think I know what this is, but you know me. Why must you be so cold about it?" Greyson asks.

"It's just a formality. I'm sorry. I must be going. I am sorry to have unloaded my past on you all. But can I ask that you don't tell anyone, please? Can we just pretend that we didn't even have this conversation today? I would appreciate it very much," Colton says in hopes that they will keep quiet and not say anything to anyone.

"Sure thing. And I know that you we're just doing your job. Don't take my craziness to heart. Sounds like you have enough to deal with," Greyson says as he shows Colton to the door. "Try to have a better day, Colton."

"I will try. Thanks," Colton says as he turns quickly to head to his car.

"Colton?" Greyson calls out to him.

Colton stops and turns and says, "Yeah?"

"We are here if you or your wife ever need to talk. Your secret is safe with us. Please stop by anytime," Greyson says to let Colton know they care deeply for them in their time of sorrow.

Colton nods and turns back toward his car.

Greyson returns inside and shuts the door.

"Well, honey, can we go to the kitchen and read our letters?" Greyson says as he puts his hand on Allison's back as they walk together into the kitchen.

Sydney is very curious as to what the letters are for, so she tries to get Sophie to help her listen without letting Eliza know what they are doing because she would just foil their plan. Sophie waits till Eliza isn't looking, and she mouths with her lips that she has a plan... just watch.

Sophie says to Eliza, "You want any drinks or snacks? I'm headed to the kitchen to get some."

"Yes please!" Eliza says excitedly.

"Okay, but you have to promise to be quiet and go wash your hands. Then come back out here and sit and wait for my return, okay?" Sophie asks if she understands.

Eliza nods, and Sophie motions for her to go wash up. As Eliza walks away, Sophie whispers to Sydney, "I'm gonna go listen up closer, then I will go in the kitchen and get us some treats, and I will dance around acting like I'm listening to my music, so they won't think I am listening and stop talking just because I am in the room. I just need my earphones out of the coffee table." Sophie grabs her phone and earphones and makes her way closer to the kitchen.

Sydney sits and watches to see what happens. Sophie stops just outside the kitchen and listens.

"I figured we were gonna get these," Greyson tells Allison.

"I'm just glad that we already made plans to be off on Friday," Allison says.

"I have to take this into my boss. I told him if I got one, I would bring it in," Greyson shares. "Can you make a copy of it?" he asks Allison.

"Sure thing, honey." Allison takes it to make a copy.

"I'm gonna call Parker and let him know that we got ours," Greyson says.

Sydney watches Sophie put in her earphones and makes her way into the kitchen just as Eliza returns.

"Where's Sophie?" Eliza whispers.

"She didn't come out yet. Just sit here and wait with me, okay?" Sydney tells Eliza.

In the kitchen, as Sophie walks in, Allison sees her and asks, "Is everything okay, Sophie?"

Sophie hears her mom but acts as though she doesn't and just goes about her business and is getting drinks and snacks for the girls and herself as she looks and dances like she's listening to music.

"Okay, you and those headphones. You never can hear what's going on around ya!" Allison laughs and shakes her head. "One day, you are going to be listening to those things and you are gonna miss out on some important info, young lady!"

Sophie hears her mom but tries to remain calm and unfazed like she didn't as she continues to get goodies for her and the girls.

Greyson calls Parker. "Parker? Hey, man, just wanted to let you know that Allison and I got our subpoenas for Friday." Greyson stands at the island, looking over the paperwork as Parker talks.

"Oh, okay, yeah, so are we working with the DA, or do we need our own attorney?" Greyson asks. There's a moment of silence. "Okay, I will come over there then to talk with you more. Let me just talk with Allison, and then I will be headed over. Okay, good to know. See you soon. Bye." Greyson hangs up as Allison returns. "Hey, I'm headed to Parker's. We need to chat with him about Friday. I'll back as soon as I can I love you!" Greyson says as he kisses Allison. "I love you, Sophie."

Sophie still acts as though she can't hear them.

Allison returns the kiss and says, "I love you too! And she can't hear you. She has her music in her ears again."

"Okay, will you let her know then? Thanks," Greyson says as he leaves the kitchen and goes out the front door.

CHAPTER 19
Didn't Say a Word

Sophie returns with enough snacks and drinks for an army.

"Dang, we are only watching a movie, maybe two! When do you think we are gonna eat all this food?" Sydney asks as she gives Sophie a *'Oh no, you didn't'* look. "Oh, by the way, your dad left outta here in quite the hurry."

"Yeah, I know!" Sophie smiles.

Sydney knows that she knows something. So, she moves in close and whispers, "So spill it then!"

"He is headed to your house to talk with your dad," Sophie whispers back.

"Really?" Sydney says curiously.

"Yep! It has something to do with the sheriff being here and something happening on Friday," Sophie relays to Sydney.

"That's Dylan's court hearing," Sydney says.

"Mommy, Sophie's whispering again!" Eliza shouts out.

"Sophie!" Allison yells from the back of the house.

"Sorry, Mom!" Sophie replies.

"I think I have a way to fix this," Sydney whispers to Sophie.

Sydney gets up off the couch and goes over and sits down next to Eliza.

"You know what?" Sydney whispers to Eliza.

"No, what?" Eliza whispers back with a giggle.

"You are so sweet and special to me!" Sydney continues to whisper. "I do not know what I would do without you in my life!"

Eliza nods and whispers, "Really?"

"Yes really! And do you know what else?" Sydney adds.

Eliza stares at Sydney with such a beautiful twinkle in her eyes as she whispers, "No, what is it?" She tries to quietly giggle.

"I have something special for you at home. But you have to promise to stop thinking that your sister and I are hiding things from you. I promise I will tell you when I whisper to your sister next time too, okay? When we whisper something to someone, it's something special just for them to hear," Sydney promises Eliza.

"Syd, what do you have for me?" Eliza wonders.

"It's something that was given to me when I was just about your age. I promise next time I see you; I will give it to you. But it will be our little secret. You know what else?" Sydney asks her again.

"No, what?" Eliza asks.

"Come here, let me get closer so I can whisper it to you, so Sophie doesn't hear," Sydney says as she moves in closer to

Eliza. "You are my very best friend!" Sydney puts her index finger to her lips as she quietly acts as though she is telling Eliza *'Shhh.'*

Eliza winks and nods as Sydney gets up and goes back to her seat.

Sophie just looks at Sydney like, *'What did you just do?'*

Sydney carefully winks at Sophie and looks down to her phone as she starts a text to Sophie.

Sydney: I do not think she is gonna be such a Tattle Tale anymore.

Sophie: Why?

Sydney: I told her people whisper special things to special people and it's not always for others to hear. So, when we whisper to each other one of us will have to go to her if she's near and whisper something special to her too!

Sophie: You are so cool I will be amazed if it works.

Sydney: We shall see! Wink wink.

"I'll be right back, ladies. I have to use the little ladies' room," Sydney says as she excuses herself from the living room.

"Want me to pause the movie, Syd?" Eliza asks.

"Sure thing, sweetie!" Sydney yells back over her shoulder as she heads to the bathroom.

While Sydney is in the bathroom, Sophie gets a text.

Lucas: Sophie is Syd with you?

Sophie: Yes, why what's up?

Lucas: Isn't Sydney's birthday later this week?

Sophie: It's the 24th of June. Today is... wow! It's the 19th. Where has the time gone?

Lucas: Exactly! I know she's only gonna be 15 but I still think that we as her friends should do something special for her. Got any ideas?

Sophie: Agh! She's coming I will get back to you a little later, okay?

Sophie quickly puts her phone down and tries to act normal as she feels her phone vibrate from a notification.

"You can start the movie back up, Eliza," Sydney tells her.

"Okay," she says in her cute, little, spunky voice.

"I think that you will like this movie, Syd," Sophie tells Sydney.

"Yeah, *Flicka* is my favorite, Syd," Eliza shares with a mouthful of popcorn.

"I heard about this movie! Isn't Tim McGraw in this one?" Sydney asks.

"Yes, he is!" Sophie quickly replies as she smiles.

"I love his music!" Sydney states happily.

"We do too!" Eliza adds.

Part way through the movie, Sydney passes out and seems to be sleeping pretty hard. Sophie decides to take advantage of the moment and messages Lucas.

Sophie: Lucas are you busy?

It takes a few minutes before Lucas responds.

Lucas: No not busy what's up?

Sophie: Syd fell asleep beside me, so I wanted to message you back about Syd's birthday.

Lucas: She's beside you?! Are you crazy?! What is she wakes up?

Sophie: She won't trust me, I know her once she falls asleep, like this, you really gotta be super loud for her to wake up. So, what were you thinking?

Lucas: Well, how about we do dinner and a movie? Or like bowling or something?

Sophie: I mean I guess so just the three of us?

Lucas: Actually, if it's okay, I would like to bring a friend.

Sophie: Sure who? Jaxon and Camden?

Lucas: No not those clowns my other friend.

Sophie: Clowns? Lol I thought they were your friends?

Lucas: Not like they used to be.

Sophie: Ok well yeah sure bring your friend.

Lucas: Maybe if we talk to Parker and Emma maybe we can just do something at her house? What's you think?

Sophie: Oh yeah that works too! Do you want me to speak with them?

Lucas: If you don't mind, I would like to talk with them since you spend more time with Sydney than I do. I think it would be a bit of a challenge for you to talk with them.

Sophie: Oh, sure good point.

Lucas: Ok I will talk with them and let you know what we come up with

Sophie: Oh, cool thanks

Lucas: No problem

Sophie: Ok ttys

Sophie and Eliza sit and finish the first movie, then they put in another movie when Allison comes into the living room.

"Hey, girls!" Allison says loudly till she notices that Sydney is passed out on the couch. "Oh, sorry. I didn't know she was sleeping," Allison whispers.

"Yeah, she's been out for a while," Sophie whispers to her mom. "Mom, can I talk to you in the kitchen please?"

"Sure, sweetheart. Is everything okay?" Allison asks as she and Sophie get up and go to the kitchen.

"Yes, everything is good. I was wondering about Syd's birthday. Lucas is going to ask Parker and Emma if we can throw a party over there for her. I would like for you and dad to be there. Can you make it?" Sophie asks while trying to look past her mom to make sure that Sydney is still sleeping.

"Do you know a time, date, and place yet?" Allison asks.

"Lucas is checking with the Ashcraft's for the place. We haven't decided on a date just, yet we have just started discussing it. Once we do then we will worry about a time. Hopefully, though, we should know very soon. I am just waiting for Lucas to contact me again."

"Well, as long as we don't have anything else planned for said day, I don't see why we can't be there," Allison says as she gets a message on her phone.

Greyson: I'm on my way home. Do we need anything?

Allison: Can you please grab some milk? Oh, and be very quiet when you come in the house. Sydney fell asleep on the couch.

Greyson: Yes, ma'am I will get some and okay I will try my best.

Allison: I love you honey.

Greyson: I love you too babe.

"Your dad is on his way back. Did you need anything?" Allison asks Sophie.

"Maybe some tea?" Sophie responds.

"Well, text your dad quick before he gets to the store," Allison quickly says.

Sophie: Dad can you please get some tea?

Greyson: What kind?

Sophie: I guess green.

Greyson: Sure, sweetheart I love you.

Sophie: Love you too dad.

"I'm going back in to finish watching the movie," Sophie says, yawning.

"It looks and sounds to me like you are headed to lie down next to Sydney." Allison quietly chuckles.

"You are probably right! Sophie says as she hugs her mom and continues with, "I love you, mom!" and sends her an air kiss.

"I love you too, sweetie," Allison says, yawning too. "Oh, it's contagious."

"Well, it is almost 11 o'clock," Sophie tells her mom.

"Yes, I see that. I guess I know where I am headed just as soon as your dad gets home," Allison states as she gets up off the stool. "I guess I will come watch the movie with you for a few minutes."

When Greyson gets home a few minutes later, he enters the house only to find that all the girls are passed out on the couch including Allison. He takes the milk and tea and puts them in the fridge.

He then walks over close to Allison and gives her a slight nudge. She just mumbles and stays asleep. Greyson decides to start softly kissing her, first on her forehead then down to the side of her face and on to her lips. She again mumbles something along the line of "When did we get a dog?" but her eyes never open, and she doesn't move other than that.

Greyson chuckles for a moment, then he decides that he is not going to bed alone, and if she won't get up, he will just have to pick her up and carry her. He leans in close and picks up her arm and wraps it around his neck as he slides his arm in under the middle of her back. He then takes his other arm and puts it under her legs and carefully picks her up.

He slowly and carefully walks back the hall to their room. As he passes through the door to their room, he lifts his foot and catches the door to close it behind himself.

He lays her on the bed and tries to make her more comfortable. He slips off her shoes then her slacks. Before he does anything else, he makes sure that their door is closed. Then he looks for a nightgown for her, and then he continues getting her ready for bed.

He unbuttons her blouse and pulls her one arm back through the sleeve. Then he rolls her over just enough to open her bra. And he pulls the strap down over her arm and lays her back on the bed as he continues removing her blouse and bra. Then he picks up her nightgown and slips it over her head as he tries to sit her up just enough so he can put each arm through its armhole, then he rolls her over just enough to pull it down in the back then rolls her over on to her back as he pulls her nightgown down over her front and pulls the covers up over her.

Greyson is not quite ready to go to sleep, so he goes out to get a bottle of water from the fridge. On his way back to the bedroom, he stops off at the living room and turns the TV, DVD player, and the lights off before he heads back to bed.

Greyson walks back to his bedroom, goes in, turns off the lights, walks over to the bed by the way of the light from his phone. He turns on his bedside light and sits down on the bed when suddenly he screams and jumps right up outta bed! He quickly covers his mouth as he quietly screams at Allison, "I thought that you were asleep!"

"Well, apparently, I was because the last thing I remember was sitting on the couch watching a movie with the girls. Then I wake up here in bed and not in my clothes that I was wearing. Honey, did you take advantage of me while I was sleeping?" Allison asks, knowing better.

"No, I would never even think about doing that, sweetheart," Greyson jokes.

"I know, honey. I was just picking with you. So how did it go over at Parker's?" Allison wonders.

"Apparently, Parker talked with the district attorney, and there is some kind of conflict, so they are pushing back the hearing date a few days. We are supposed to get a letter in the mail with the new information in it. But while I was there, Lucas and Claire showed up," Greyson tells Allison.

"Oh, I bet I know why!" Allison smiles and giggles like a little girl.

"Oh yeah, why do you think?" Greyson playfully teases.

"Because of Sydney's birthday. He wants to have a party for her. Lucas was chatting with Sophie today, and they want to have a little party even though she will only be fifteen," Allison says like she is the queen of knowing everything.

"Well, you are partly right. So, since the hearing got moved, want to go to Sydney's party on Friday?" Greyson quickly adds.

"Sure, do you have any other details?" Allison asks.

"Parker said he would see that we knew the rest tomorrow. They were working out the rest of the details when I left," Greyson tells her.

"Oh, okay, awesome. I told Sophie we would try to go if we could," Allison says as she sits there thinking for just a moment when she quietly yells out, "Wait! What? What's this partly stuff?"

"I do not know if I should say or just let you wait and find out for yourself?" Greyson sits and waits for the moment to get more intense.

"Really, Greyson?" Allison says sternly. "I would tell you if I knew something. Come on, spill it!"

"Okay, but you cannot say a word to anyone! Because if you do and it gets back to me, I'm just gonna say that I didn't say a word!" Greyson tests her.

Allison jokingly punches Greyson on his arm and says, "Greyson, just tell me already!"

"Oh-kay! Oh-kay! Holy cow, woman!" Greyson laughs until he sees Allison give him the hairy eyeball. So, Greyson mumbles that Claire asked Parker to dinner!

"Wait, did I hear you right?" Allison asks.

"Well, I guess that depends on what you think you heard." Greyson laughs.

"What I think I heard is Claire asked Parker to dinner? Aww, that's so cute. They would make a very cute couple," Allison says, feeling nostalgic thinking back to her and Greyson's first dinner.

"Please, you cannot say a word!" Greyson politely demands.

"I won't!" Allison says all giddy-like.

"Allison, promise!" Greyson sternly says.

"I promise, honey. You know we should get some sleep, it's getting late," Allison suggests to him.

"Good point! Good night, dear. I love you!" Greyson says as he turns out his light.

"Good night, honey. I love you too!" Allison says as she cuddles up next to Greyson.

CHAPTER 20
We Got This

Sydney wakes up before everyone else, so she decides to go on Facebook, and she is looking through her notifications. There doesn't seem to be much going on. She sees today, June 20th, birthdays. She clicks on it to see if anyone she knows has a birthday today. *Oh, cool, it's Miss Dixon's birthday*, Sydney thinks to herself. She wishes her a happy birthday and then she gets off her phone and turns on the TV to look for something to watch till someone gets up.

About thirty minutes go by when Greyson comes out from his bedroom.

"Good morning, Greyson," Sydney greets him.

"Oh, good morning, Sydney! Are you the only one who is up?" Greyson asks.

Sydney chuckles, "I was till you came out."

"Are you hungry? Want some cereal?" He politely asks.

"I can wait for Sophie and Eliza, sir," Sydney responds even though she is very hungry.

"You're not home. I appreciate your respect, but please don't call me sir, and are you sure? It could be a while till they get up," Greyson notifies her.

"Sorry, and I am hungry, but I don't want to be rude and eat without the girls. But it's okay. I can wait. I'm sure it won't be much longer," Sydney says, trying to patiently wait.

"Oh, it sounds like your mind is made up, so I'm sorry to push. I won't bother you anymore about it," Greyson states. "I hope you don't mind me grabbing a quick bite to eat because I have to meet with your dad this morning. We have some errands to run together."

Greyson tries not to be rude and eat in front of her.

"Oh no, please go ahead. I have to use the ladies' room anyway," Sydney says as she heads quickly for the bathroom.

When Sydney is finished, she comes out to see that Sophie is awake.

"Hey, bestie! You're up!" Sydney says happily.

"Yes, I am, but how did you sleep?" Sophie asks as she tries to stretch and rub achy body parts.

"I slept okay. Didn't you?" Sydney says, watching Sophie as she dances around or exercises or whatever it is she is trying to do.

"*No!* Not really. We need to sleep in my room on my bed next time, Syd. I am aching all over," Sophie says, still trying to stretch. "So how long have you been up, Syd?"

"Long enough to go online and see its Miss Dixon has a birthday today! I didn't know her birthday was close to mine!" Sydney says, surprised and excited.

"Wow, really? That's cool! Did you wish her a happy birthday?" Sophie wonders.

"Yes, ma'am! I did! Are you going to?" Sydney asks.

"Well, duh! Of course! I'm not sure if you know it or not, but she is one of my favorite teachers!" Sophie says happily.

"That's awesome! I like her too! So, what are we doing today?" Sydney asks to see what Sophie would like to do.

"I can help answer that. Last night, Parker said that after we run our errands today, he was stopping by to pick you girls up for some training time," Greyson informs the girls.

"How long do you think you will be, Dad?" Sophie asks.

"Hopefully not too long. I can message you when we are headed back. But for now, I must go. Please come here, Sophie." Greyson meets her halfway, and he hugs and kisses her forehead then continues, "Please tell your mom and sister that I love them."

"Will do, Dad!" Sophie says.

Greyson leaves, and just as he goes out and shuts the door, Eliza wakes up.

"Sophie?" Eliza yells as she jumps up on the couch.

"I'm right here, sissy," Sophie says as she comes out from the kitchen. "Are you hungry?"

"Yes, please!" Eliza says as she jumps up off the couch and runs for the kitchen.

"Syd, Eliza, what do you want for breakfast?" Sophie asks.

"I'm good with cereal. Whatcha got?" Sydney asks, hoping to hear soon.

"We got Cinnamon Life, Cinnamon Oat Squares, Fruity Pebbles, Lucky Charms, Cinnamon Toast Crunch," Sophie says, listing off what they had.

"I think I will have what Eliza is having," Sydney says, looking at Eliza and waiting for her response.

"Sissy, I want a hurricane cereal!" Eliza says while acting very silly.

Sydney looks at Sophie and has a very strange look on her face.

"Oh, what kind of hurricane cereal do you want?" Sophie asks, pretty sure she knows which ones but just wants to make sure.

"I want Life, Oat Squares, and Toast Crunch all together! Please!" Eliza says, watching her get the boxes so she can mix them.

"Okay, one bowl of Cinnamon Life Square Crunch coming up! Syd, you still want what she wants?" Sophie asks.

"Actually, yes! Yes, I do! It does not sound all that bad now that I think about it!" Sydney says, sticking to her word.

"Okay, here is your bowl, Liz, and now for Syd's bowl." Sophie pours out a bowl for Sydney and pushes it over to her.

Sophie pours herself a bowl of cereal and sits down to eat with Syd and Liz.

"You know what, Liz?" Sydney asks.

"What, Syd?" Eliza stares at her with the cutest green eyes.

"This is good! Thanks for the breakfast experience," Sydney shares.

They finish up their breakfast and get ready for the day. They decide to sit and watch TV till Parker gets back.

A few hours passes when Sophie gets a text.

> *Greyson:* We are headed back.
>
> *Sophie:* Ok we are already ready.
>
> *Greyson:* Ok love you.
>
> *Sophie:* Love you too dad!

"Okay, they are headed back. Do you think Eliza will be coming with?" Sophie asks.

"Let me message Emma and see if she can hang with her," Sydney replies.

"Okay, I will ask Mom to make sure too," Sophie adds.

"Well, I will wait till you ask your mom," Sydney says before bothering Emma.

Sophie goes back to her mom's room and knocks. She says through the door, "It's me, mom. I have a quick question for you." Sophie opens the door and goes in.

Sydney hears the door open as Sophie comes out saying, "Okay, mom, thanks. I love you!" She nods as she comes walking out then says, "She said it's okay with her if it's okay with Emma."

"Okay, let me see what she has planned," Sydney says as she starts to text Emma.

> *Sydney:* Emma what are you doing today? Can Eliza come over while we train?

"Okay, now we wait. Hopefully she gets back to me before our dads get back," Sydney states.

> *Emma:* Sure, she can! I'm not that busy.

Sydney: Ok cool! Love and miss you Em!

Emma: Love you too.

"Emma said it's okay!" Sydney shares.

Eliza gets excited, so excited she can't sit still.

Then the front door opens, and Greyson and Parker come in. "Are you ladies ready?" Parker asks.

"Yes, we are!" Eliza says with enough excitement for them all.

"Oh, are you coming too, Eliza?" Parker asks, not quite knowing whether she is definitely coming along.

"Yes, dad. Emma and Allison said it was okay," Sydney tells him.

"Okay, well, let's go get loaded up, everyone," Parker instructs them. "I will talk with you soon, Greyson." He walks out the door and shuts it behind himself.

As Parker gets in the truck, he tells the girls, "I have one more stop on the way home."

"Where's that, Dad?" Sydney wonders.

"I have to get Lucas," Parker shares.

They get Lucas and head to the ranch. As they pull up, Emma is outside waiting for them.

"Come in for some sandwiches quickly before you guys go to train," Emma suggests.

"You kids go ahead. I will be in just as soon as I talk with Obee," Parker says to them.

Parker goes to the stables to look for Obee. He walks out to the training ring and no Obee. He turns around then walks back into the stables and runs hard right into Obee! Their heads hit, and they almost knock each other out.

"I was looking for you, Obee. What a way to find you," Parker chuckles.

"Yeah, I know the kids told me. I was inside waiting for you to come in to eat with us. So, what did you need me for?" Obee wonders.

"While I was out with Greyson, I got that spa gift certificate we wanted to give to Emma. When do you think we should give it to her?" Parker asks for Obee's opinion.

"We should put it in a nice card and just lay it in on the counter like later tonight and just let her find it tomorrow morning. What do you think?" Obee says, liking his idea a lot.

"Well, I did get her a nice thank you card. Let's sign it, and we can do that later after she retires for the night," Parker says, agreeing with Obee and his idea.

They sign the thank you card for Emma and head inside for a quick lunch. They wash up and go seat themselves at the table. "Sorry, we are late. We just had something to take care of quickly. Did we miss grace?" Parker asks.

"Yes, I am afraid that you did, but we will forgive you this one time," Emma says as she smiles.

"I need to speak with Lucas and Sophie after we eat and before we head out to train," Parker informs them.

Sydney and Sophie look at each other like it was odd that her dad didn't include her. But Sophie has a good idea why, he wants to see them and not Sydney.

Sydney excuses herself from the table to go use the ladies' room. While she is out, they all quickly whisper and discuss the party for Sydney. Lucas, Sophie, and Eliza offer to do decorations. Emma says she will make the cake and some food. Parker and Obee offer to do something with Sydney to distract her from everyone else getting the house ready for the party. They get everything planned out just in time before Sydney returns.

Lucas finishes by saying, "It's okay. We got this! She will be so shocked."

Just as Lucas completes his comment, Sydney comes back into the kitchen and asks, "Who will be shocked?"

"Your dad!" Lucas says hoping she buys it.

Sydney looks at her dad and then around the table at everyone else. "Why would you be shocked, dad?"

Parker quickly tries to think of something believable. "I'm sorry. I went ahead and talked with Sophie and Lucas while you were in the ladies' room. I basically told them that I need them here as much as possible so we can train hard so we can get a bunch of trophies this year."

Lucas chimes in, "Yeah, and I said we would get so many he would be shocked!"

They all laugh as Sydney states, "Oh, it sure won't be hard! And speaking of training, we should get on it."

"Yes, you are right. We have to go get training. Come on, kids, let's get out there and see what you got for me today!" Parker says, very excited about how well they will do today. "Obee, are you coming with?"

"Yep, for sure! I'm right behind you."

They go out and saddle up the horses and head out to train. Eliza stays back with Emma. Eliza and Emma work on party details. They go shopping to get supplies to make the cake and other food supplies that are needed. By the time Emma and Eliza get back, the mail has gone, so Emma stops to check it and then comes in the lane and to the house. As Emma and Eliza empty out the car, they hear laughing and giggling coming from the stables.

"Eliza, we need to hurry and get these items in the house before Sydney sees. Quickly, help me grab everything and let's get it inside," Emma quickly and quietly tells Eliza.

Eliza helps Emma grab all the goodies and get it inside before anyone realizes that they even left. Once they get inside, they quickly rush around, putting everything away so no one can see what they bought.

"Okay, let's make some dinner. Hang out at the island, and I will cook up some burger and some noodles. Would you mind helping me make some lasagna? You can help me make layers with the noodles then cheese and sauce. Sound like fun?" Emma asks.

Eliza lights up as she says, "Yes that sounds fun!" as she claps. "My mommy is too busy to let me help her cook."

Emma smiles as she prepares everything so they can start making dinner while everyone else is out at the stables, where there seems to be some excitement.

Everyone is laughing and having a great time.

"That was just hilarious when he reared up and you went flying off the back, Lucas! And we already knew that it isn't your first time either except usually you go up over the top of his head!" Sydney laughs at Lucas.

"Well, your ride was awful moody today, wasn't she? Just stomping and kicking like that!" Lucas laughs back.

"It's like it's a full moon or something." Sophie chuckles.

"All I know is once we got these beautiful creatures under control, you guys had one heck of a training day. But let's get them cleaned up, fed, and taken care of for the night because I do not know about y'all, but I am famished!" Parker says to hurry them along.

They all work together to get everything done and head inside to wash up. When they get inside, Emma comes out of the kitchen to see what all the ruckus is.

"Hey, Emma! It smells awesome in here. How much longer?" Parker wonders.

"Just a few more minutes. Sounds like y'all were having a good time out there," Emma smiles.

"Yes, we had an extremely good day worth of training and a bunch of fun!" Parker expresses.

"Oh, good. When you are done washing up, you have some mail," Emma informs Parker.

Emma goes back to the kitchen to check up on dinner and gives Eliza plates and utensils to set the table with. The kids come running into the kitchen and pick their places at the table and wait for dinner to be ready.

Parker comes into the kitchen and looks through the mail and sees the letter from the district attorney's office. He opens it and reads it then excuses himself from the kitchen to make a phone call to Greyson. When he's done talking with Greyson, he heads back to the kitchen.

The food is on the table, and everyone is ready to eat. Everyone is looking at Parker as he has a confused look on his face as he starts to ask, "Did someone already..." Parker stops as he gets interrupted by Sydney.

"Yes, dad. Grace has already been said." Sydney smiles.

They all eat and talk about the day's events. When they are done, Sophie and Lucas make plans to get rides home.

"Lucas, if you want, I'm sure we can take you home to save your mom a trip out here," Sophie says, winking at Lucas so that no one else can see.

"Oh, yeah. That would be totally awesome. Thanks. I will let my mom know." Lucas catches on quite quickly to what Sophie is up to.

A few minutes later, Greyson and Allison stop by to get Lucas and their girls. They don't stay long, but Parker, Emma, and Sydney see them off while Obee leaves the card and gift certificate for Emma on the island in the kitchen.

Obee then leaves the kitchen and heads for the front door as he exits as Parker, Emma, and Sydney come back in.

Sydney heads to the living room, and Parker follows her as Emma goes into the kitchen to finish cleaning up.

Suddenly, Parker hears screaming coming from the kitchen. He gets up quickly and rushes in to see what's going on with Sydney hot on his heels.

"Emma? Are you okay?" Parker shouts out as he runs to the kitchen. When Parker enters the kitchen, he sees Emma crying. "Are you okay? Did you cut yourself? Did you fall?" Parker asks, concerned.

"No, no, no, I am just fine," Emma gushed.

"But you are crying! So, something has to be wrong! So, what's up?" Parker searches for why she is crying.

"These are tears of complete joy! Parker, you and Obee and you too, Sydney, are all so amazing!" Emma exclaims.

Just then, Parker feels so silly that he never even noticed that Emma had opened the gift that they got her.

"You are so welcome, Emma. We felt you so deserved a day of pampering, so whenever you want to go, just let me know, and I will take care of your duties," Parker offers.

"I will definitely take you up on that offer, Parker," Emma states with certainty. "For now, I am calling it a night. Thank you again!"

"Okay, good night, Emma. We will finish up here," Parker reassures Emma. "Come on, Syd, let's finish cleaning up the kitchen.

When they finish, Parker heads off to his room, and Sydney goes to hers to watch a little TV before she goes to bed.

CHAPTER 21
Happy Birthday

The last four days have been a blur of excitement. Sydney, Sophie, and Lucas had so much fun that the time literally just flew by. They had two more great days of sales at the boutique, another amazing day of training, and they even took some time with Eliza to go out to the lake to go fishing.

Sophie, Eliza, and Lucas all get a ride together to head home, or at least that's what they want Sydney to believe. They all say their goodbyes before leaving.

"Syd, I had such a great time fishing today. I can't wait to do it again very soon!" Sophie beamed.

"Thank you, Syd, for inviting me to come with y'all fishing. I had a lot of fun too!" Eliza chimed in.

"Oh, you guys do not ever have to thank me. You are my friends, and I really enjoy your company. Anytime you want to come, spend some time with me no matter how little or how long!" Sydney expresses from the heart to them.

"Well, I too had an amazing time! Every time we hang out lately, it just seems that we can always find a way to have even more fun than the last time we hung out. I really wish that we could just never sleep and hang out 24-7!" Lucas insisted.

"Oh, okay, Lucas. Yes, we love you very much, but even I need some sleep to reset from our current fun adventures! And you wanna hang 24-7? I think you would seriously get very tired of me very quickly if that ever happened. But yeah, if I could go without sleep, yeah, I think that I could probably hang out a lot more too! Maybe not 24-7 though," Sydney says mostly in agreement with Lucas.

"But are you guys all really sure that you have to leave this early?" Sydney begged, hoping that someone would want to stay just a little longer to hang out with her. After all, it is her birthday tomorrow, Sydney thinks to herself.

"I would love to, Syd, but I have been slacking big time on my chores at home, and I just keep promising my mom that I will do them, but then I just keep leaving and coming back here. So, I am so sorry, but I just can't. I mean if I can get home and get my chores done quick enough, maybe I can come back over," Sophie says, hoping that's where Sydney leaves it.

"I would love to come help you. That's if you wanted me to," Sydney noted.

"It's okay, Syd. I am not asking. But I will work as hard as I can to make it back over, okay?" Sophie explained.

"Yeah, okay, it's fine. Don't worry about it. I'm sure that I probably have some chores to do too," Sydney says, kinda bummed out.

"I probably have some chores too, but I also kinda had plans with my friend this evening! Which I honestly almost forgot about. But I did have a g-gr-gr-great time, though," Lucas says, acting like he's that cereal critter.

"Oh, okay, okay, I get it. Well, I hope to see all or some of you soon!" Sydney cheered. "I'm gonna miss y'all!" She reaches out for hugs from each one of them.

Lucas jumps at the chance to hug Sydney first. He tries to subtly kiss her quietly on her cheek so as not to arouse suspicion from anyone else.

Next, Sophie and Eliza give Sydney a big hug from them both at the same time.

They all collect into Allison's car as Sydney stands there waving goodbye just in time for her dad to come around the corner of the stables, smiling.

"Dad, what are you doing?" Sydney asks.

"I'm sorry. I was waiting for everyone to leave. I had something special I wanted to ask you for tomorrow evening," Parker says as he continues to smile.

"Really? I'm intrigued to know what it is that you want to ask me?" Sydney wonders.

"I was actually wanting you and I to go out for dinner together. Since your mom was so brutally taken from us, you and I haven't really been out together and I thought, why not? So, you want to accompany me for a nice, quiet dinner? Just the two of us. And maybe a little shopping too?" Parker suggests.

Sydney rushes to hug her dad. "Oh, dad, I would love to accompany you to dinner. Where are we going?" Sydney asks with excitement.

"Sweetheart, that is completely up to you, but I do not need to know right now!" Parker quickly expresses. "Give it some thought, okay? I want it to be special for my special little filly." He smiles as he reaches out to pull her in for a hug.

They both embrace in a long hug like neither wants to let go. Parker smiles as he thinks back to the last time that he has had such a loving connection with Syd. He just wishes she would never have to grow up.

When they are done sharing their gentle, loving hug, they both have tears in their eyes as they pull away from each other. They both quickly wipe them away as they chuckle.
"You are now sworn to secrecy that you seen me crying!" Parker swears to Sydney.

"My lips are sealed with super glue!" Sydney laughs.

"I guess we should go see what Emma is into," Parker suggests.
"Sure, dad!" Sydney says as she puts her arm around her dad to walk into the house together.

Parker puts his arm around Sydney too as he acts as if he wants to say something to Sydney. "You know...ah, never mind."

"Pardon me for my crazy heart and thoughts, dad, but I really miss Mom!" Sydney mourns as she wept. "I miss her hugs and life talks with me."

Parker stops and turns to Sydney. "Sweetheart, you are absolutely amazing! I didn't want to bring it up, but I am so glad that you did! That is exactly what I wanted to say. I was just afraid to." Parker sobs as he starts to apologize.

"I'm so sorry for my weak heart!" He hangs his head in shame.

Sydney puts her hand on his cheeks and moves his head so she can look him in the eyes, and she cries as she says, "Dad, I love you so much, just as mom did, and I am so sure she still does. Please do not ever think your heart is weak! What you and mom had was something so special, you are not weak! You are a broken-hearted man, father, and husband who desperately needs to express himself openly and freely so you can properly grieve. I will never look down on you for doing the only thing that feels right. Remember what mom always said too! *Crying builds character!* I love you so much, dad. You are the most important person in my life, and don't you ever forget it!" Sydney sobs harder as Parker wipes her tears.

Parker chuckles. "Sydney, you are so wise beyond your years. I am so proud of you, and I know that you probably get a lot of your knowledge from your grandad, Jack." Parker pauses for a moment as he begins to cry more. "I'm sorry, Syd. I miss him so much too! I'm so glad that you took after him and your mother."

"I know I do too! But let's take some deep breaths and collect ourselves so we can go inside and see what Emma is up to." Sydney stops and thinks for a moment.

As Parker wipes tears away, he sees the look on Sydney's face and states, "Oh, I know that look! Just what are you scheming now, my little filly?" Parker curiously asks.

"Dad, would you be into maybe going to a movie this evening?" Sydney hopes he says yes.

"To be honest, that sounds like a really good idea! Let's go check with Emma. Then we can get ready and just go see what's playing. How's that sound?" Parker offers.

"That sounds like a great idea!" Sydney responds as they hurry into the house to see Emma.

As they run up the front steps, they hit the door so quickly that it flies open. When Emma hears this, she quickly comes outta the kitchen to see what all the commotion is.

"Y'all in a hurry?" Emma starts to scold till she sees them, then she quickly chuckles when she sees them laughing and giggling.

"We are good, Emma. Sorry, we need a little father-daughter time. Would you mind if we went to the movies?" Parker asks.

"That would be awesome! Yes, you two please go have some fun! I have some things that I really must get done, and I really do not need any distractions," Emma says then restates her comment. "Let me rephrase that—y'all are not a distraction, but this is very important, and if y'all were out having a great time, then I would be happy, and everything would just work out so much better." Emma sighs.

"Okay, we understand, Emma. Syd, go get ready!" Parker says. Just after Sydney takes off up the stairs, he hollers up after her, "Carefully, my little filly."

"Was that your idea to go to the movies?" Emma questions Parker.

"Actually, no. It was Sydney's, and I just wanted to check with you first," Parker replies.

"Well, I must say it's perfect because I need to get her cake made, and I was really concerned about how I was gonna get her outta the house so I could," Emma exclaims.

"Well then, it all worked out. I better go get ready so we can get outta here soon. Listen, I said I was taking her somewhere nice tomorrow evening, but since you need us, well Syd, to be gone for a little while, I think I will try to take her for a bite to eat and maybe some ice cream after the movie as well. If that helps at all?" Parker volunteers.

"Oh yes because I would like to see if Eliza can come over to help. I promised her that she could," Emma says happily.

"Okay, consider it done! I must get my rear in gear! I'll be right back, Emma," Parker says as he takes off towards his room.

Emma messages Allison, hoping that Eliza could come over.

Emma: Allison hello! I was wondering if Eliza could come over to help make Sydney's cake? I told her if it was ok with you that she was more than welcome to come help to make it.

Just then, Sydney comes bouncing down the stairs. Emma says out of concern, "Sydney, what will it take for you to slow down on those stairs?"

"I honestly do not know, but I am excited to get to spend some much-needed time with my dad!" Sydney says ecstatically and outta breath.

"I know that you don't wanna be spending it with your dad in a hospital ER with a broken leg or an arm. I'm sorry, I don't mean to be naggy like I am your mother, but I really do care for you like you are my daughter," Emma tries to relay to Sydney. "Please have a great time this evening. You both deserve some great private time together, just the two of you."

"Oh, I plan to." Sydney moves closer to Emma as she whispers, "I am gonna try to talk to him into taking me out for a burger and some ice cream too!" Sydney smiles and winks at Emma.

Emma chuckles. "I think that sounds like fun, and he will probably be glad to!" Emma states, remembering just a few moments ago when Parker said the same thing. Emma smiles as she thinks to herself, *they are so in sync with each other.*

Then quickly but quietly, Parker sneaks around the corner and scares Sydney when he shouts out, *"Boo!* I got you!" Parker starts laughing.

"*Agh!*" Sydney screams as she starts laughing hysterically, "Dad, you are so crazy!"

"Still works!" Parker cried out. "I remember doing that when you were much smaller! Do you remember, Syd?"

"Yes, absolutely I remember! I used to be so scared to go around corners for fear that you would be there waiting to scare the absolute life outta me," Sydney remembers.

"Good times is all I remember!" Parker laughs as he continues, "Okay, my sweet little filly, are you about ready?" Parker tries to hurry them along.

"Yeah, I am good to go!" Sydney sings out. Just then, Emma gets a text.

> *Allison:* Yes, that is great I just got a call, someone would like to see one of my listed properties. Sophie is going to Lucas's. I will drop of Eliza just after I drop off Sophie.

> *Emma:* Ok great be safe see you soon.

"Everything okay, Emma?" Parker asks.

"Oh, yes! No worries! Allison just had someone who wanted to see one of her listings. So, she needs to show it and wanted to know if I could keep an eye on Eliza for a bit," Emma cleverly states.

"What about Sophie?" Sydney wonders.

"Oh, apparently, she has something else she needed to do. I'm not exactly sure," Emma cautiously states.

"Oh, okay. Well, it's father and daughter time, so can we get going, dad? I would love to get a burger before the movie," Sydney says as she winks at Emma quickly before her dad sees and catches on.

Parker gives Emma a confused look. Emma shows him her phone and says, "Have fun and please text me when you are headed back." Parker nods and replies, "Will do! Let's go, my little filly." Emma messages Parker.

Emma: I did not say a word!

Parker: Well, how did she know?

Emma: She mentioned to me that she was hoping that y'all could get a burger and ice cream while you were out. I said that you would probably be glad to.

Parker: She is so amazing! Okay I will text you when we are getting ready to head back.

"That must be Allison," Parker notices as he and Sydney head out the lane when he sees a car turning in.

As they pass each other, Parker, and Allison wave at each other.

Like it has the whole past week, the day quickly turns to night, and they are headed home. Parker texts Emma and lets her know that they are headed back.

When Parker and Sydney get home, it's almost bedtime. Parker parks his truck and says softly, "Thank you, Syd!"

"For what, dad?"

"For being such an amazing young lady, for your kind heart, for an amazing evening!" Parker lists off some of the ways Sydney amazes him. "Just to name a few!"

"Dad, I love you! Thanks for the amazing night of fun! It was much appreciated! Not to mention much needed!" Sydney confirms. "Would you like to do something tomorrow together too!"

"I sure would, but we already have dinner planned. What else would you like to do?" Parker asks.

"I do not know just yet, but I will definitely think about it and let you know in the morning!" Sydney says as she starts now thinking about it.

They get out of the truck and head inside as they talk about the movie. When they get inside, Emma hears them come in and comes out to greet them.

"Yeah, it was awesome!" Sydney says to Parker.

"Hey, there you are! What was awesome? Did you have a good time?" Emma quickly questions them.

"Yes, here we are! The movie was awesome! Absolutely! We had a blast!" Sydney shares.

"It was definitely some much-needed time with one of the most beautiful young ladies that I know!" Parker praises.

"That is so great to hear! So, what did y'all go see?" Emma wonders.

"We saw *Venom*!" Sydney exclaims.

"Eww, *Venom* sounds like a snake movie!" Emma says as she shudders like she just seen a snake. "I am not a fan of snakes! It gives me the heebie-jeebies just thinking about it."

"Well, it's definitely not a snake movie! It's a Marvel movie," Sydney states.

"Is that one of those comic book movies?" Emma asks curiously.

"Yes, and there's a guy named Eddie Brock that is a reporter, and his body gets overtaken by a jelly-like glob of goo critter from outer space. It wants to eat constantly, and it talks to Eddie, the guy whose body it overtook. The critter's name is

Venom. When Venom takes over Eddie's body, he turns Eddie into a black critter with a bunch of sharp, pointy teeth, and he can do all kinds of cool stuff. He helps an Asian lady in her shop when a bad guy comes in," Sydney says with excitement. "But the movie does have some mild violence with fights, and it likes to eat but not regular food!" Sydney describes in a bunch of detail but not fully because she knows that Emma probably won't like it or even approve of it. Sydney respects her opinion, but this was a date with her dad, and he approved, which is all that matters.

"Aliens? That doesn't sound like my kind of movie. I am still so glad that y'all had such fun," Emma comments.

"Yeah, it's probably not your kind of movie, Emma. But it definitely was funny with the silly puns. It was very cleverly written with lots of action," Parker adds.

"Any plans for tomorrow?" Emma asks, hoping that they talked about something so that Lucas, Sophie, Eliza, and she could decorate for her party.

"Actually, Syd had so much fun that she asked if we could continue a little fun over into tomorrow. I said sure!" Parker says as he looks at Sydney as she smiles at his comment which means even more fun to come.

"I expect tomorrow to be as fun as today, so I am headed off to bed so I can get plenty of rest!" Sydney says as she hugs her dad and Emma before heading to bed.

"Good night, my little filly," Parker says as he hugs Sydney.

"Night, dad. I love you!" Sydney states.

"Good night, Sydney," Emma shares.

"Night, Emma. I love you too!" Sydney says as she smiles and turns to go up the stairs.

"Sweet dreams, my little filly," Parker says behind her as she ascends the stairs.

Emma motions for Parker to follow her into the kitchen. She whispers so that Sydney can't hear, "So I will message Lucas, Sophie, and Eliza about coming over to help decorate. Can y'all be back by two o'clock?"

"Sure thing. I did say we would go out to dinner, but I can make that up to her at another time. I will treat her to a special breakfast and whatever else she wants to do. Can you text me saying that I need to come home early because of an emergency. About thirty minutes before so we can make it here by two?" Parker asks, putting the plan into motion.

"I can do that. Okay, I will text the kids early tomorrow to have them here just after y'all leave. But for now, I am off to bed. Good night, Parker," Emma says as she heads to her room.

"Sounds like a good idea. Good night, Emma." Parker heads to bed as well.

After what seems like the longest night ever, Sydney lies there, waiting to get outta bed. When she hears what sounds like a soft knock on her door, she wonders who it could be as she crawls outta bed to go see. As she opens her door, there stands her dad.

"Dad? What are you doing?" Sydney asks, confused.

"What is the date, Sydney, do you know?" Parker asks excitedly.

"It's June 24th, why?" Sydney wonders.

"Well, I was wondering if you would like to go for a special birthday breakfast? Before we do whatever, it is that you wanted to do together today," Parker whispers.

"Ah, sure, but what time is it?" Sydney asks, thinking it's still early.

"Sweetheart, it's seven o'clock," Parker shares.

"Oh, really? Yeah, give me a few minutes to get ready!" Sydney says with more spunkiness than when she opened the door.

"Okay, I will be downstairs when you are ready," Parker assures her.

A few minutes later, Sydney comes downstairs. She finds her dad talking with Emma in the kitchen. "Don't mean to interrupt, but I am ready whenever you are, dad," Sydney says with enthusiasm.

"I guess that's my cue. I will see you later, Emma. Have a great day!" Parker says as he and Sydney head out for the day.

"Have fun, guys!" Emma yells to them as they leave.

Emma decides it's never too early to get everyone here to get the decorating done. So, she messages Lucas, Allison, and Obee all at once.

Emma: Good morning, everyone! Sydney and Parker have left. You are clear to come over as soon as you would like.

Obee: Was just headed over, be there soon.

A few minutes goes by when Allison responds.

Allison: Greyson, the girls, and I will be leaving in a few to head over.

Obee makes it to the house. As he comes in, he shouts out for Emma.

"I'm here, Emma! Where might you be?"

"In the kitchen, Obee," Emma yells back.

"The Abbotts will be here shortly," Emma shares.

Emma gets a message.

Lucas: Mom and I will be over. We just have to make a stop first.

"And that was Lucas. They will be here after they make a quick stop." Emma says.

Lucas: Emma is it ok that I bring a friend to help decorate?

Emma: Sure, Lucas the more the merrier.

Lucas: Ok cool.

About 30 minutes later, everyone has finally arrived.

"Okay, everyone. We need balloons filled, blown up and hung around, food prepped, and decorations put up. Who wants to do which?" Emma asks.

"What do you mean by fill the balloons?" Sophie wonders.

"I would like some glitter put in them," Emma instructs.

"I don't mean to interfere with your decorating ideas, but isn't that going to be super messy?" Allison asks, concerned about the potential mess it will make.

"It's okay. I have an easy solution for that," Emma reassures Allison.

The girls with Lucas and his friends help do the balloons and decorations while Greyson and Obee oversee Allison, Claire, and Emma in the kitchen.

It's now getting close to 1:30 p.m., so Emma does a quick walkthrough and is very pleased with the kids' decorating abilities. Everything is ready as far as food is concerned. Everyone is already present for the party. Emma asks for Claire and Greyson to move their cars out behind the stables where Sydney can't see them as she messages Parker.

Emma: Parker, I'm sorry to interrupt you and Sydney's fun but I need you home asap.

Parker: Is everything ok?

Emma: Well not really.

Parker: Oh, what's wrong?

Emma: It seems that we have a broken window from a bird in the living room.

Parker: Oh yeah that sounds serious. Olay I will tell Sydney and we will get straight home.

"Everyone, they are headed home. Let's take our places in the living room," Emma quickly instructs them.

"What did you tell them?" Greyson asks out of curiosity.

"I told them that we have a broken window from a bird in the living room." Emma chuckles as she prays out loud,

"Lord, please don't let a bird break our window."

"That's pretty good because Sydney will be intrigued and come running into the house before Parker and surprise!" Sophie states excitedly.

About 15 minutes later, Emma sees them coming in the lane. "Here they come, everyone! Get ready!"

Everyone hides in the living room and waits. They can hear a faint sound of a car door closing and slight mumbles of voices that are gradually getting louder. Then the door! Sydney is the first one through the door.

"Sydney, wait up. We don't know what kind of bird we are dealing with. I don't want you to get hurt!" Parker yells from behind Sydney as she runs into the house and right into the living room.

"*Surprise, Sydney!*" they all shout as they jump out from their hidden places.

"Guys! Aww, really? This is awesome! I had no idea. Whose idea was this? I seriously want to hug them!" Sydney says as she starts to cry tears of joy.

"Well, technically, it was all Lucas, and he asked for my help, so I agreed," Sophie shares.

"Aww, come here, you two!" Sydney says as she reaches to hug them each. "This is beyond awesome! I have the best of friends." Sydney pauses for a moment as she notices someone new in her home. "Stanley? Is that really you?" Sydney is shocked to see him there.

"Yes, me it is," Stanley replies in his favorite sci-fi character's voice.

"Come here," Sydney says as she meets him halfway to share a hug with him.

"I am serious, guys. I am so blown away by this amazing gift!" Sydney shares.

"Speaking of gifts, we have a few here for you to open," Lucas points out.

"This was a gift enough," Sydney says so happy about their generosity.

"This one is from me," Lucas states.

"Well, I will open this one first. Wonder what it can be?" Sydney wonders as she unwraps it. "Cool, a country mix CD, a cinnamon apple candle, and a hand-drawn picture of SOT! Thanks, Lucas. That's awesome!" Sydney smiles.

She opens the rest of her gifts. She gets a gift certificate for the mall, a new purse, a horse coloring book, horse notepads and utensils for school, a watch, and some new jeans.

Parker asks everyone to please follow him outside. When they get outside, everyone is confused as to why they have to go outside. Parker waves for Obee to give him a hand. They walk into the stables and come back out with kayaks.

"Happy birthday, my little filly!" Parker surprises Sydney with kayaks for her and two of her friends.

Sydney's eyes light up and get so big. She is so shocked as she tries to find the words. "I'm sorry, Dad, but all I can say is thank you so much. We all were just talking how we wished we could have kayaks for the lake! Thank you, thank you!" Sydney says, full of joy.

"Okay, who wants food?" Emma asks. "Meet in the kitchen, and we shall eat."

Everyone heads in to eat. After everyone eats, Emma says, "There is just one more thing to do!" Emma turns around and picks up the cake and walks over to Sydney as everyone starts to sing "Happy Birthday." Sydney makes a wish and blows out the candles.

Everyone has cake and ice cream. The adults are just sitting there chatting about a little bit of everything. The kids all go in the living room to hang out.

"That cake really was amazing, Emma!" Allison expresses happily.

"Well, thank you! It's an old family recipe." Emma shares.

Just then, Sydney comes running into the kitchen frantically screaming, "Come quick! It's Eliza. Something is wrong—she's vomiting everywhere."

Greyson and Allison take off for the living room with everyone else following close behind them. Emma goes for towels and rags to clean up, as she also grabs a small bucket.

"We need a...oh, thanks, Emma!" They take the bucket from Emma.

"I'm gonna go get some clean, dry clothes for her," Sydney offers.

"Emma, do you have a thermometer? So, we can see if she has a fever," Allison asks.

"Yes, be right back." Emma heads for the half bathroom by the kitchen and gets the thermometer and sleeves then returns to Allison. "These little sleeves go on, then tear off the paper and it's ready to use," Emma instructs Allison.

"Eliza, honey, I need a few seconds to take your temperature. Are you gonna get sick again?" Allison calmly asks Eliza.

Eliza shakes her head no, so Allison takes the quick opportunity to get her temperature. She waits till it beeps, and she doesn't have a temperature.

"Hmm, that's odd," Allison says.

"What's that, Hun?" Greyson asks, trying to stay calm.

"She doesn't have a high temperature. It's like she's fine," Allison says, confused. "Was she jumping around a bunch before she got sick?" Allison asks the other kids.

They all reported that she was just sitting there coloring in Sydney's new coloring book.

"Okay, that's just weird. Honey, just calm down and sit still for a little bit, and if you feel like you are gonna get sick, just use this bucket." Allison walks away to talk privately with the other adults.

Sydney returns with clean, dry clothes for Eliza. "Thank you, Sydney!" Allison praises her.

"Well, I think we should be headed home soon and get her settled down for the night," Allison mentions to Greyson. He agrees. They say their goodbyes and prepare to leave as soon as she is redressed in clean clothes.

Emma gets a bag for Eliza's clothes. "Here you go, Allison, and you may take the bucket with you as well."

Sydney says goodbye to Sophie, and the Abbotts leave to head home.

CHAPTER 22
Court: Day One

It's been almost a week since Sydney's party, and time just keeps flying by. They still haven't figured out why Eliza got so sick. She hasn't gotten even sick at all since. Everyone seems to think that she either just ate too much or was extra excited and bouncing around, but she wasn't really her regular bounce-around, excited self. She was much calmer than normal. So, they wanna say that she just ate too much or something that didn't agree with her.

Today, Lucas and Sophie are going over to the ranch to hang out for a little bit. They are supposed to get their class selection forms so they can pick the classes that they want to take as their electives. As Sydney lies there deciding if she wants to get up or just stay in bed just a little longer, her tummy has different objectives for her. She decides she is gonna shut it up by going and having some breakfast.

As Sydney gets motivated and out of bed, she hopes that Emma is up and made something yummy for breakfast. She quickly gets dressed and heads to the kitchen, but she doesn't have to get very close when she can tell that Emma most definitely is awake and it smells like she has prepared something very yummy! This is more than enough reason for her to hurry a bit quicker to the kitchen.

Before she nears the kitchen, she thinks about shouting out to Emma how amazing her food smells, but she gets distracted by the voices she hears coming from the direction of the kitchen. She pauses for a moment to make sure that she wasn't heard. Then she quietly moves in closer to the kitchen to get a better listen to what's being said.

"Okay, Greyson, I will see you and Allison at the courthouse. Thanks again, guys. It means a lot! Okay, talk to you soon," Parker states as he hangs up his phone and continues talking with Emma. "This day I think is going to be almost as hard as that night. I just hope that I can keep my composure, Emma!" Parker says, concerned that he won't be able to.

"Just remember this verse, 1 Corinthians 10:13: 'You will not be tested or tempted with something that another man has not experienced,'" Emma starts when Parker takes over.

"Yes, I know that God will be faithful, and he won't let me be tested or tempted beyond what I can handle. But when you are tested and tempted, he will provide a way to handle it so it can be endured," Parker recites from memory. "I also believe in God with all that I am, but I still can't help but feel like I am gonna lose it today! What am I gonna do, Emma?" Parker is frustrated from fear of having to relive that night all over again.

Emma walks over closer to Parker and looks him deep into his eyes and states, "Parker, I know you think that this is going to be the hardest thing that you have ever had to do, but I can guarantee you that you will be just fine. Just do your best to remain cool, and when you feel the anxiety building, just think to yourself that you have to breathe, then count to 10, take a deep breath, and think happy thoughts. But not too happy—you don't want the judge seeing you smiling." Emma chuckles. "I would be there if I could, but I am going to have a full house of kids later."

"It's okay, Emma. I will have Greyson and Allison there. And I will do my best to take your advice. Well, I must get going. Thanks again." Parker thanks Emma as he pushes his chair back to get up.

"Anytime, Parker," Emma says so sweetly and understanding.

Sydney ceases the moment to say goodbye to her dad, so she quickly goes running into the kitchen and runs right into Parker. She puts her arms around him and just squeezes Parker so hard that he can feel his breathing a bit constricted as she says, "I love you, Dad! Get Mom justice!"

Parker hugs Sydney back till he hears what Sydney says. Then he takes her arms and pulls them off from around himself when he states, "Whoa, back up there, little filly! What do you mean by 'Get Mom justice'?" Parker says sternly. "Have you been eaves dropping on my conversations?"

"No, not intentionally," Sydney says, hoping he drops it.

"Not intentionally? If it was something that I wanted you to know, I would tell you. What makes you think that you can just listen in to my business whenever you want?" Parker says as his voice begins to get gradually louder.

Sydney shouts back, "She's my mom, and I have a right to know! How dare you keep something like this from me?"

"Don't tell me what you have the right to know! You are my child, and if I don't want you to know, then I will not tell you!" Parker continues to shout more angrily now. "Did you ever think maybe there was a reason why I didn't say anything to you? *No! I am sure you didn't!*"

Emma tries to intervene. "Parker!" Emma quickly shouts to get his attention and snap him outta his current mood. "That is your only child who you are acting a fool to!" Emma pauses for a moment to calm herself down and collect her thoughts. "Now you need to apologize to her right now before you regret it," Emma states more reasonably.

"I have to go. I do not have time for this bully party." Parker pushes past Sydney and goes out the front door, slamming it on his way out.

Sydney turns and takes off running up the stairs to her room, slamming her door behind her.

Obee comes into the kitchen, shocked. "Wow, what just happened?"

"Whatever do you mean, Obee?" Emma says like she knows absolutely nothing.

"I know you know what I mean, Emma. So quit playing coy and come clean," Obee begs.

"Apparently, Sydney overheard Parker talking about the court hearing today. She came into the kitchen and made mention of it to him. He went off the deep end. Sydney stood up to him and fought back. He got ticked off and left, slamming the front door. She tore off upstairs, slamming her bedroom door," Emma states, catching her breath. "What a day this is going to be." Emma sarcastically laughs.

"Sounds like it's a case of like father like daughter," Obee says like it's nothing new.

"Today I would agree with you," Emma agrees.

"Well, Emma, Parker tore off too!" Obee informs her.

"Oh, is that right?" Emma asks curiously.

"Let's just say stones were flying everywhere when he went out the lane," Obee shockingly reports.

"I hope he holds his temper better than that in court," Emma strongly hopes.

Out of nowhere, the doorbell rings.

"Help yourself to some breakfast," Emma tells Obee while she goes to see who's at the door.

Emma opens the door, and Allison is standing there with the girls. "Good morning, Allison. Come in," Emma offers. "Sydney is in her room, girls."

The girls run past Emma and head upstairs.

"Thanks, Emma, but I'm sorry this is a drop-and-run," Allison politely states.

"Oh, you are fine, and good luck today, especially with the hot wire," Emma says jokingly.

"You mean Parker?" Allison asks as she rolls her eyes.

"Yep, that would be the one. I take it he ended up at your house?" Emma asks, knowing that he most likely did.

"Yes, ma'am! But let's just let it at that," Allison states shortly.

"Ah, yes, I completely understand. I just hope that he can get it together before court or it won't only be not good for Dylan, but he could end up in the hot seat," Emma promises.

"Greyson is trying to calm him down. That's why I am just a little early. I wanted to give them some time. But I don't want to be too long. They wanted to go into the DA's office just a bit early. I will keep you posted," Allison says as she turns to leave.

"Okay, no problem," Emma says as she quietly shuts the door.

Sydney hears a soft knock on her door followed by "Syd? You in there."

Sydney just lies there and doesn't say a word. Again, she hears the knock but this time a bit louder followed again by "Syd? It's Sophie and Eliza. May we please come in?" Sydney buries her head under her pillow.

Sophie whispers to Eliza, "Can you please go get Emma?"

Eliza nods and sits on the bare wooden stairs and slides all the way down to the bottom on her bum. She cautiously looks around for Emma. She walks into the kitchen, and Emma is sitting at the table, drinking tea.

Emma sees her and asks, "Hey there, Eliza! Is everything okay?" "Sophie sent me to come get you," Eliza quietly says.

"Oh, okay. Let's go see what she wants." Emma reaches for Eliza's hand. Eliza puts her hand in Emma's, and they head upstairs.

They get to the top of the stairs to find Sophie standing outside of Sydney's bedroom door.

Sophie whispers, "I knocked, but she won't answer the door."

"Is it locked?" Emma asks.

"I don't know. I haven't tried to open it," Sophie tells Emma.

Emma tries the door, and it opens. They see Sydney lying on her bed with her pillow over her head. Emma signs to Sophie and Eliza to wait just a minute. Emma walks over to Sydney's bed and sits down. She puts her hand on Sydney's back.

Speaking softly, Emma talks to Sydney. "Sydney, you, okay?"

From through the pillow, they hear a muffled response: "Please go away and let me be. I don't want to be bothered right now."

"Your best friend is here. Don't you wanna say hello?" Emma asks.

"Can everyone please just give me some time to myself!" Sydney screams from behind her pillow.

Emma gets up and says to the girls so that Sydney can hear, "Come on, girls. Let's go have some breakfast! There's a feast in the kitchen sitting there just waiting to be devoured. Kitchen closes in 30 minutes. Come on, girls. I am famished!" Emma says cleverly, knowing that Sydney can't resist her breakfast.

"Me too! I feel like I could eat a horse. But not any of yours at your farm." Eliza giggles.

Sophie shouts across the room, "I can't wait to see you when you are ready to come downstairs, bestie."

Sophie stands in the doorway for a moment to see if Sydney responds, and when she doesn't, Sophie quietly closes the door, turns around, and heads back downstairs to the kitchen for some hot breakfast before it gets cold.

Meanwhile, at the Abbott's

"Greyson, what the heck is my issue? I can't believe I acted like such a jerk toward Sydney." Parker hangs his head out of disbelief. "I mean things this past week have been the best since Ivy's passing. Now I'm afraid I done screwed that all up," Parker says as he wipes his eyes.

"Listen, Parker, I think you are being way too hard on yourself. So, let's work on your current demeanor for court. Then later before you go home, you can worry about how it's gonna go when you get there. But I honestly think everything will be just fine. You are just so stressed. I can guarantee you that after court, you will feel better about right now, and you will have different feelings that you will have to contend with," Greyson says, hoping he can get Parker to calm down some and relax.

"I know that you are probably right, but I just can't help but feel..." Parker says when Greyson interrupts.

"Just please do me a favor and just stop thinking about what happened this morning, okay?" Greyson asks.

"Okay, I will try," Parker says quietly.

"Okay, now let's breathe. In and out. Nice, deep, long breaths." Greyson guides Parker into breathing with him.

The front door opens, and Allison has returned.

"Hey, babe!" Greyson greets Allison.

She walks over to him and hugs and kisses him and responds, "How's everything here?"

"Better now," Parker says.

"Okay, are we ready to head to the courthouse?" Allison asks.

"No but yes. I just want to get this over with," Parker says painfully.

They gather themselves, their belongings and needed paperwork, then they head out to Greyson's truck to head to the courthouse.

Meanwhile, back at the Ashcraft ranch

Emma, Sophie, and Eliza are sitting in the kitchen just chatting when they get a visitor.

Sophie catches out the corner of her eye that Sydney has finally come down to the kitchen.

"Hey, beautiful bestie! We saved you some breakfast!" Sophie says cheerfully.

Sydney says a bit grumpily, "Thanks," as she slumps down in a chair.

Emma sits a covered plate down in front of her with a fork. Sydney sits there and just stares at the plate. Everyone remains quiet as they watch Sydney to see if she is gonna eat or say something. Sydney continues to sit and stare at her covered plate of food when her eyes start tearing up.

Sophie gets up and goes to Sydney and rubs her back while she softly asks, "Do you wanna talk about anything? We promise to listen and not judge."

Sydney looks up and sadly sobs, "I miss Mom!" as she begins sobbing harder.

Emma says from across the table, "We all do, sweetheart. We miss her dearly!"

"Dad has a strange way of showing it! I just simply asked for him to get her justice, and he basically chews my head off!" Sydney angrily shrieks.

"That's why he acted like that this morning, he's hurting so bad he left his anger get the best of himself. I promise you that he will come home with a slightly different attitude. I am also sure that he will want to sit down with you and explain himself and apologize for this morning. But for now, can we just put all of that to the back of our minds and eat so we can try to get through this day, hopefully with a little less sadness?" Emma asks hopefully.

"Yeah, also because we have classes to pick! Did you get your class form?" Sophie asks happily, trying to lighten up Sydney's mood.

"I will try, but I'm not making any promises," Sydney says as she uncovers her plate of breakfast.

Eliza gets the bright idea to try to make Sydney hopefully at least laugh by telling a few jokes. "Hey, Syd, what do you call a pig that takes karate?" Eliza chuckles as she folds her hands and swings her legs from her chair.

Sydney looks up at Eliza and says, "I don't know, maybe chop chop?" Sydney guesses.

"No, silly!" Eliza chuckles as she says, "A pork chop!" Everyone laughs, and Sydney smiles. "At least you smiled. Okay, here's another one. Why did the golfer bring two pairs of pants?"

Sydney shrugs as she says, "I don't know."

Just then, the doorbell rings. Emma gets up to check to see who's at the door.

"In case he gets a hole in one." Eliza chuckles as Sophie laughs and Sydney smiles.

Then Lucas pops out around the corner and tries to scare everyone. "*Hey!*" he shouts.

Sydney and Sophie jump while Eliza about falls off her chair when Lucas startles her.

"Careful, Eliza. Sorry, didn't mean to make you about fall off your chair," Lucas apologizes.

"It's okay! Okay, one more," Eliza says while she tries to think of a good, funny one.

"One more what?" Lucas asks.

"Joke. She's trying to make Sydney laugh," Sophie says as she shakes Sydney a bit with her arm around her shoulder.

"Ah, okay, cool," Lucas says with a smile.

"So, I know I said one, but I have a few more. Are you ready?" Eliza says, looking around the room. Everyone nods. "What's the difference between the bird flu and the swine flu?"

Lucas thinks and quickly responds, "One is a light flu, and one is a heavy flu?"

"Nope! One requires a tweetment, and one needs an oinkment!" Eliza laughs as does everyone, including Sydney, who gives a small chuckle. "Okay, let's do another one!" Eliza says excitedly and with determination to get Sydney laughing. "Why do seagulls fly over the sea?"

Everyone shrugs that they don't know.

"Well, if they fly over the bay, then they would be bagels!" Eliza laughs.

"Ah, I heard that one before, but I forgot how it went. That was cute," Lucas chimes in. "Got any more?"

"Yes, sure. How do you stop a bull from charging?"

"Hmm, wave a different color flag than red?" Sydney guesses.

"That's a good idea, but no, goofy! You cancel his credit card!" Eliza chuckles with silliness.

"Duh, that was a good one," Sydney laughs with everyone.

"See, it's working!" Eliza says proudly. "Okay, how about another one?"

"Yes! Sure!" They all say almost in unison.

"Okay! Why did the mushroom go to the party?" Eliza quizzes everyone.

"This is an easy one. Because he wanted to be the highlight of the party!" Lucas says confidently and positive that he has the right answer.

Eliza starts laughing because she knows that his answer isn't right, and he is so sure as she tries to give the answer. "Sorry, not the right answer Lucas. It's because he was a fungi!" Everyone laughs, and Sydney high-fives Eliza.

"Okay, one more. Why do chicken coops only have two doors?" Eliza asks.

Everyone just looks at Eliza, waiting to hear the answer.

"Okay, I have joked y'all out." Eliza chuckles. "It's because if it had four doors, it would be a chicken sedan." They all laugh.

"Thank you, Eliza. That did make me feel a little better," Sydney says as she motions for her to come closer. When Eliza moves closer to Sydney, she hugs Eliza.

Sydney finishes her breakfast and puts her dishes in the sink as she excuses herself for a moment.

"I'm headed to my room quickly to get my course form. Lucas, do you have yours?"

"Yes, I do!"

"Okay, I shall be right back," Sydney says as she runs out of the kitchen.

Sydney returns quickly and sits back down at the table with Lucas and Sophie to pick their classes.

Meanwhile at the courthouse

"Now that you all know how this is going to go, do you have any questions?" the district attorney asks.

"I'm sorry, but what happens if I can't keep myself together in there? I mean, if I lose it, will that be bad?" Parker asks, concerned about affecting the outcome.

"If you mean breaking down and crying, it will only help show how distraught that you are. But your temper and outburst can and most likely won't be good," informs the district attorney.

Parker nods.

"Okay, please wait here till someone comes to get you. Shouldn't be too long," instructs the district attorney.

A few minutes pass as they sit there quietly and patiently wait. Then an assistant comes and takes them to the courtroom. She whispers just before they go in the room, "Please silence your phones, and sit where I direct you when we enter." She takes them into the courtroom and directs them to sit directly behind the district attorney by pointing. Once they get seated, she leaves the courtroom.

"Next case?" asks the judge.

"Your Honor, next on the docket is the county with the Ashcraft's and the county verses, Dylan Hutchins," the bailiff responds as she hands the case folder over the judge's desk.

"This is a preliminary hearing. Today we will assess that we have sufficient evidence to proceed, and we will hear the defendant's plea. May I hear what we have as current evidence?" the judge requests.

The district attorney stands and proceeds to show their evidence on Dylan. "First, Your Honor, we have the car used in the hit and run registered most recently to the defendant. We have a confession from the defendant. We also have a confession from the one witness who saw the crime that was committed," the DA states as he sits back down.

"Defendant, what is your plea?" the judge asks.

Dylan stands, clears his throat, and responds, "Your Honor, I plead not guilty." As he sits back down, there are some hushes, grumbles, and outbursts from the courtroom.

The judge bangs his gavel on his bench as he shouts, "Silence in my courtroom! Now, Mr. Hutchins, I'm a bit confused. There is a confession from you, which makes you guilty, so why the 'not guilty' plea now?" the judge wonders.

"To be honest, Your Honor, I was drunk when I supposedly confessed, and I don't believe I did the act nor that I even confessed," Dylan states like he's not guilty and thinks he even has the right to think he isn't guilty.

Parker makes a fist and looks at Greyson for support. Greyson sees Parker making a fist, and he puts his hand on Parker's to try to stop him from doing anything stupid like punching the pew or worse.

"Are you sure this is how you want to plead?" the judge asks Dylan.

He stands and says, "Yes, Your Honor. I want a trial."

"Okay, it's your future. Is this your council's advice?" the judge asks, double-checking that this is the route he wants to take.

"It is against my better judgment that he wants to go this route despite my plea with him to go with the guilty plea, Your Honor," Dylan's council reports.

"Okay, I pray you get your fair judgment, Mr. Hutchins. I believe that we have sufficient evidence to proceed," the judge says as he directs his attention to the DA. "Who are your witnesses?"

"Your Honor, we have the husband of the late Mrs. Ivy Ashcraft, Mr. Ashcraft. Mr. and Mrs. Abbott were present the evening of said hit-and-run. Our other witness would like to remain anonymous. They are willing to do a video from another location, to provide evidence if we can do that?" the DA reports.

"Yes, we can talk about that in my chambers when we are done here. Okay, Mr. Hutchins, we will set up a trail for you even though I still think it's against your better judgment to do this. But in the end, it is truly your decision. I will get a date and get it sent out to everyone who needs to be here. Thank you all. You may be dismissed," the judge announces.

Greyson gets up and waits for Parker to go first, then he follows him out of the courtroom, while Allison follows from behind Greyson. They make their way out of the courthouse and to Greyson's truck. They all stay quiet till they get in. That's when Parker can't bite his tongue any longer.

"I'm sorry, but what is that fruit cake smoking? To think he's gonna get off with less especially with making statements like he was drunk! Like that makes it okay?" Parker spouts off angrily.

"It's okay. He's making his bed, and he will be sleeping in it for quite a while. I don't think he even comprehends that he...pardon me, Parker, for saying this, but that sorry excuse for a life killed a good person! At the very least he should get manslaughter charges!" Greyson vents furiously.

"Well, can I please make a suggestion?" Allison calmly asks. "After this morning, how about I make some dinner and you stay with us to eat, then that will also give you some time to cool off before going home," she suggests.

"Yeah, I agree. Parker, please come have dinner with us," Greyson pleads.

"Oh, okay. I hate to put you guys out to make dinner. But I will come over to calm down some," Parker agrees.

"Don't you even think that you are putting us out! After all your family does for us. It's the least we can do for you," Greyson states proudly.

"Exactly! It's not a big deal. I would be happy to make some dinner. Now I can't in good faith guarantee you that it will be anywhere near as good as Emma's," Allison jokes.

"It's okay as long as it's warm," Parker says.

They head to the Abbotts' for time to calm down and relax.

CHAPTER 23
Please Forgive Me

Buzz. Buzz.

"Good morning, Lexington!" says the radio announcer. "What a beautiful day! Temps will be in the high 80's today with all the sun one could want. Traffic is normal today with no accidents to report."

"In other news, yesterday started the trial for one Dylan Hutchins, the suspected driver in the hit and run accident which killed one of Lexington's up and coming ladies of the community, Ivy Ashcraft. It turns out he skipped out on the guilty plea and said he was innocent! What a shock this must be, not just to the community but to the Ashcraft family. My condolences to the Ashcraft's who are already hurting enough then to have to deal with this new blow!"

Sydney grabs her alarm clock and throws it across the room as she screams at the top of her lungs, "Ugh! This just isn't fair!" as she sits on her bed and sobs.

A few minutes later, Parker knocks quickly on her bedroom door as he blows through it at the same time. "Are you okay? Emma said she heard a crash come from up here!" Parker says while he catches his breath.

Sydney jumps outta bed and runs over to her dad and grabs him and hugs him dearly. "I just heard on the radio that Dylan pleaded not guilty! Is that true?" Sydney sobs.

"Yes, he did, and I really need to talk to you first thing today. Can you please come down and have some breakfast with me so we can talk? I really have a lot I must tell you," Parker says wholeheartedly.

"Sure, Dad, I can. I have something that I need to tell you too!" Sydney professes.

They go down to the kitchen to have some breakfast and talk about the happenings from yesterday.

"Emma, Syd, and I would like some breakfast please. Let's sit next to each other, my little filly," Parker says as he selects where he wants to sit, and then Sydney sits down next to her dad.

"Okay, I will make some eggs, bacon, and toast. Coming right up!" Emma says happily.

"Syd, I want to say how sorry I am from the bottom of my heart! I am sorry for treating you like a child, for snapping and ripping you apart like I did yesterday. I'm sorry for not coming home last night and for anything else that I may have missed! Can you please forgive me?" Parker assures her.

"Yes, I can, and I am sorry too, Dad! I love you!" Sydney exclaims.

"So, listen, I am sorry that you had to find out the way you did. I really meant to be home last night to talk with you, but I don't have a good enough reason as to why I wasn't. But what I can tell you is I want you to do me and your mother the biggest favor! I think this will help you too! It's probably going to be a while till I need it completed, but if you could write a victim impact statement for court, I may just let you come to court for that, to voice your thoughts on how this has affected you and your life. What do you think?" Parker asks, hoping that she agrees.

Sydney thinks about it, and then she says, "That sounds like a great idea! I'm not sure how much it will help me and my feelings, but I will do it!"

Parker smiles. "That's great! I will be doing one as well. Again, I am so sorry for my behavior yesterday, but you know as well as I do how hard it has been. I know that doesn't give me the right to act like I did, nor does it excuse it. So together, I would like to work on our feelings about this whole situation. I think it will help me, and I am sure that you will benefit from it as well," Parker openly suggests.

"I do think we can arrange that, dad! I also think we should do more time out like we did the other week. I really feel that we need this," Sydney requests.

"I will make time for that with you for sure!" Parker assures her. "I will also do my best to include you more in things that I know about, especially pertaining to your mother. I keep forgetting that you are growing up and even though you are still my baby. So enough of this. What are your plans for today?" Parker wonders.

"Lucas has football tryouts, and he asked Sophie and I to go watch him today. So, we will be doing that if that's okay with you?" Sydney asks.

"Ah yeah sure I guess you may," Parker says, giving his approval.

"What are your plans for today?" Sydney asks.

"At some point, I need to get with Greyson, but other than that, nothing too pressing. Why, what are you thinking?" Parker wonders.

"I was thinking that maybe you may wanna come to watch Lucas at football tryouts too? I mean his dad should be there, but since he obviously doesn't have one and you have been trying to be like a dad to him, I thought maybe you might wanna come give him some support too," Sydney thoughtfully suggests.

"That does sound very doable. As a matter of fact, I think I am gonna call Greyson and see if he would like to join us," Parker adds. "If you don't mind, I'm gonna go call him now. I'll be back." Parker leaves the kitchen for more privacy.

Sydney decides she will confirm with Lucas.

> *Sydney:* Hey Lucas I will be at your tryouts later.

> *Lucas:* Oh, awesome sounds like fun. Can't wait.

> *Sydney:* I hope it's okay I asked my dad to come with too!

> *Lucas:* Oh yeah cool!

> *Sydney:* Ok cya l8r!

> *Lucas:* You betcha!

Sydney heads to her room to get ready. When she gets to her room, she texts Sophie to see if she's up yet.

> *Sydney:* Hey bestie you awake yet?

Sydney gets dressed in her normal jeans and t-shirt. She pulls her hair up into a small ponytail.

Sophie: I am now.

Sydney: Sorry did I wake you?

Sophie: No, I didn't even have my ringer on so what's up?

Sydney: Dad said that I could go to Lucas's tryouts today.

Sophie: Cool I didn't ask yet.

Sydney: I also asked my dad to come along. He said sure! He was gonna talk to your dad to see if he would wanna come along too!

Sophie: Oh nice! Well, I guess I better get myself around for today, so I am ready when it's time to go. Lol.

Sydney: Okay, for sure cya soon Sophie!

Sydney heads down to the kitchen to see if her dad is ready yet. When she gets to the kitchen, he is not in there, so she goes into the living room to wait. Parker ends up following her into the living room.

"I saw you headed in here. Are you ready?" Parker asks.

"Yes, can we leave early? Because I would like to hang out with Sophie a little before we head to the school," Sydney explains.

"That's what I was hoping you would ask. Let's get going," Parker says excitedly.

On his way out, he yells for Emma. "Emma, we will be back! We're headed to the Abbotts' then over to the school."

"Okay, have fun," Emma yells back out from her room.

Parker and Sydney get in his truck and head to the Abbotts'. It doesn't take them long till they pull up to the Abbotts'. When

Parker stops and shuts off the engine, Sydney quickly jumps out and runs up to the door and rings the doorbell. After about a minute or so, Eliza flings open the door.

Eliza just about jumps into Sydney's arms as she shouts, "Syd! I didn't know that you were coming over!"

Sydney smiles and says, "Yep! I didn't know for sure. But here I am! Where's your sissy?"

Eliza takes Sydney's hand and takes her to Sophie.

Greyson is sitting in the living room when he calls out, "Come on in, man! What time do you think we should leave?"

"Let me check with Lucas to see what time he has to be there," Parker says while he takes out his phone and starts texting.

Parker: Lucas, what time do you need to be at school by?

Lucas: Oh, hey Parker! I have to be there in about an hour.

Parker: Do you need a ride?

Lucas: Actually, mom can but it would probably help if she didn't have to leave. But let me just double check with her.

Parker: Oaky just let me know because if you need us to Greyson and I can stop and get you.

"Greyson, I may have to pick up Lucas, so we can take my truck," Parker thoughtfully suggests.

"Oh, okay. When do you have to pick him up?" Greyson wonders.

"I'm just waiting for his response. He has to check with his mom," Parker responds.

After a few minutes, Lucas responds.

> *Lucas:* She said it would help her immensely if you could pick me up.

> *Parker:* Okay sounds great we will be by to pick you up soon.

Lucas: Ok I will be ready.

"Okay, everyone. We will be leaving in about 10 minutes," Parker informs everyone.

"You want to take your truck or mine?" Greyson wonders.

"We can take mine," Parker replies.

"Well, you did drive here. I wouldn't mind taking mine," Greyson suggests.

"Are you sure?"

"Yes, for sure! It's only fair," Greyson adds.

"Okay, well, let's get going then if that's good for you?" Parker requests.

Sydney, Sophie, and Eliza run out and jump in the truck to the positions that they want to sit in. Parker and Greyson follow them out as Greyson locks up on his way out.

When they get to Lucas's house, he is outside waiting already. Claire is standing on the porch and waves to them as Lucas gets in, and then they prepare to leave. Lucas waves as they pull out to leave.

"So, are you excited, Lucas?" Greyson asks.

"Eh, not really." Lucas sighs.

"That was a big sigh, Lucas. Is everything okay?" Parker asks, concerned.

"Yeah, I guess so," Lucas reluctantly responds.

"If you need to talk with either of us, we are available. We aren't your dad, but we would be happy to be your go-to dad if you need us to be," Greyson offers. "Ain't that right, Parker?"

"Definitely!" Parker happily accepts.

"Well, here we are. Do we need to drop you off anywhere in particular?" Greyson asks as he pulls up outside of the football field.

"No, this is good, thanks," Lucas says graciously.

"Okay, let me get parked. Good luck today!" Greyson says, trying to boost Lucas's mood.

"Definitely, for sure. Good luck. We will be in the stands quietly cheering you on," Parker respectfully adds.

"Thanks, guys. It means a lot," Lucas says as he gets out of the truck to go to tryouts. The girls, Greyson and Parker, head to the stands to watch. They sit up as high as they can so they can see everything.

As they sit and watch, they keep noticing that the coach keeps having discussions with Lucas, that don't look like they are going very well. They are too far away to be able to hear what's being said. After about the third time, the coach waves his arms up in the air and points for Lucas to do laps.

Lucas looks up at them in the stands as he unwillingly goes to the edge of the field and starts running laps by himself. They watch him run laps for what seems like forever before the coach waves him back over to participate with the others.

At the end of the tryouts, the coach pulls everyone in together and talks with them. When he is done, he disperses everyone, and as they all make their way off the field, he holds Lucas behind. He looks as though he is really laying it to Lucas while he just stands there and takes it.

When he finally lets Lucas go, everyone comes down out of the stands to meet him at the gates to the field. They all walk quietly to the truck together. Once they are all in, it's very quiet.

Greyson breaks the silence by saying, "Lucas, pardon me for saying so, but it didn't seem like you had a very good day on the field. Do you wanna talk about it?" Greyson says, trying to let it up to Lucas if he wants to talk or not.

"Not now, maybe later. Can you please just take me home?" Lucas requests.

"Sure thing, Lucas," Greyson says with disappointment but understanding.

As they pull in Lucas's driveway, Greyson and Parker look at each other as Parker says, "Text us later, and we can chat. You can do it as a group of just us men. The ladies are going on a school shopping spree in a few days, and we still wanna do one with you for school, so think about what time of the day you would like to go."

"Yes, sir," Lucas says with respect.

Parker smiles. "No need to say *sir* to me, Lucas. Okay, we shall see you later and talk to you soon?"

"Ah, yeah, I can do that. Talk to you soon. Thanks, guys, for the lift," Lucas says quickly like he just wants to get inside.

"Bye, Lucas!" Greyson and Parker say as Lucas quickly shuts the door and walks quickly to his house.

They wait till he's inside, then they leave.

"I wish I knew what that coach's issue was today. It just seemed like he was just picking on Lucas," Parker says with a bit of irritation.

"Hopefully he will group message us later and explain," Greyson adds.

When they get to the Abbotts' house, Parker and Sydney get out and head to their truck to head home.

Greyson walks over to Parker's window. "Thanks for including us today. It was nice to get out with all the kids. Just wish I knew what was up with Lucas today."

"No problem. It was nice, I agree. Yeah, something is up with him. Hopefully he even tells us. Well, see you soon," Parker says.

"Yep, definitely!" Greyson says as he steps back while Parker backs out of his driveway.

Parker drives Sydney and himself home for the evening. They get home and eat. After they eat, they both take off in their own directions.

Sydney goes to her room and decides to message Lucas.

>*Sydney:* Hey.

He almost immediately responds.

>*Lucas:* HEY!!

>*Sydney:* You seem happier.

>*Lucas:* Eh maybe a little so what's up?

>*Sydney:* I just wanted to check on you to see how you are doing.

Lucas: I'm ok. Thanks for asking.

Sydney: We have 2 days at the Boutique this week and a day of practice here at the ranch. With football practice will you be able to make it?

Lucas: I wouldn't miss it!

Sydney: Ok good night.

Lucas: Sweet dreams Syd good night ttys.

CHAPTER 24
School Shopping Spree

It's been a super busy at the boutique this week. So much so we had to put in an order for more products. It should be here soon.

Training on the track is good, but something is up with SOT. She isn't acting like her normal cool and easy self. She keeps shaking her head, and when Lucas and Loads of Luck are close to her, she just stomps her feet and tries to pull away from him besides being very moody. Parker is going to have a vet come by and check her out.

Today is a very special day! Sydney, Sophie, Emma, Allison, and Eliza will carry on the *'Someone Else's Laundry Shopping Excursion.'* This is a regular event with Ivy and Allison. They spend most of the day going to all the thrift stores in a tri-county area, looking for awesome deals while spending money and saving more.

Buzz. Buzz.

The radio announcer says, "Good morning', Lexington, and what a beautiful day it is so far! It's so bright and sunny you will definitely not want to forget your shades if you head out today."

Sydney hits the alarm clock to shut it off. She stretches and gets outta bed with a smile. She gathers her outfit for the day and heads to the shower.

In the kitchen, Emma makes a big breakfast for everyone. Parker comes in the kitchen with a little extra pep in his step.

"Good morning, Emma! Breakfast smells amazing! I am so happy that you are here," Parker praises.

"Good morning to you too, Parker. Are you feeling, okay?" Emma asks, unsure where all this chipperness comes from.

"Couldn't be better!" Parker says with a huge smile.

"Huh, okay. You did stay home all-night last night?" Emma quickly questions him.

"Yes, ma'am. What kind of silly question is that?" Parker chuckles.

"To be honest, if I didn't know any better, I would have thought that you got lucky last night. Wait, is she still here?" Emma questions jokingly.

"Emma, you are a crack! No, I didn't go out, and no, I didn't have anyone over. I just woke up feeling quite good, and I'm sharing my happiness with whomever I encounter. Unless they don't want any," Parker says as he gets serious for a moment till, he sees Emma smile, then he laughs.

"Parker, you just like to keep me on my toes." Emma laughs.

They hear thumping from the stairs. Just then, Sydney comes bouncing into the kitchen.

"You're awful bouncy today?" Emma points out.

"Emma, do you think maybe she got lucky last night?" Parker jokes.

Emma whips Parker with a dish towel as she scolds him, "Parker! There are little virgin ears here!"

"Who, me?" Sydney asks as she looks around the room like there could be someone else there.

"Yes, you!" Emma shrieks.

"I can definitely say nope, not lucky here!" Sydney says proudly. She continues with a whisper, "I'm still a virgin!" She winks.

"There must be something in the air that missed my bedroom then this morning," Emma states, kinda bummed. "Y'all are just so giddy today compared to normal. Now don't get me wrong... I like y'all this way much better. Not to mention I love seeing y'all so happy."

"You know what I think it is?" Sydney asks like she has the answer. "I will tell you... it's waking up to the smell of this amazing, smelling breakfast! You don't get that option, Em, because there's no amazing food being cooked when you get up," Sydney says like it's the only possible answer.

Emma walks over to Sydney and hugs her tightly. "I love you, young one!"

"I love you too, Emma!" Sydney replies.

"Okay, let's eat! We have a huge day of shopping to get done!" Emma pushes on to get the day rolling.

"I'll text Obee," Parker offers.

They all eat and clean up as a team so they can get going sooner. When they are done, they head over to the Abbotts'.

When they pull up to the Abbotts', Sophie is waiting outside for them, she opens the door and alerts Allison and Greyson.

When the car stops, Sophie runs over to the car to greet Sydney.

Sydney opens her door. "Hey, bestie! I am so excited!"

Sophie starts geeking out. "I know, me too!"

They start to go off hand in hand when they get stopped quickly in their tracks.

"Don't go too far. We need to leave almost immediately so we can get all our shopping done!" Allison says.

"Mom, what car are we going in?" Sophie questions.

"That's what we are discussing now, then we will be going. Can you please just be patient?" Allison says, trying to settle down the girls a bit.

While the adults discuss the plans for everything for the day from travel accommodations, stores they are shopping at, and lunch options, Claire pulls in with Lucas.

The girls go up to greet Lucas as he gets out of his mother's car.

"Hey!" Sydney and Sophie say in unison.

"Hey girls," Lucas says shyly as he runs his hands through his hair and sticks his hands in his pockets.

Allison waves for Claire to wait up for a minute as she walks over to her car. "Thanks for bringing Lucas over and allowing him to go with us today!" Allison states with excitement.

"I should be the one thanking y'all for your generosity. It truly means so much to our family." Claire generously thanks Allison.

"Well, we wanted to help after all Lucas is a great kid! He deserves it," Allison brags.

Claire looks around and says shocked, "you have to be talking about someone else's kid, because I know my boy are you sure you don't have mine confused with somebody else," Claire jokes.

"Nope, we mean Lucas!" Allison says proudly.

"Huh, well, you must tell me your secrets to get that child at my home," Claire whispers and jokes.

Allison laughs. "Anytime. Since we are not exactly sure when we will be back would you like us to drop him off later?"

"Please? Thanks! Well, I must get going," Claire says as she starts to back out.

"No problem!" Allison responds before Claire gets out the driveway.

"Are we ready?" Allison asks, trying to get going.

The kids all nod!

"Sure thing!" Parker says, excited to get going too.

"Give me a kiss, love!" Greyson asks Allison.

When Allison goes to Greyson, he grabs her, turns her, and kisses her as he dips her down! Then quickly puts her vertical as quickly as he dipped her. When he goes to let her go, she grabs her head from the rush.

"Thank God you are driving, Emma, because I just got a brain rush from Greyson's kiss!" Allison smiles and shares.

"Oh my, that must have been some kiss!" Emma chuckles.

All the ladies get into Emma's car and the guys get into Parker's truck.

They head out for a day of shopping with no worries, cares, and responsibilities except paying for whatever cool things they find.

In the back seat, the girls talk about what they want to look for.

"So, we should look for some dresses. I know it's not really your style, but I think this year you should give it more of a chance," Sophie says, trying to get Sydney to follow suit.

"As far as dresses are concerned, sure, I'm game, but do you wanna go to any school dances this year? If so, maybe we should look for some we can wear to those?" Sydney suggests.

"Oh, definitely, without a doubt, bestie!" Sophie agrees.

"But since I agreed to get a few dresses to change it up, can you maybe try to find an outfit or two that's not dressy like some khakis or jeans and some T-shirts?" Sydney wonders.

"Sure, I think I can do that!" Sophie smiles as they continue talking about all the things they would like to try to find.

Meanwhile, in the truck

Lucas finally gets to tell Parker and Greyson what's been up with him.

"So, this does kinda have to do with a girl?" Greyson asks to clarify that he heard Lucas correctly.

"Yes, kinda. The other part is since I have been hanging out with Sophie and Sydney, I like the person I have and am becoming compared to the rude dude I once was," Lucas states proudly.

"Well, that makes total sense. You wanting to be a better person is good in so many ways!" Parker chimes in.

"Yeah, when I hang out with the jocks per se, they just think that it's cool to be mean to other kids. And to be honest, I got super showed up and teased like crazy when Sydney kicked my rear. So that made them want to get even nastier, which I really wasn't a fan of to begin with. I was raised to have manners and treat females with respect, and when I hung out with the jocks, they just had this expectation that went against my beliefs. But to have them as friends, I had to sink to the lows of peer pressure to fit in," Lucas willingly shares.

"You learned something important through all of this, though. It has made you a better man for it. I'm proud of you!" Parker assures Lucas.

"Yeah, I'm just sorry it took me being so mean to your girls to wake up! But they have been way nicer to me than I deserve, but I am so grateful for it! I have so much more fun with the girls than I ever did with the jocks. People seem to like me better too!" Lucas happily shares.

They morning goes by quite quickly, and it's time for lunch. Allison contacts Greyson to see where there are and if they are ready for lunch.

Allison: We are ready for lunch how about y'all?

A few minutes later, Greyson replies.

Greyson: Sure, we are good for lunch.

Allison: Okay we will meet y'all at the steakhouse. We should be there in about 10 minutes.

Greyson: We should be there in about 10 minutes give or take as well.

When everyone gets to the steakhouse, they go in and get seated. The waitress takes their order and brings them their drinks and some starter bread.

As they wait for their food, they all discuss what their finds were for the day. The men were done for the day, but the girls still have one more place that they wanted to go to before they call it quits.

After a few minutes, their appetizer is brought out to their table. They all pick at the appetizer and continue chatting about the day's events.

A few minutes later, their food is served. They all enjoy their food as they talk about things they want to do yet for the remainder of the day.

When they are done, they pay, and the guys fix to go back to Greyson's while the girls fix to go to their last store that they want to stop at. The girls go to their last store and get their shopping done, and then they head to the Abbotts' too.

When they get home, they get inside and are home for just a few minutes when the girls yell out from the living room.

"Mom! Eliza is getting sick again!" Sophie screams.

Allison and Greyson come running with Parker and Emma right behind them.

"Greyson, I need the basin from the bathroom closet. Please hurry. Sophie, can you please get the mop and bucket? Emma, can you please grab me some towels from under the kitchen sink?" Allison instructs everyone.

Everyone comes rushing back to Allison with the items she sent them for. She gives Eliza the basin as she tries to wipe her up a little.

"What was she doing before she got sick?" Allison asks the girls.

"Nothing, Mom. She was just sitting on the floor," Sophie says, scared.

"I know she didn't eat much. Greyson, honey, can you please go get the thermometer from in the medicine cabinet?" Allison kindly asks. "Are you done, sweetheart?"

Eliza tries to talk. When she gets sick again a few minutes later, Eliza replies, "I think I am done, Mommy," as she makes a sour face.

"Greyson, can you get her a drink please?" Allison asks as she prepares to take Eliza's temperature. "Open up. Let's get your temperature. Then you may have a drink," Allison instructs her.

She takes Eliza's temperature, and once again, it's in the normal range, nowhere near a fever range. Allison is confused at why she is getting sick when she has no fever, she hasn't overeaten, nor has she been carrying on or acting crazy.

"I'm sorry. She is going to need a bath, and this needs cleaned up. Is there anyone who would like to help?" Allison asks those who are there.

"If you don't mind, Allison, I could give you a hand and bathe her if Sophie can show me where everything is," Emma offers.

"Thanks, that would be absolutely perfect. Sweetheart, do you mind Emma giving you a bath?" Allison asks Eliza.

"It's okay, Mommy," Eliza says as she stands to go with Emma to the bathroom.

Sophie follows to show Emma where everything is. Then she goes to get some clean clothes for Eliza.

"Is there anything I can do to help Allison?" Sydney asks.

"Actually, if you could please get me the trash can from the kitchen, that would be great!" Allison informs Sydney.

"Yeah, sure, I can do that," Sydney says as she goes to the kitchen.

"Allison, do you mind if I steal your man for a little bit? I have a veterinarian coming to the house, and since I rode with Emma, I was wondering if Greyson could take me home?" Parker hates to ask with everything that's going on.

"Oh, yes, sure, not an issue, Parker. I love you, dear. See you when you get back," Allison says patiently.

Greyson leans down to give Allison a kiss as he says, "I love you. I will hurry back."

"Oh, honey, take your time. I'm good here," Allison says understandably.

"Okay, love you, dear!" Greyson says as he walks out the door with Parker following him.

"Thanks again, Allison," Parker says right before he walks out the door and shuts it.

After the men leave, Allison gets the living room cleaned up and sanitized where Eliza got sick. Emma has Eliza all cleaned up.

"Sophie, honey, can you please take this trash bag out to the can outside?" Allison asks.

"Sure, Mom!"

Emma sits down for a moment to talk with Allison. "How long has this been happening with Eliza?"

Allison thinks back and says, "I think the first time was at your place. And I believe this was only the third time. Why do you ask?"

"This is totally my opinion, but I would definitely not let this go. If she gets sick like that again, I will make an appointment and get her to a doctor or the hospital. But that's just my opinion and what I would do," Emma offers.

"Oh, yes. I don't think I wanna wait for the next time. I may just make an appointment in a little bit. I would rather take her and find out it's nothing than not take her and wait then wish I had done something sooner!" Allison says proactively.

"That sounds like an even better idea!" Emma agrees. "I hate to run, but I think I am gonna head out. I have some things to get done back home."

"Yes, same here. I am sorry about Eliza! I hope that you had a great day with us," Allison hopes.

"Yes, I had a great time. I will pray for Eliza. Sydney, are you ready, young one?" Emma asks.

"Yes, ma'am! Bye, bestie!" Sydney says as she hugs Sophie. "Feel better, Eliza!"

"Thanks for your help, Miss Emma! And Syd! Goodbye till later." Eliza thanks them as they leave.

CHAPTER 25
New Family Surprise

Greyson gets Parker home just before the veterinarian gets to the ranch. Greyson sticks around to see what's up with SOT!

Greyson notices a van coming in the lane, so he shouts out to Parker. Parker leaves Obee with SOT as he goes to see what has Greyson in such an uproar.

"What's up, Greyson? Did you see a mouse?" Parker laughs.

"Yeah, you wish! But no, I think the veterinarian is here." Greyson points down the driveway.

"Awesome! We made it here in good time then," Parker says, pleased.

They both stand there, waiting for the veterinarian to get close enough to park. Once they are parked, Parker walks closer to greet them. When the door opens, Parker notices it's a female.

Parker gets nervous as he introduces himself.

"Hello, ma'am! I-I am Parker," he says, stuttering his way through his greeting to her.

"Hello, Parker. I'm Alyssa, and I was told that you have a more stubborn than normal horse that you are concerned about?" The veterinarian reads from her notes.

"Ah yes, way this right! Agh, sorry. I meant right this way!" Parker tries to act like he didn't just stutter through his words. "Obee, the veterinarian is here."

"Hello, Obee, was it?" Alyssa asks as she puts out her hand to shake his.

Obee puts his hand out and shakes her hand.

"Okay, so which one of these beautiful animals is the reason I am here?" Alyssa asks curiously.

Obee points out to SOT.

"Thanks! So, what is her issue?" she asks. When she asks, SOT starts shaking her head up and down and back and forth. "Oh, I guess she's trying to show me?" Alyssa laughs.

"Yeah, that is something new that she recently started. She's stomping her feet, along with shaking and rearing up her head. She just seems more moody than normal," Parker says, concerned.

"Ah, okay, I see, and just how long has this been happening?" Alyssa asks like she's pretty sure that she knows what the issue is.

"Let me think." Obee scratches his head and counts on his fingers as he mumbles under his breath then says, "Boss, when was that storm?" Obee tries to remember back.

"Hmm, I think it was like maybe about a month ago?" Parker stumbles through his thoughts.

"Oh, you mean that big and nasty bunch of storms that came through most recently a few weeks ago?" Alyssa asks.

"Yes, it was during that last bunch of storms. It was a short time after that," Parker says.

Greyson stands back, just taking in all this comic show of love at first sight for at least one of them but maybe both.

"Oh, okay, great. Well, I have a few tests to do, but I am about 90% sure I know what her issue is, but I don't wanna say till I run my tests. If you don't mind, I just need about 20 minutes to run them," Alyssa informs them.

Obee smiles as he stands there watching her. Parker just stands there watching and waiting to find out what it is. Greyson just slowly steps further away, picking up on the fact that she needs her space to do her job.

Alyssa stops for a moment then says politely, "If you have something else to do, you may want to go do it. This is a bit boring and not the prettiest thing to watch."

"I can get you a lemonade or a water?" Obee offers.

"Umm, sure, a water would be great! Can you bring it out to me in about 20 minutes? Thanks." Alyssa gets to getting everything prepared to run her tests.

Parker grabs Obee by his arm and pulls him to follow him. As they head for the house, they pause at the end of the stables and both look back, and as they do, they notice she is looking their way too! She smiles at them, and they return the smiles. Then Greyson decides to push them both before they fill the stables up with drool. Then they quickly scurry off to the house.

While they are in the kitchen, Obee keeps trying to look out the window, when he's not, he's pacing the kitchen from one side to the other and back.

"Obee, if you keep pacing back and forth, I'm gonna have to replace the kitchen floor from you wearing a hole through it!" Parker says, laughing.

"I'm sorry, boss, but Alyssa has my heart! I'm so drawn to her. I think I found the love of my life!" Obee says as he breathes heavily. "I can't wait to go and take her this water!"

"Obee!" Parker snaps his fingers at Obee. "Earth to Obee!" Parker tries to snap Obee back to reality.

"Man, he's really out there somewhere!" Greyson points out.

"*Oliver Beavin!*" Parker quickly shouts with a loud clap right in front of his face.

"Oh yes, boss! What's up?" Obee responds.

"Seriously?!" Parker chuckles, "set your timer to count down the time."

"That's a great idea, boss!" Obee takes his phone and sets a timer for 20 minutes and then waits.

Greyson thinks of something to distract Obee for a few minutes to help him pass the time.

"Obee?" Greyson says to get his attention.

"Yeah, Greyson, what's up?" Obee replies.

"I have an idea! Parker, of course you have to approve it first," Greyson says, putting it out there and gaining the attention of both of them.

"What's that, Greyson?" Parker wonders where he's going with this.

"So, what do you guys think about doing something here for Halloween? Like you have plenty of land and I think we should do a haunted or spooky trail? What do you think?" Greyson happily asks. Just then, Sydney and Emma come walking into the house.

"Let's keep this on the down low," Parker quickly whispers and winks to Greyson in approval.

"Wow, a kitchen full of men!" Emma says, shocked to see them all there. Are y'all hungry?"

"A snack would be nice, but we are waiting for the veterinarian to run some tests on SOT. She said that she needed some time to complete and run them. So, we came in here for Obee to get her a drink and wait," Parker says as he chuckles.

"Oh, that's not funny. Obee, if you offered her a drink, why are you just sitting in here?" Emma wonders as if Obee is being rude for making her wait.

"If he had his way, he wouldn't be just sitting here. He would've already taken it out to her," Greyson jokes and laughs.

"I'm sorry. I'm very confused," Emma states.

Then the doorbell rings.

"I'll get it!" Sydney says as she runs for the door.

When she opens the door, there stands a very beautiful young woman.

"Hello sweetheart! Is your..." Alyssa gets cut off when Obee hears her speaking from in the kitchen and comes running out to the door.

"Hi, Obee! Is your..." Again, Alyssa stops in midsentence because Parker has followed Obee out to see what was going on and she notices him trying to hide behind Obee.

"Here's the water that you wanted," Obee says as he hands it to her.

Alyssa takes the water and says, "Yes, thank you, Obee. But I have the results of my tests, and I wanted to tell your boss." Alyssa tries to look around Obee to see Parker.

Parker sees her and locks eyes with her as he steps out from behind Obee while Greyson and Emma just stand there, smirking at the craziness from Obee and Parker over Alyssa.

"Are you talking about SOT?" Sydney softly asks.

"Yes, little lady, I am," Alyssa says, smiling.

"Oh, cool, so what's wrong with my horse?" Sydney asks, concerned.

Alyssa looks worried about telling Sydney, but Parker nods that it's okay.

"Well, I have some hopefully great news!" Alyssa starts to say, dragging out the suspense.

"It's great news? She's acting very different or off from her normal! And that's great?" Sydney says, freaking out. "What is so great about all that?"

"Yes, definitely! I will say that an addition to your stables will make it much easier to handle though!" Alyssa says, smiling from ear to ear.

Everyone gets quiet for a few moments when Sydney thinks she is picking up what Alyssa is putting down.

"Wait! Are you saying what I think that you are?" Sydney says super happy and surprised.

"That I am! It's such happy news!" Alyssa shares.

"Oh my! Dad, SOT's pregnant!" Sydney says, jumping up and down and running around.

Parker stands there for a moment, just letting it sink in. Then he says a bit confused, "But how?"

The look on Greyson's face is priceless as he says, "Parker, please tell me that you are kidding about your last comment? It seriously hasn't been that long for you." He chuckles.

"Greyson, I'm the one who should be asking you seriously? I know how it works, but what I mean is we keep the horses separated unless we are riding them. So how is this possible?"

Obee thinks, and when the lights go on, he lights up. "Boss, I think I know when," he says cautiously.

"Well, don't leave us hanging Obee. Come out with it already," Parker says as he tries to think when it was even possible.

"Dad!" Sydney says like she knows when it happened.

"Yes, Syd!"

"The storm!" Sydney spills.

"Ding ding ding! We have a winner!" Obee blurts out.

"Oh da... sorry... oh, shucks! You are so right! Oh, man. Well, it's great news! So, when is she possibly due?" Parker asks. "I mean how much time do I have to get an addition added to the stables?"

"I would be safe saying you should plan to have it done by the end of March. Just because you want some leeway in case of building issues. But it should be completed by the middle of April," Alyssa informs them.

"This is so awesome. I have to message Sophie and Lucas!" Sydney says excitedly, and as quickly as she was excited for the new addition to the family, she stops dead in her tracks and her emotion turns sad.

"Syd, you, okay?" Parker asks.

"But what about the track? How will I race?" Sydney asks, freaking out.

"Okay, so she should still be okay to race in October, but for April, I would advise against that," Alyssa informs Sydney and the rest of the family.

"That's okay. We have Tall Leaps you can use if you would like?" Parker suggests to Sydney.

"Oh, okay. I guess so," Sydney says, slightly bummed.

"Or since we will be making the stables bigger, maybe we can just buy another horse?" Parker slips out that little tidbit of information.

"We will see. It's a lot of work training a new horse. I'll think about it, Dad," Sydney says emotionally.

"That works for me, Syd," he says, hoping she'll change her mind eventually. Then he turns his attention to Alyssa. "Now, Alyssa, what do I owe you for your time and services?"

"How about dinner and a movie?" Alyssa quickly answers.

Parker and Obee just look at each other, shocked. Parker redirects his attention to Alyssa and says, "Seriously?!"

Alyssa laughs, "I'm sorry. I have always wanted to say that! I got the feeling that y'all would find it as a funny joke. I'm sorry. I don't know what I was thinking. That was very unprofessional."

Obee steps forward and clears his throat. "Alyssa?"

"Yes, Obee?"

"Umm, I was wondering." Obee pauses for a moment till he gets the courage to continue. "So, I don't know if I will get this opportunity again." He looks around then back to her. "I guess what I am trying to say... no, I do mean to ask if you maybe one night if you aren't busy and if you could maybe see yourself with..." Obee stops when Alyssa takes his hand.

"Obee?"

He takes a big, hard swallow. "Yes, Alyssa," Obee says, trembling.

"Aww, would you just look at you. Well, I am certain that I am reading all the signs correctly, and if I am, I want you to know the answer is yes! Yes, I will have dinner and do a movie with you!" Alyssa says as she feels completely out of her element.

You would have thought that Obee won the lottery. When he hears her answer to his partially asked question, his eyes light up, and he grabs Alyssa and hugs her and dances around with her. Then when he realizes that he is making a complete idiot of himself, he stops and lets Alyssa go as he carefully straightens her vet coat that he wrinkled up.

"I'm sorry, Alyssa! Yes, that is exactly what I wanted to ask you. When would you like to have a dinner and a movie on me? I don't mean on me... I mean with me. I will pay!" Obee stumbles through his comment and hopes she isn't scared away or offended by his clumsiness.

"You are all good, Obee. How about I give you my number, and when you want to go, give me a day or two's notice and we will go out? Is that okay?" Alyssa says, smiling such a beautiful smile, so beautiful that Obee can't take his eyes off her lips and her smile as he hands her his phone. She puts her number in his phone and hands it back to him.

"Okay, I must be going soon, so Parker, if you don't mind, I will just send you a bill?" Alyssa asks.

"Yes, that would be just fine. Thank you again for your services. Will you be back to do check-ups regularly?" Parker wonders.

"I tell you what I can do for you. When I stop by to see your employee, I will check in on her and make sure she is doing well," Alyssa promises.

"Okay, that works. Thank you," Parker says gratefully.

"Can I ask you for a huge favor, Sydney? Is that right?" she recalls from her memory.

"Yes, ma'am!" Sydney responds.

"I need you to please make sure that SOT has fresh, clean water every day, good quality hay, and some horse vitamins! Can you do that for me?" Alyssa instructs and kindly asks.

Sydney looks at her dad. He responds with, "I will make sure that she has everything she needs to do that for not just SOT but her baby and per your instructions."

"Okay then, everyone. It was very great meeting y'all. Obee, I will be waiting for your text! Goodbye, everyone," she says as she leaves for her next appointment.

"Look at you, Obee! You got yourself a date!" Emma says proudly.

Obee rubs his head and says, "Yeah, I still don't know how because I wasn't able to ask her myself." He giggles. "But I am a lucky guy that she was smart enough to know what I wanted."

"Yes, you are very lucky, Obee!" Greyson adds.

"Well, we have a bunch to celebrate. What do y'all say about us going out on a buggy and catching some fireworks when they set them off?" Parker asks everyone.

"In all the excitement, I almost forgot that it was the Fourth of July!" Obee says.

"Dad, I'm gonna call it a night if you don't mind," Sydney sighs.

"Is everything okay, Syd?" Parker wonders.

"Yeah, everything is good. It's just been a super eventful day, and I am tired. I'm sorry. I love you!" Sydney professes.

"Oh, okay, good night. I love you, my little filly," Parker replies.

Sydney heads to her room, while the others go outside.

Sydney decides to message her friends and tell them about the end to her exciting day.

    Sydney: HEY BESTIE! Have I got something so awesome to tell you!

    Sydney: HEY Lucas! I have something to tell you that is super awesome!

She waits for just a few minutes for responses.

    Lucas: Sounds like your day was better than the rest of mine.

    Sydney: You wanna talk about it?

Lucas: I mean basically I wasn't sure about joining football this year and today just made it even more clear! But I don't wanna drag down your happy mood so let's talk about your day so I can hopefully be happier.

Sydney: Well, I don't know how to say this without sounding... well confusing so I'm just gonna say it. We are gonna be parents!

Lucas: Syd I know that you are joking. We for one aren't dating to even do what needs to be accomplished to even be a parent.

Sydney: No silly! SOT is pregnant and Loads of Luck is the dad!

Lucas: WHAT? How?

Sydney: Seriously? Do you remember the storm?

Lucas: Duh yeah, my bad! Wow! This is so cool I'm gonna be a dad in a sense.

Sydney: Well, I am headed to bed, so I just wanted to share the awesome news!

Lucas: Thanks, good night, Syd! Ttys

Sydney gets changed for bed when Sophie responds.

Sophie: Hey bestie! What's so awesome?

Sydney: We are gonna be adding onto the stables.

Sophie: Yeah, wow that is cool.

Sydney: Am I sensing some sarcasm?

Sophie: Maybe lol

Sydney: Well, think what you like but I am gonna need room for my new baby!

Sophie: New baby? Is your dad getting you a new horse?

Sydney: No silly goose SOT is pregnant!

Sophie: Really? How cool! Congrats!

Sydney: Thanks! Well, I just wanted to let you know the awesome news. Now I am off to bed. Night bestie!

Sophie: No problem good night! Ttys

Sydney falls asleep looking out her window and listening to the fireworks.

CHAPTER 26
Preparing For the First Day

It's been a very busy and eventful last month. The boutique has been doing so well. We have raised a nice bundle of money for the cancer research. But with school starting soon, the hours at the boutique will be cut to select hours on Friday, Saturday, and Sundays. Over the summer months, we weren't open on Sundays, but with school starting, we decided it would be okay for the school months to be open for our customers.

SOT is doing so well! She is slowly starting to swell up just a little. You can't tell by just looking at her, but we have a piece of twine that we try to place around her belly as close as we can to the same spot each time so we can track her growth. Alyssa has been keeping a good eye on her when she comes to see Obee.

Yes, you heard correctly! Alyssa and Obee have hit it off like a major bang! They are like two peas in a pod. They have been together more than not. When Alyssa is not around, Obee has been talking about possibly marrying her. They, together, have been bouncing around the idea of possibly having Alyssa move to the ranch. Even though Alyssa says she has found heaven when she met Obee, they still wanna wait before they do decide to just have her give up her place and make the living together commitment. She is basically at the ranch for 90% of her free time.

But it makes complete sense.

Training has been a bit different since SOT is pregnant. We still have them, but we just don't train as hard. We have been also training with one of our other horses. Classy Steps is a five-year-old Tennessee Walker. She is a Cremello-colored Tennessee Walker, which is basically white with a hint of yellow on top. She almost looks like a trophy—that's probably how she got her name because gold is classy. Her mane and tail are a little more cream colored.

SOT seems unhappy that Classy Steps goes out when PB Cup and Loads of Luck go out for training. But she is young, and we don't wanna take any chances of a miscarriage. Lucas has not missed a training session yet. He seems very devoted.

Ah, yes, Lucas. Where does one start when it comes to him? He's so devoted to training with Loads of Luck it's truly amazing. But there's only so much time in a day, and he hasn't missed any time at the boutique either. So, he has decided to slack on his school football career. The coach being so hard on him and singling him out probably has a lot to do with it.

Rumor has it that he and Stanley have become very good friends this summer. He's made mention several times of hanging out with Stanley and gaming on the Xbox together.

Emma is so excited for the new school year to start. She has been gathering items for her new classroom and getting her classes planned. It's hard to believe that the new year starts very soon. Besides her getting her classes planned, we have been busy getting alarms set and making bedtimes. This week, we have a shopping trip planned to get food for lunches and some food for easier and quicker meals for after school.

Parker made it easier to care for the horses since our days are shortened by school starting. He didn't want to add more stress and workload to Obee. So, he got some self-watering devices and had them hooked up. With that said he has had the planning done for the new stable.

They should be breaking ground just before school starts in the next week! He tells the contractor that he wants it done in time before winter when it gets cold, and the ground gets too hard.

Tonight, is the back-to-school event where we get our schedules, make sure that they are correct, pick our clubs, and meet our new teachers. Emma will be meeting many of her new students for the first time tonight.

Sophie and Eliza want to come over today at lunch, while Allison goes to show one of her properties. She wants to coordinate our outfits for the first day. After all, being a sophomore is a big deal. So, we have to our bring game! Like either of us are even looking for or are even interested in boys.

Sydney gets a text, and it interrupts her thoughts.

Lucas: Hey good morning!

Sydney: Hello! Good morning. What's up?

Lucas: Just wondering what you are up to today.

Sydney: Umm I believe Sophie and Eliza are coming over around lunch time. What are you up to?

Lucas: Besides talking to you? Not much I may go to Stanley's today. He wants to hang out before we have to go to the back-to-school event. Are you going tonight?

Sydney: Of course, I would not miss it for the world!

Lucas: Ok well I will hopefully see you there later tonight?

Sydney: I will be there, but you may or may not see me lol.

Lucas: Oh, ok well I really hope I do get to see you ok ttys! Sydney. Ok l8r!

Sydney lies there, not wanting to get out of bed, wishing she had more summertime to hang out and just have fun. She decides to message Sophie.

Sydney: Hey bestie! Are you up yet?

Sophie: Hey I sure am! How are you? Are you excited for later tonight?

Sydney: Eh I would rather have more summer! Lol hey I was wondering if you think your mom would be able to bring y'all over earlier than lunch time?

Sophie: I don't know but I can ask quick! Mom would probably be extremely happy to get rid of us sooner rather than later.

Sydney: I hate to be such a pain, but can you ask? Sophie. Sure! Be right back Sydney. Ok!

Sydney decides to get up and grab a shower while she waits.

Meanwhile, at Lucas's house
Lucas messages Stanley.

Lucas: Hey Stanley!

Stanley: Hey Lucas! How are you?

Lucas: Would you mind if I came over in a little bit?

Stanley: Sure, that should be just fine.

Lucas: Ok cool see you in a bit.

Stanley: Ok sounds great!

Lucas: It'll probably be in like 30 minutes give or take.

Stanley: That works then I'll have time for breakfast! Ok see you then Lucas, thanks!

Meanwhile, back at Sydney's house

Sophie: Mom said yes! So how soon you want us to come over?

Sydney: As early as you can talk your mom into bringing y'all over!

Sophie: 10-4 bestie! I'm all over it!

Sydney: Sweet! See ya soon!

Sophie: Most definitely!

Sydney runs downstairs to alert Emma of Sophie and Eliza coming over sooner.

"Emma!" Sydney shouts as she hits the bottom of the stairs. "I have to talk to you!"

Just as Sydney goes to run into the kitchen, she runs hard into Emma, who is headed out from the kitchen when she hears Sydney yelling.

Emma thinks quickly and grabs hold of Sydney when they collide so they can balance each other and not go crashing on to the floor when she says, "Seriously, Sydney! One of these days, child, you, or someone else is gonna get seriously hurt with you and your friends zipping through this house like you are on speed or something!" Emma tries to scold her, but she's so happy, and she isn't letting any monkeys throw wrenches in to mess that up. She hugs Sydney then releases her and asks, "So what has you in such an uproar?"

"Sophie and Eliza are coming over earlier than originally anticipated," Sydney says with excitement.

"Oh, okay, good to know. But please be careful before you get hurt running through this house," Emma pleads with Sydney.

"Okay, I will try harder to not run," Sydney repeats.

"Thank you, Sydney!" Emma yells after Sydney as she shuffles into the living room to wait for Sophie and Eliza.

Meanwhile, over at Stanley's house

There's something stirring. In Stanley's room, he and Lucas are cooking up a plan for the first day of school.

"I have been thinking! And I think you and I are going to be an amazing team this year," Lucas states to Stanley.

"Oh, how's that Lucas?" Stanley curiously asks.

"I know you have your eyes on a specific special lady, right?" Lucas points out.

"Yes but..."

"No! There's no buts here! I won't hear it!" Lucas takes action, stomping out Stanley's doubt.

"Okay, well, what if she doesn't feel the same way as me?" Stanley questions.

"That's where we will be a team! We are going to help each other get the woman we want! So, you game?" Lucas prays he says yes.

"Okay, I'm listening."

"Well, I don't have everything worked out just yet, but one thing is for sure: that what we have to do is to talk up each other to the lady that the other one wants! You got me so far?" Lucas tries to explain.

"Yeah, I talk to your lady friend telling her good things about you, and you return the favor for me!" Stanley words it his way to make sure he's got it right.

"Yeah, that was said quite nicely and exactly what I mean! So, we will work on other little things to help entice them," Lucas adds.

"So do we, or will we have a time frame of which we hope to have our lady by?" Stanley asks.

"Well, I was hoping we'd have them by the homecoming dance. I think it's doable," Lucas says, setting an initial date for their plan.

"Well, that's not a lot of time, and we have to be careful not to over push or over intrude," Lucas warns.

"Because when we lose that for which we strive to have, then it will be twice as hard to regain our place which we lost," Stanley riddles to Lucas.

"Okay, I think I know what you said, but enough with the riddles. So tonight, I need you to try to say something awesome about me to Syd! Can you, do it?" Lucas asks, setting the plan into action.

"I will conquer that! Will you do the same for me?" Stanley asks, hoping that this plan of Lucas's works.

"I have your back, Stanley!" Lucas assures him.

"Okay, so you wanna do a little gaming before we head to school later?" Stanley asks happily.

"Sure!"

Back at the Ashcraft ranch

Sophie and Eliza have arrived, and they are in Sydney's bedroom picking out Sydney's first day outfit while Allison talks with Emma in the kitchen.

"So will you be able to make it to the back-to-school night?" Emma asks.

"Well, I hope so, but I have a settlement late this afternoon. If it goes off without a hitch, I will definitely be there, but there have been a few stumps in the road for this family, so let's pray it goes well," Allison relays. "Greyson was gonna try to make it, so he could bring the girls home afterward, but I think he had something come up that may overrun into tonight as well. So, we may need them to be dropped off?"

"I can do that. If you like, I can drop the girls off at the house on the way back through town," Emma offers.

"That would be great! But only if Greyson doesn't show up. So yes, please. But only if he doesn't make it, could you?" Allison graciously asks.

"Not a problem!" Emma accepts the possible favor.

"Okay, sounds great! Well, I hate to go, but I have a few errands to run before my showing at noon. Thanks again, Emma!" Allison says gratefully.

"You're welcome. Good luck later!"

Upstairs, the girls have finally completed Sydney's day one outfit.

"Syd, you are gonna look so irresistible!" Sophie shrieks.

"You know, I'm not going to school looking for anything or anyone from the opposite sex! So, what's it matter how good or bad I look?" Sydney says, stomping on Sophie's thoughts of finding a man.

"Well, you never know whom you might run into and how they could change your mind." Sophie continues to push the issue.

"Look, bestie, I love you to the ends of the earth but no! I don't want to date anyone! What you want is up to you, but I just hope he doesn't come between us! End of story so can we please just drop it already?" Sydney fiercely strikes down Sophie's idea again.

"Okay, bestie, I will drop it," Sophie softly says.

"Can we please play Uno?" Eliza asks.

"Sure, it's downstairs in the living room. Let's go play. But don't run down the stairs because Emma has really been on me about that lately," Sydney says informing them of Emma's wishes.

They go down and play Uno till lunch. After lunch, they continue playing card games till it's time to get ready to head to school.

After a few hours, it's time for them to make their way to school.

"Girls, are you ready to go? I like to be leaving in about 10 minutes please," Emma shouts out to the living room from the foyer as she heads into the kitchen.

The girls clean up their game and go to the kitchen to be ready for when Emma is ready to go.

"We are ready whenever you are, Em," Sydney says as they look for a quick snack.

"I just need a few minutes, then I will be ready," Emma replies.

"Okay, can we go out and wait in the car?" Sydney asks suggestively. "Sure, I'll be right out in a bit," Emma says.

The girls head out to the car and are super excited to get to school.

Emma finishes up and meets the kids out in the car. On the way to the school, the girls are very chatty and excited. As they pull in, the excitement level rises with them.

"Okay, girls, here we are. Have a good time, and can you please wait for me in the lobby at the end of the night please?!" Emma requests.

"Yes, ma'am!" Sydney responds for them all.

When the girls get out of the car, they head into the school and head to the schedule table to pick up their schedules. On their schedule sheets is their homeroom number, locker number with combination code, and their class schedule. The girls find their lockers and try to open their locks. When they hear some familiar voices, they turn to look, and there stands Lucas with a young boy they don't recognize, but his voice sounds very familiar.

"Sophie, who is that with Lucas?" Sydney asks curiously.

"I don't know, bestie! But if I have to guess, I would say it kinda sounds like Stanley, but that is not Stanley. That is a fine hunk of a man!" Sophie says, almost drooling.

Sydney gives Sophie a look of disappointment and punches her on her arm when she says, "Sophie! Umm, I thought we weren't doing the boy thing just yet?"

Sophie rubs her arm and gives Sydney the evil, hairy eye and says, "Well, I never said it was set in stone. And that is definitely a situation that I would love to get to know better! Even if we are just friends."

"Well, you may just get your chance because here they come!" Sydney says quickly as she reduces her voice to a whisper.

"Hey, Sydney, Sophie, and Eliza. How are y'all?" Lucas asks eagerly.

Sophie bounces forward and tries to get the attention of the new guy that was with Lucas and says, "Hey, Lucas! How are you? And who's your friend?"

"Hey, Sophie!" Stanley states as he watches the look on Sophie's face change when she goes from confused to an aha moment. "It's me, Stanley."

"Stanley?" Sophie says confused and tries to figure out what was going on. "Wow, umm, you look great! When did you... I mean how did... words cannot express how truly shocked I am that I didn't even know it was you! Just last week, this was not you!"

"It's okay, I understand. But I decided that I needed an overhaul and makeover before school. I got rid of the glasses for contacts, got my hair cut, frosted, and styled, and had a facial done for my acne. I've been working out. Not for any reason other than I personally wanted to feel better about myself," Stanley happily reports.

"Well, you are looking quite good! If you don't mind me saying so," Sophie says, trying not to let on that she is crushing on him so much at the moment.

Sydney tries to change the subject. "So, did y'all find your lockers? And did you get them open yet?"

"I didn't find mine yet. Did you, Lucas?" Stanley replies.

"No, I had just picked up my schedule when Stanley ran into me and he spotted y'all over here," Lucas states. "Did y'all find yours?"

"We both found our lockers, but we only got one opened. We were just gonna open the other one," Sydney says.

"So where are you gals' lockers at? If you don't mind me asking?" Stanley questions.

"Ours is actually together right here," Sophie offers.

"Okay, well, we will meet up with you later. Bye, gals," Stanley says as he motions for Lucas to follow him.

"Okay, bye!" Sophie waves and winks to Stanley.

After the boys walk away, Sydney hammers on Sophie, "Sophie! What are you thinking?"

"I'm sorry, I couldn't help myself!" Sophie smiles and responds like a child being scolded.

"Come on, we gotta get to our first class," Sydney says, ignoring Sophie and what she was just saying.

Meanwhile, the boys are back to scheming to get the gals.

"Stanley, it looks like it's gonna be easy for you to hook up with Sophie! But for me, it looks like you will have your work cut out for you!" Lucas stops and says, thinking about how Sophie acted versus Sydney to each of them.

"We will get through this and get our gals!" Stanley assures Lucas.

CHAPTER 27
Sophomore Year, First Day

Buzz. Buzz.

"**G**ood morning, Lexington," the radio announcer says, drawing out the greeting. "What a beautiful first day of school for the local kiddos! It's so beautiful that it's gonna be so hard for any of them to wanna even go to school! But take it from me... get a great education and you can do anything that you want when you grow up! In other news..." Sydney hits the alarm to shut it off.

She quickly jumps outta bed and gathers her outfit to grab a quick shower just to wake up and to feel a little fresher. After her shower, she gets dressed in the outfit that she and Sophie picked out a few days ago. As she admires herself in the mirror, she can't help but feel overly excited about her first day as a sophomore.

"Mmm, Emma's at it again!" Sydney says to herself out loud as she is still admiring herself in the mirror.

"Breakfast is ready!" Sydney hears Emma shout out from the kitchen for everyone to hear.

"Coming, Emma!" Sydney quickly yells back. Sydney carefully goes down the stairs to the kitchen because falling from rushing on the first day and getting hurt just isn't a great way to start off the first day of sophomore year.

"Oh, Em! I was smelling your breakfast all the way upstairs and it smells ah-maz-zing as usual!" Sydney hungrily states.

"Well, eat up so your brain can function properly," Emma says as she tries to quickly get cleaned up before they leave. "Not to rush you, but if you could eat quickly, I would like to be at school a little early today please."

"Okay, so will we have time to stop and pick up Sophie?" Sydney says with a mouthful of eggs.

"Sydney, please do not eat with your mouth open. Not only is it quite rude but it's disgusting and not safe. But if you get done eating soon enough, we should have time if she is out waiting for us," Emma caringly says.

Sydney swallows her food and responds, "Sorry, Em. I was trying to hurry, and okay, I will let her know. I'm done. I will save the rest for after school," Sydney says as she gets up to get the plastic wrap and wraps her food for later. She puts her plate in the fridge and texts Sophie.

Sydney: Hey bestie be ready we are gonna be leaving in a tiny bit.

Sophie: Ok no problem I will be ready! See ya soon!

Sydney: Love ya!

Sophie: Love you too!

"Sophie will be ready!" Sydney excitedly exclaims.

"Okay, I just need to grab my bag, and we will be on our way if you wanna tell her?" Emma informs her.

"Got it! I will text her on my way to the car," Sydney says as she grabs her book bag and heads out the door to the car.

Sydney: We are leaving can you please be outside waiting? Thanks, love you.

Sophie: 10-4 bestie love you too!

Just as Sydney gets in the car and closes the door, Emma comes out of the house.

Then Sydney jumps because someone knocks on her door window and scares her. She turns to look and sees her dad. She quickly jumps out of the car and gives him a huge, tight hug.

"I love you, dad!" Sydney wholeheartedly expresses.

"I love you too, my little filly," Parker says as he holds back the tears.

"I'm sorry, dad, but we have to go!" Sydney says as she gets in the car again. As she gets in, she put down her window and says, "I love you and will see you after school!"

"I'm gonna hold you to that, my little filly!" Parker says as he waves to her as Emma pulls away.

Sydney watches from the side mirror and waves till she can't see him anymore.

Parker stands there tearing up as he also waves till, he can no longer see her, not knowing that Obee has walked up behind him and scares him.

"Obee! Watch it," Parker says, chuckling as he wipes his face quickly.

"It's okay, boss. She'll be back later," Obee kindly says.

"Yeah, I know. It's just she is growing up so fast! I'm not ready for her to move away!" Parker says as another tear slides down his face.

"Come on, let's go eat and get your mind on something different," Obee quickly says.

Meanwhile, at the Abbott's

Sophie stands outside waiting for Emma and Sydney. Then she sees Emma's car. Her heart starts racing, and her breathing gets faster as the excitement of her being at school in just a short few minutes hits her. When Emma pulls up, she waits till she stops so she can get in.

Sydney gets out and hugs Sophie, and they get into the back seat together.

"That sure was quick, Emma! Thanks again for picking me up," Sophie happily states.

"Not a problem, Sophie. I'm happy to pick you up," Emma reassures Sophie.

"You look so good, Syd! You are gonna catch a couple eyes today!" Sophie says while licking the tip of her finger and touching Sydney's shoulder while making sizzling noises. "Smoking!" She smiles.

"I do have you to thank! After all, you picked it out for me. You also are looking quite fine yourself! I betcha you will turn more heads than I will," Sydney thoughtfully says.

"Okay, we are here, girls! Have a great day! I will meet you out her after school," Emma tells the girls.

They quickly get out of the car and say "Okay, see ya" simultaneously as they head for the front doors.

They get into the school and head for their homeroom; awesomely, they have the same one this year. They go in and find their seats, and on their desks are the updated schedules. They sit and quickly start comparing their schedules.

"Yes! We have almost every class together!" Sydney states with excitement.

"That is beyond awesome!" Sophie expresses enthusiastically.

They are in absolute heaven when they get interrupted by Stanley and Lucas.

"Hey, ladies! Good morning. How are you?" Stanley beams with happiness.

"Stanley, Lucas, good morning. Are you guys in this homeroom too?" Sydney regrettably asks as she turns to focus back to Sophie.

"Actually, yes, Syd, we are! Isn't that cool?" Lucas exclaims with a hint of hesitation.

Sydney rolls her eyes then faces Lucas and barely smiles. "Yeah, that's just great," she states sarcastically.

"Okay, class, if I may get your attention, can we all take our seats?" Mr. Skaggs requests. When everyone is seated, he continues, "Good morning, all! Welcome to the first day of the new school year. I am Mr. Skaggs. On your desk are your updated schedules for the year. If you have a class that is just a semester, the current one is what you are scheduled to take for now. If you need something fixed, please see the guidance office. You will be here every morning. Please just come in and take your seat. You will not have assigned seats, but please be respectful of your classmates," Mr. Skaggs reports.

They do the pledge of allegiance and watch the morning announcements on the TV. Then they are dismissed just after Mr. Skaggs leaves them with some words of encouragement. "My students, please have a great day. If I don't have you in a class later, then I shall see you tomorrow morning. But till then, please remember this: Vince Lombardi said, *'Confidence is contagious. So is lack of confidence.'* Go in confidence, my students," Mr. Skaggs shares.

The students get up and head to their next classes. It turns out that Sophie and Sydney have Emma's class first. As they make their way to her class, Lucas and Stanley try catching up to the girls.

"Hey, Syd, where are you headed?" Lucas wonders.

"We are headed to Ms. Howard's class," Sydney says, unfazed at Lucas's attempts to bother her.

Lucas looks at his schedule and responds, "So am I! How awesome is that?"

Sydney and Sophie look at each other, and Sydney sighs, "Just great! Oh, look, here we are!" Sydney says as they get to Emma's room, where she stands at the door waiting for her first class.

Emma nods and smiles as each student enters her room. Once they all arrive, she comes in the room and closes the door.

"Good morning, class. I am Ms. Howard. It's very great to meet you all! You may sit where you wish unless I see an issue within class, then I will pick your seat for you. Okay, we will be doing a bunch of journal work in this class, but also, there will be a bunch of teamwork assignments. So I would like for you to think about whom you would like to pair with as a team of two and four partners. I do not need to know this now, but please keep it in the back of your mind," Emma says, preparing her class for future assignments. "This is a team building class. In this class, we will learn not just team building but how to be respectful toward others," Emma states as she hears some grumbling coming from different areas of the room.

"Okay, for those of you who grumbled, I have a question for you." Emma thinks for a moment and rephrases her question. "Nah, how about we go around the whole room and find out from everyone. I don't wanna point out anyone in particular, and I think it'll be good to hear from everyone. So let's go around the room and do what I like to call *classification diversification*. So please tell us your name and what or how you think people classify you as a person. For example, at my home, I feel I am classified as the cook or maybe the maid. Is it true? It could be, but it's only what I think I am classified as. The rest of you, as you wait for your turn, I want you to listen closely because I have something that I need y'all to do after we hear everyone's opinions. So let's start at the beginning of this row and work our way around the room. Will you start us off, Miss Sophie?" Emma requests.

"Hello, I am Sophie Abbott. I feel people think that I am preppy but friendly." She smiles.

"Hi, I'm Sydney Ashcraft. I feel people think I am weak and quiet. But possibly daring," she says, looking at her desk.

"Hey, how are y'all? I am Ellie Clark. I feel people think I am pretty and sassy," she says as she flaunts her hair and winks at those who care to look at her.

"Good morning. I am Clay Woodward," he says as he takes a bow. "I think people think I'm a comedian."

"Hey, everyone! I'm Lucas Devinshire. I think people think of me as a bully and a jock," he says, cool and collected.

"Hi! I'm Stanley Melman. I think people think that I am a nerd or geek," he says kinda in a flat tone and a bit robotic.

As she drags out her words slowly, she says, "I'm Chasity Hayden! I think people think I am emo," she sighs.

He nods before saying, "I'm Roscoe Newcum. Hello, all. I think people think I am a punk rocker." He flips his long pink and lime green bangs back away from his face. "And they would be right!" He winks.

She stands and very flirtatiously says, "Hel-lo! I'm Roxie Tiller! I think that people think I am flirty and a teacher's pet." She smacks her lips and cracks her gum.

"So I am Lora Dillman, and I would just love to wish everybody a great day, and I think people think I am classy, unique, and sweet. Thank you!" She states softly and sweetly.

"I'm Scotty Goss!" he says while chewing gum and making tiny popping noises with it as he continues, "I know people think I'm a grease monkey and it's definitely true."

"I-I-I am sorry. I-I-I am...ugh!" she says, frustrated.

"It's okay. Take your time, think it through, and try again, dear." Emma kindly states.

She thinks for a minute as she looks around to see all who are looking at her. She closes her eyes and says, "I'm Layla Burkhead." She takes a deep breath and continues, "I think people think...think I am shy, plain, and weird." She finishes and opens her eyes as she looks around, and the class claps for her!

Emma claps with the class as she comments to the class, "First, I would like to say that you did very well, Layla! And what a diverse class we have!" Emma states this proudly. "Okay, now for part two. So I want you to pick two people in the room to tell them something about them that you think, whether it's something about their outfit, appearance, attitude, whatever you want, but I pray you all have something nice to say as well. So take a moment to think, and I will call on you one at time to reveal your comments. Go ahead. I will give you like 5 minutes. Start now!" Emma instructs them.

After about 5 minutes, she looks around the room and sees a few students still writing, so she waits for a few more minutes.

"Okay, do we all have our two classmates picked?" She looks around, and most are nodding, so she starts, "Okay, here we go. Clay, will you please start us off?"

"Sure, Ms. Howard. I would like to say that I picked Sydney and Scotty. Sydney, I have to say that I look up to you! I think you are very brave and fearless! Scotty, my man, what can I say? You are the best mechanic a dude could ask for!" Clay shares.

"Thank you, Clay. Now how about we have Chasity share with us?"

"I picked Roscoe for his awesome hair! Love the colors, man. I also picked Lucas for his awesome football skills!"

"Okay, thanks, Chasity! Next, Roscoe, let's hear your choices."

"Thanks. I picked Chasity and Sydney. Chasity for her awesome jewelry. And Sydney for her man jewels to ride like she does. Can I get some lessons sometime?" He winks and smiles at Sydney as she blushes and looks away quickly as she puts her hand up to block her face from Roscoe's sight.

"Okay, thanks, Roscoe. Now how about we hear from Roxie?"

"Oh, I thought you would never ask," she says with a little giggle. "Okay, I picked Stanley and Layla. Stanley, you are looking quite fine. Did you get contacts? And Layla, sweetheart, you have very beautiful eyes."

"Very nice, Roxie. Next, can I have Stanley share with us please?"

"Certainly! First I would like to say to Roxie, yes, I did get contacts. Thanks for noticing. Now the two I picked are Sophie and Clay. Sophie is sweet and pretty. While Clay is funny. He makes me laugh." Stanley says as he tries to look toward Sophie without making it seem apparent to her so he can catch her reaction.

"Wonderful, Stanley! Thank you! Let's hear whom Layla picked."

"Umm I picked... I," she mumbles under her breath and tries again. "I picked Ellie and Lora because they are both so pretty and nice." She says quickly as she sighs that she made it through.

"Very good Layla. Next Lucas who did you pick?"

"Well, one of mine was picked already, so I will pick Roxie and Stanley. Roxie is misunderstood. In my opinion, I think she is very nice, almost overly nice. I know Stanley outside of this class, and he is a good listener," he says, smiling at Sydney's direction as she catches notice and rolls her eyes.

"Good job, Lucas! Yes, if you know someone outside of this class or school, you may use how you know them as well. Okay, next on the list will be Scotty."

"I chose Lora and Lucas. Lora, I think, is sweet and smart. Lucas, I think, has done a three-sixty. He used to be cocky and quite the bully. But so far, he seems nice this year."

"Scotty, what a nice thing to say. Thanks. Now next, we have Lora." Emma smiles.

"Yes, ma'am. I picked Sophie for her amazing voice. And Ellie for her fashion sense. I mean Sophie has great fashion sense too, but I love her voice!" she says kindly.

"Great. Thank you, Lora! Next, Ellie, you're up!"

"Thanks, Ms. Howard. So, like, I picked Scotty and Roxie. My reasons are as follows: Scotty, I like a man who knows his way around a car, so that to me makes you very smart. Roxie, you are very pretty," she says respectfully.

"Thank you, Ellie. Next, Sydney could you please share your list with us."

"Absolutely! I picked Roscoe and Layla. Roscoe, I picked you because you seem very sweet considering your choice of outer layers and disguise. Also, if I may say, yes, I would love to give you some lessons sometime. Layla, I picked you because I think you are very pretty."

"Okay, great, Sydney. Now lastly, let's hear Sophie's choices. Sophie, can you please share with us your choices?"

"Yes, I chose Chasity and Clay. Chasity, I think you are very bold, and whether you are trying to or not, you make black look sexy! Clay, I think you are very caring because you go outta your way to try to make people laugh so they feel better. Or at least that's how I see it."

"Great job, everyone! So now you can see what people do and don't feel about you as you necessarily think. Okay, that's the end of our class for the day. Have a great rest of your day, everyone," Emma says as the bell rings and the students head to their next classes.

Sydney and Sophie are some of the first students out the door. As they walk down the hall. They hear a commotion behind themselves. When they turn around, they see Roscoe trying to quickly make his way through the crowded hallway.

"Excuse me. Excuse me please. Thanks. Excuse me," they hear as he makes his way closer to them. When he sees Sydney standing there watching, he shouts out, "Sydney, please wait up!"

Sydney blushes as she looks at Sophie, and Sophie gives her a wink and smiles. When they look back, there stands Roscoe.

"Hey, Syd! May I call you Syd?"

"Hey Roscoe. Umm, sure, yeah, what's up?"

"I was wondering if I could walk with you to your next class?"

"Umm, sure," Sydney says happily.

Meanwhile, Lucas stands back just watching as Roscoe walks away with Sydney. Stanley comes down the hall and sees Lucas just standing there, and he says, "Hey, man, whatcha doing?"

"Watching my girl get swooped up by another dude!" he says angrily.

"Lucas, I know you like Syd, but that doesn't make her your girl. Have you expressed your feelings to her yet?" Stanley asks, trying to help.

"Well, no," Lucas says sadly. "But..."

"There's no buts! Lucas, if you don't say anything, how is she to know?"

"How can I? Every time I try, someone interrupts us, and I can't tell her!" he snaps.

"We can talk more after school. I gotta get to class," Stanley says as he takes off for his next class.

The day flies by, and it's the last few minutes of the school day. When the bell rings, everyone quickly pushes from the classrooms to the hallways to get outta school as quickly as possible.

Sydney gets outside and waits for Emma and Sophie. Lucas spots her and runs over to her.

"Syd, there you are! Hey, I need to talk with you about something important really soon. Can I come over today?" he asks, hoping she agrees.

"Oh, Lucas, I'm sorry. I can't today. I have a lot going on. Maybe another day this week?" Sydney says, shutting Lucas down.

Before he can say anything more, Sophie and Roscoe come out and distract Sydney from Lucas.

"Syd? Can I just have a minute of your time please?" Lucas carefully asks. He waits, and when Sydney doesn't acknowledge him, he touches her arm. "Syd?"

"Rude! Ugh, what, Lucas?" Sydney growls just as Emma comes around the corner and sees how aggravated Sydney is.

"Hey there, everyone. Is everything okay?" she asks, hoping to intervene before something bad happens.

"Oh, hey. Yes, we are just waiting for you, Em," Sydney cleverly states.

"Oh, okay, great. Are you girls ready to go?"

"Yes, ma'am." Sydney smiles.

"Okay, let's get to the car I have to get home and make dinner," Emma says, trying to hurry them to the car.

As the girls head for the car, Roscoe follows, and Lucas just stands there confused as he shouts out to Sydney, "Goodbye, Syd!" but she keeps walking like she doesn't hear him.

While Lucas stands there, watching with his heart in his hands, Stanley comes up and spooks him, and he jumps. "Dude, thanks for the warning!"

"Sorry, I guess you were in deep thought there just now?" Stanley asks.

"Yeah, I guess so. Hey, can I come over later?" Lucas wonders.

"Sure, see ya then. I got to go!" Stanley says as he quickly walks away.

At Emma's car, the girls get in, and Sydney tries to get Emma to let Roscoe come home with them.

"I'm sorry, Sydney, but not tonight. How about another day?" Emma suggests.

"Okay, bye, Roscoe. See you later. Here's my number. Text me," she says as she shuts the car door and Emma drives away. Sydney waves as they leave.

Emma drops off Sophie, and they head home.

CHAPTER 28
Please Say Yes

The first week of school has been a challenge for most of the students with settling back into getting up early and going to school, the new teachers, new friends, new classes, and for most, advancement into a higher grade with harder classes. Sydney has started off a bit moody but has since come around, and Lucas seizes his moment to ask her to the homecoming dance.

As they stand outside after school, Lucas walks up to Sydney and prepares to have a conversation with her. He clears his throat and begins, "Syd?"

"Yeah, Lucas, what's up?"

"I was hoping to have a minute of your time. I have something I wanted to talk with you about and something I would like to ask you. So could you please spare a few minutes before Emma comes out?" Lucas asks, trying not to sound desperate.

"Umm, yeah, sure. Walk with me to Emma's car," Sydney starts to walk, and Lucas follows. "So, what's up?"

"I do not know where to begin." Lucas gets nervous as he is about to pour out some of his heart into Sydney's hands. "So, I would like to ask you to the homecoming dance. Has anyone else asked you yet to go?" He prays the answer is no.

"No, not yet."

"So would you like to be my date?" He prays she says yes.
"I...umm..."

"I am sorry. I don't mean to put you on the spot, but we only have like a little over two weeks till the dance, and I want to make sure that we have time to coordinate our outfits if you would say yes and go with me."

"Well, what else did you need to speak to me about? Because Emma is headed this way," Sydney asks, curious as to what else he wanted to talk to her about.

"Oh, it's nothing. It can wait, but only if you say yes to accompanying me to the dance?"

"Sydney, are you ready to go?" Emma asks.

"In one second, Em," Sydney assures her.

"I am sorry. I do not mean to bug or make you think that I am trying to be pushy, but I was really hoping to have an answer today. If you can do me that favor at least."

"Oh yes, sure, why not? I am sorry, Lucas, but I must get going before Em beats me. See you later. Text me, okay?" Sydney says as she hurries off to Emma's car and gets in.

"Okay..." Lucas says as he watches her run off and be gone as fast as she said yes.

Suddenly, Lucas feels a sharp jab to his side. When he turns to look, he sees Stanley standing there. "Easy, man, before you take out a rib!" Lucas jokes.

"Sorry, man, my bad. So, I seen that you were out here talking to Sydney. So come on, spill it. How did it go?" Stanley asks, excited that he finally asked Sydney out.

"It went good enough for now."

"Good enough for now? What did you do, Lucas?"

"Well, Stanley, I asked her to the dance so I can talk with her more then about going out. So that's what I mean by it went good enough for now."

"So, she said yes?"

"Yes, Stanley, she said yes!" Lucas smiles.

"Well, that's a start. Now Roscoe can't ask her. Good job!" Stanley is proud of Lucas and his achievement.

"Roscoe?"

"Duh! Haven't you noticed those two together? I am surprised that he didn't already ask Sydney to go to the dance with him," Stanley says like he's the only one who is paying attention lately.

"Actually, I haven't noticed, but I am glad one of us is paying attention."

"Well, do you need a ride home, neighbor?" Stanley offers.

"Actually, yes, I could use a ride because I do not feel like going to football practice today. The coach has been rubbing me the wrong way. I am about to say screw it and just quit the football team," Lucas says, irritated by the coach and his shenanigans.

"Okay, well, come on. My mom is waiting over here for me," Stanley says as he heads for his mother's car. "Hey, Mom!"

"Hello, Stanley! Hey, Lucas! Do you need a ride?" Stanley's mom asks.

"Please, ma'am?"

"Sure thing, Lucas, just climb on in here."

"Thanks, Mom. I appreciate you helping my friend."

"Well, he is our neighbor. How rude of me would it be to not include to him to ride along with us?" Stanley's mom asks.

Stanley and Lucas get into the car, and Stanley's mother drives them home.

"Ma'am, I was wondering if I may I stay and visit with Stanley for a while?"

"Well, for starters, please call me Oliva. And yes, you may. Will you be staying for dinner?"

"Ah, no, Oliva. I just need a few minutes to speak with Stanley about the dance and our evening's agenda."

"Okay, sure, no problem. Well, here we are, boys. Have fun. I will let you know when dinner is complete, Stanley," Oliva states as they park, and all get out of the car.

"Okay, Mom. I will be in my room," Stanley says as he waves for Lucas to follow him.

Once they get to Stanley's room, he pulls Lucas in and quickly shuts the door.

"Dude, what were you thinking just now out there?"

"Stanley, you are gonna have to be clearer on what you mean. What did I do wrong?"

"How about telling my mom about the dance?"

"What's wrong with that?" Lucas asks, confused how that can be a bad thing.

"Well, for starters, my mom won't let me live it down!" Stanley says all frantically.

"I still don't see why it was a problem."

"Dude, I have never been to a dance, and she is gonna go crazy on me after you leave!" Stanley says sternly but with aggravation.

"Would you just calm down? It will be all right. So, are you gonna ask Sophie to the dance before Clay does? Or I am gonna be the only one with a date here?"

"Yes, I am gonna ask her. But what do you mean by Clay?"

"Seriously, dude, this again? Obviously, we are both blind to our own fate. Okay, just ask her then. I do have something that I want to do for you though."

"You want to do something for me? Like?" Stanley says, very confused.

"I will tell you as soon as you have your date's confirmation! So, get to asking her and let me know when you are secured with your date for homecoming. But for now, I must roll. I have much to start planning. I only have just a little over two weeks to get this done! And if you secure your date, that is even less time I have. So, I must get stepping, dawg!" Lucas says as he gets up and heads for the door.

"Dawg? What's with this *dawg* stuff?" Stanley thinks that Lucas is outta his dang mind.

"It's all good, dude. D-a-w-g! It's a cool dawg, not like the furry kind." Lucas chuckles as he opens Stanley's bedroom door and starts to walk out. He looks back over his shoulder and says, "Text me soon so I can plan for you too!"

"Okay, I am on it," Stanley says like he's just super drained.

Meanwhile, back at the Ashcraft ranch

Sydney is texting with Sophie.

> *Sydney:* So, then he walked with me to Emma's car and asked me to dance. Originally, he said that he needed to talk to me about something else but then he didn't feel like there was more he wanted to either ask or say to me,

> *Sophie:* Well, what do you think it is?

> Sydney: I have no clue. Maybe it was just nothing. You know like him being nervous to ask me to the dance.

> *Sophie:* Yeah possibly. Hold on I just got a text.

> *Sydney:* Really from who?

Sydney waits and waits some more, but Sophie doesn't respond.

> *Sydney:* Sophie? Don't hold out on me! Come on who messages you?

> *Sophie:* Sorry I am back it was Stanley.

> *Sydney:* Stanley? What did he want?

> *Sophie:* He asked me to the dance.

> *Sydney:* SO, what did you say?

Sophie: I told him yes because I can't have you going to the dance all by yourself.

Sydney: Oh yeah duh cool! But what about Clay?

Sophie: Well, I could ask you the same thing? What about Roscoe? I am sure Clay is going and I can dance with him there. I don't have to go to there with him to dance with him. Besides we are just friends.

Sydney: Roscoe? Yeah, same we are just friends. And we don't have to go together either to dance together.

Sophie: I think that he wants to be more than friends.

Sydney: Nah I don't want a boyfriend. I told you! Just Friends!

Sophie: Ok well I must be going you picking me up in the morning?

Sydney: Yeah, sure I can have Em pick you up.

Sophie: Ok good night I am gonna get ready for bed and relax for a bit.

Sydney: Ok sounds good. Good night love you bestie!

Sophie: Love you too!

Meanwhile, at Lucas's house

Lucas sits as his desk and draws out Sydney's dress when he gets a text.

Stanley: Lucas dude! Are you up?

Lucas: Yeah, what's up? Did you ask her?

Stanley: Yes, I did!

Lucas: And?

Stanley: I am sorry I am still shocked that she said yes! This is the 1st dance I have ever gone to, and I am so nervous.

Lucas: Great! Now I will be making her dress for you to give to her so do not let her buy one!

Stanley: You? Are making her dress?

Lucas: Yes, what's wrong with that?

Stanley: Are you in sewing class?

Lucas: No!

Stanley: Then can you please explain to me how you are gonna make Sophie's dress?

Lucas: Not just Sophie's but Sydney's too!

Stanley: I am so confused right now.

Lucas: Well, I hate to cut this short, but I have a ton of work ahead of me. You are more than welcome to come over and talk to me while I work on these, but I can't keep texting.

Stanley: Okay I will see if I can come over for just a bit.

Lucas: Okay but I must go now. If you can just come in and come to my room.

CHAPTER 29
Dress Design

"**O**kay, where was I? Oh yes, Sydney's dress." Lucas says as he draws out her design for her dress. As he sits and thinks about what he wants to do, he hears a soft knock on his bedroom door. "Come in."

"It's just me." Stanley tells Lucas.

"Yeah, I figured as much because my mom wasn't home. She could be by now, but I doubt it."

"So what are you doing there?" Stanley asks curiously.

"I'm drawing out what I want Sydney's dress to look like."

"Can you explain to me what I am looking at?"

"Sure, so this is Sydney's dress. It's going to be pastel purple lilac in color. It's going to be full length, and this style is called the mermaid. It shows off the female's shape. I am going to have the top of the bodice and straps be satin as is the rest of the dress. I will have a thin layer of beaded tulle over the top. It will be modest instead of showing off the breasts as most of these style of dresses do. I will make it, so that no cleavage is showing. I will have the bodice go almost straight across with a band of satin ribbon separating it from the skirt at the waist. The bottom will flare out from about the knees down. Most of these style of dresses drag on the floor, but I will have hers stop at about the floor. I will need to get some measurements to have this fit just right, but that will be tomorrow."

"Ah, yeah, and just how will you accomplish that?" Stanley wonders how clever he can be trying to get this piece of info not just from Sydney but Sophie too.

"Well, to be honest, I had not even thought about that just yet, but I am sure I will come up with something. I mean, how hard can it possibly be?"

"For you and I? Seriously? You have got to be kidding me, right?" Stanley says, shocked that he would even make such a statement.

"So wanna help me design for Sophie now? Since you are here," Lucas wonders.

"Really, you would let me do that?"

"Well, I asked you, didn't I? Yes, so here are two ideas I have. So I can do one kinda like Sydney's, or how about this," Lucas says with excitement as he starts to draw out a different design for Sophie's dress.

Stanley hovers over Lucas, watching him draw out Sophie's design.

"Okay, I am liking it so far, but can you elaborate as you draw so it makes it more understandable?"

"Sure! So this style of dress is called a maxi."

"Wait! Wait one minute! I cannot have my girl wearing a dress called something she may use every month for her lady issues."

"Ha, funny. Most people our age at school won't even know what it is called, and it's not like it's gonna have a license plate saying *Maxi* or anything. It's just the style of dress. You got me?"

"Yeah, sure, if you say so," Stanley says, not so sure.

"Just trust me, dude. Okay, so underneath will be a beautiful satin aqua-blue skirt with a slit up to her knee."

"A slit? Up to her knee?"

"Yes! Would you rather I go up to her thigh or higher?"

"No!" Stanley says with disgust like Lucas is trying to say he's some kind of pervert. "No, you're right. The knee is great!"

"Okay, let me finish then. Next, the bodice will have satin as well. Then around what would be the neckline, which is this part will be like Sydney's dress. Instead of the material just covering each breast and having cleavage showing, we will make it more modest and leave most of her breast bone open, but we will come across just where the breasts start to make shape." Lucas draws out to show Stanley.

"Then the neckline will be satin as well. But coming out from under that satin neckline will be various shades of color. Probably like three shades should be good of tulle that will be cut in maybe four- to five-inch wide sections the length of her dress. You with me so far?"

"Ah, yes!"

"Okay, just checking. You got kinda quiet on me. Okay, then, there will be a wide satin band around her waist, and the tulle will come down under the waistband and hang to the floor. A few of the pieces can have some sequins to sparkle it up a bit. And for her straps, she too can have satin straps, I would say about an inch to maybe two inches wide. So what do you think?" Lucas checks for Stanley's approval.

"Well, I am impressed. But why does it matter on a specific color of satin underneath? You won't even see it, will you?" Stanley says, a bit confused.

"No, you will. That's why those strips hanging down will only be a few inches wide so as she walks, they will move with her movements and show the main color under the tulle. And the tulle will also cover her leg where the slit is and leave just enough to the imagination. Do you see it?"

"Yeah, kinda. I guess so." Stanley tries hard to see what Lucas has envisioned but cannot quite grasp it. "But I definitely like it so far, just can't wait to see it on Sophie."

"Same for me with Syd." Lucas agrees with Stanley. "Trust me, our ladies will be showstoppers at the dance."

"I hope so! Who knows, maybe you will be a big hit and have a new job designing dresses for the ladies at school," Stanley chuckles.

"Let's not take it that far," Lucas warns. "Okay, well, I have a lot of work to do, so I must be heading to bed, but before you go, listen, I want this to be a secret. You can't tell anyone anything! You got me?"

"Yes! Not a problem. You are doing me a huge favor for which I am most grateful for," Stanley reassures Lucas.

"Okay, one other thing. I am going to try to see if I can get the girls out to Sydney's place tomorrow after school so I can get measurements for the dresses, and then I need to go to the store to get supplies. Would you like to come with and help me? You would be like my seamstress right-hand man."

"Umm…oh…okay, sure. But what store are you able to get the supplies you need at?" Stanley wonders.

"The fabric store, of course. They will have everything I need."

"Everything?"

"Yes, sir, right down to their shoes."

"Wait, their shoes?"

"Yes, they need matching shoes for their dresses."

"Okay, so anything else I need to know?"

"Not at the moment, so I just need to draw out to female figures with lines for you to write measurements for each one I need, then I am off to bed," Lucas says as he yawns.

"Okay, I will take that as my cue to head out and off to bed myself. After all, if I am to be your right-hand man, I need to get plenty of rest from what it sounds like. So good night, dawg."

"Yep, good night, dude. Thanks for coming over and helping out. I really appreciate it."

"No problem! I really appreciate you going out of your way to do such an amazing thing for me and my girl."

"She is not your girl just yet," Lucas reminds Stanley.

"I know, but I really hope so after the dance, and I hope this helps win me some points."

"I hope so too, dude. No other guy at school would do this for their girls. So hopefully it will win us some major brownie points." Lucas hopes.

"Okay, I am out so you can get some rest, and I can get home and get some rest too!" Stanley says as he goes for the door, opens it, and starts to walk through then suddenly stops and turns to Lucas.

"Did you forget something?" Lucas asks.

"Actually, would you like my mom to pick you up in the morning to take you to school with us?"

"If you think your mom will be okay with it? But you do not have to pick me up. I can just walk over. It's not a big deal. Just text me in the morning, and let me know," Lucas says as he finishes his female drawing chart for their measurements.

"Okay, will do, night!"

"Thanks, night."

Stanley leaves to head home, and Lucas finishes up his chart before heading to bed. Just before he heads off to bed, he gets a text.

Stanley: Hey! Mom was up and she said no problem. You can ride along with us tomorrow for sure!

Lucas: Okay, thanks for the heads up, I will be at your place tomorrow morning in time to leave. Night.

Stanley: Deal! You are welcome and night to you too!

Lucas heads to bed and drifts off to sleep.

CHAPTER 30
Not Again

Lucas can barely sleep from all his excitement. All he can think about is getting to school, getting the day over with, then getting over to the Ashcraft's so he can get the girls measured for his dress designs, and then he and Stanley can go get the supplies that he needs, so he can get started on the girls' dresses. He really hopes that the girls like his designs and appreciate them as much as he did designing and making them. He also hopes that this is a generous and special enough gift to win Sydney's heart. If not, he won't give up; he will just try a different tactic.

Eventually, Lucas falls asleep. But it doesn't seem to be for long before his alarm starts blaring in his ear. He hits the snooze and tries to get a few more minutes of shut-eye. He lies there thinking; he's just resting his eyes when he hears a horn honking.

He thinks he's dreaming and tries to ignore it till he realizes that he has actually fallen back asleep and that it is Oliva honking her horn. He jumps up outta bed and grabs his phone and texts Stanley.

Lucas: I am so sorry man! I will be out in 5 or less.

Stanley: Ok mom said she can wait for a few more minutes but hurry.

Lucas puts on his socks, throws on a pair of jeans, and grabs a shirt. As he grabs his measurements sheet he made up for the girls and his book bag, he runs down to the front door, slips on his shoes, and runs out the door, through the yard, and over to Stanley's.

Stanley has the passenger side window down, and he shouts to Lucas, "Take your time. We are good!"

"I know, but I can't thank you guys enough for allowing me to ride with you to school."

"So I figured you would be so excited to get to school and that I was gonna see you standing outside of our car waiting on us. So what happened?" Stanley wonders.

"Ha ha ha, that was the plan. Seriously, though, that is also why I was late, for which I am sorry. I can't say I am sorry enough. But I was so excited last night I couldn't even sleep! Then I thought I hit my snooze, but apparently, I did not."
"Well, you are up and good now even though you look a little rough," Stanley informs Lucas.

"Rough? How rough?"

"Well, your hair is everywhere for starters, you have a red hand impression of the side of your face, and it looks like some dried drool that was running down your face. But other than that, you look the same as usual." Stanley lays it all out for Lucas.

"Well, the hair I don't care about, the red mark will eventually go away, but the drool, ugh, yuck! I must have crashed hard after I turned off my phone."

"Stanley, open the glove box, dear," Oliva instructs him.

Stanley opens it and says, "Okay, now what, Mom?"

"Is there a travel pack of makeup wipes in there?"

"Makeup wipes?" Lucas says, double-thinking about the dried drool on his face. "I am good thanks! I will try to scrape it off."

"No, don't you even think about it. Just use one of my wipes." Oliva pleads with Lucas.

"But they are makeup wipes!" he says, a bit grossed out by the thought of using them.

"Lucas, they are to clean up your face. They have nothing to do with makeup other than they clean it off your face...well, not your face but a lady with makeup on her face."

Lucas thinks about what Oliva states and says, "Oh, okay, sure. I would love to use one."

Stanley finds the pack of wipes and gets one out to give to Lucas. And just in the nick of time because Lucas can see the school just up ahead.

"Did I get it all, Stanley?" Lucas asks quickly.

"Looks like it!" Stanley chuckles.

"Okay, boys, here you are. Will you be needing a ride after school?" Oliva asks.

"I will let you know, Mom. We may be going to the Ashcraft's after school. But either way, I will let you know," Stanley assures his mom.

"Don't look now, Stanley, but Emma just pulled up behind us," Lucas nervously states.

"Well, let me go check right now, Mom. Can you wait for just a few more minutes?" Stanley asks as he exits the car.

"Sure thing, sweetheart."

"Okay, Mom. Come on, Lucas, you have to ask with me," Stanley says, trying to hurry along Lucas.

"Okay, okay, I'm coming. Again, sorry, I was late this morning, and thanks for the ride," Lucas says as he exits the car and practically gets dragged by Stanley to Emma's car.

"Good morning, Sydney, Sophie. Miss Emma." Stanley greets everyone.

"Good morning," Sydney and Sophie say in unison.

"Good morning, Stanley and Lucas," Emma says. "What are you boys up to this morning?"

"Well, Lucas and I were wondering if we may come over to the Ranch later after school?" Stanley says as he elbow-jabs Lucas.

"Ah yeah, I have something I need to talk with the girls about if that's okay?" Lucas adds.

"Sure, I don't think that would be an issue. Do you have a ride out, or would you like to come out right after school?" Emma asks.

"Actually, may we get a ride back to the ranch after school?" Lucas asks. "This is kinda important, and I am on a bit of a tight schedule."

"Sure, I can give you a ride out. How will you boys be getting home then?" Emma wonders.

"I will take care of those details, but I am sure we will be good in that area. It would just be very helpful for the ride out, thanks," Lucas gratefully replies.

Sydney and Sophie just stand there wondering just what ever does Lucas have up his sleeve this time. Sydney rolls her eyes at Sophie, and Sophie nods back.

"Yes, I can definitely help out with the ride there. Okay, boys and girls, I must go park now. I will see you in class in a few minutes," Emma states as she prepares to drive away.

"Thanks," Lucas states as he shuts the passenger side car door so she can go park.

Stanley quickly jogs over to his mother's car and relays the message. "We have a ride over to the Ashcraft's later, but I do not know what Lucas's plans are for after that, so if we need you, I will text you, Mom. Have a great day. I love you," Stanley informs his mother.

"Okay, have a great day at school, sweetheart. I love you too!" Oliva says as she drives off.

Stanley looks for Lucas and can see that he is talking with Sydney and Sophie as they walk closer to the front door to enter the school. He hurries to meet up with them.

"Ladies," Stanley greets Sydney and Sophie.

"Morning, Stanley," Sydney says like she's very tired.

"Good morning, Stanley." Sophie returns the greeting.

"Sounds like you didn't get much sleep either, Sydney," notices Stanley.

"Didn't you sleep well either, Stanley?" Sydney asks.

Lucas looks at Stanley and gives him a "Don't do it" look.

"Ah no, I didn't get very much either," Stanley says to cover for the remark he was gonna make about Lucas.

"Well, we must be getting to our lockers. We will see you guys later in homeroom," Sydney says as she tugs on Sophie's arm to get moving and follow her.

Stanley and Lucas just stop and watch them walk away as they give a quick wave.

Then Lucas sees Roscoe walk up behind the girls, and he tries to scare Sydney but grabs her around her waist and quickly gives out a scream of "Boo!"

Stanley must have been watching too because just as Roscoe scares Sydney, he looks at Lucas and says, "Dawg, did you?"

"Yes, Stanley, I did see that," Lucas states a with a bit of aggravation.

"Well, let's not worry about it for now. Besides we have already asked the girls to the dance so they can't back out now, it's not like them to be so cruel." Stanley tries to redirect Lucas's thoughts.

"You are right, Stanley. Let's just get to homeroom and get this day over with," Lucas says, trying to remain cool about what he just witnessed.

After they go to their lockers, Stanley and Lucas head into homeroom only to see Sydney and Sophie sitting beside each other as normal, but Roscoe is directly in front of Sydney, and they are engaged in a conversation that seems pretty intense. Lucas really wants to know what they are talking about, but at the same time, he doesn't want to let on that he has any kind of feelings for her or to seem jealous so he moves a row away, hoping that maybe he can still kinda hear what's being said.

"So what was up with that earlier this morning, Sydney?" Roscoe asks.

"I don't know what you mean, Roscoe," Sydney says, confused.

"Lucas? He and Stanley were over at your ride's car, and then he walked with you into school."

"Oh, that? That was nothing." Sydney tries to play it off because it really was nothing.

After all, it wasn't like she asked him to come over to Emma's car and walk with her and Sophie into school. Sydney thinks to herself before continuing with Roscoe. "We are just friends, and he and Stanley came over to say good morning. I don't know much more than that," Sydney tells Roscoe.

Then the homeroom bell rings, and Sydney motions for Roscoe to turn around so he doesn't get in trouble.

They go through all the normal homeroom business, and then they head to their next class. As Stanley and Lucas exit the room, Roscoe is standing across the hallway and just gives them an evil stare.

"Oh, I know that you just seen that!" Lucas says quickly and quietly under his breath to Stanley.

Stanley returns with, "Yep! Yes, sir, I did. And if you don't mind me saying, so I think he's bad news, Lucas. So let's just steer clear of him," Stanley wisely states.

"Not a problem," Lucas adds, agreeing with Stanley that Roscoe is up to no good.

They manage to get through the rest of the day with no major issues. Lucas and Stanley wait outside for Sydney and Sophie. When they exit the school, Roscoe isn't very far behind them.

"Don't look now, Stanley, but someone is following very close behind Sydney and Sophie."

"Let's just act like we are not aware. You just help watch for Emma, and we will move toward her and not worry about meeting up with the girls till we make it to Emma's car."

"Good idea, Stanley."

They both keep an eye out for Emma while trying not to pay any attention to Roscoe and the girls. But it looks like fate has another option for them. As Sophie sees Lucas and Stanley, she tugs at Sydney, and they head over toward them with Roscoe hot on their tails.

"Where are you headed, ladies?" Roscoe asks.

"Oh, over to wait with Lucas and Stanley." Sophie just puts out there not thinking any of her decision to do so.

"Lucas, don't look now, but I heard Sophie mention they are headed this way," Stanley whispers under his breath.

"Uh-hmm," Lucas says quietly so hopefully only Stanley can hear.

"Ah, there you boys are!" Sophie says. "Are you waiting for Emma?"

"Yes, we were actually. Sorry, we didn't see you ladies there," Lucas says and tries to act cool with Roscoe so he acknowledges him as well. "Roscoe." Lucas nods.

"Lucas. So why are you waiting for their ride?" Roscoe asks quite rudely.

"Oh, are you writing a book? Because actually I do not think that is any of your business," Stanley says without thinking as his mouth writes a check his body definitely does not wanna cash.

"If I was, I do not think you would be very enlighting for the storyline. Besides, can't a man ask?" Roscoe says, very cocky.

"Oh yes, he may, but it doesn't mean that he will get the answers he seeks." Lucas grows a pair and stands up against him with Stanley.

"Oh, look there's Em. Come on, guys, we have to get going. Emma does not like to be left waiting," Sydney quickly hurries them along as she can feel the air get so thick from tension she almost couldn't breathe.

"Oh yes, coming Syd!" Lucas says happily as he pushes Stanley ahead of him while watching that Roscoe stays put.

While they are all headed to Emma's car and not watching Roscoe, Lucas shoots him an *'I won this time'* look as Roscoe shoots back a *'You're on my list, so watch your back'* look.

Lucas quickly turns to watch where he's going as they get closer to Emma's car.

They all get in rather quickly once they reach Emma's car. Once inside, Emma asks, "What was that? Did I interrupt something?"

"Uh, to be honest, I have no idea, Emma, but I sure am glad that you came around when you did," Lucas says, not knowing what to think at this point.

Sydney says, agreeing, "Yeah, what is with him lately?"

"You mean you are finally noticing what I was trying to tell you all along?" Sophie says, shocked.

"Wait, you have noticed this behavior and not said anything to anyone?" Lucas asks, confused.

"Well, I mentioned it to Syd. Whom else should I have mentioned it to?" Sophie asks. "If Sydney wouldn't listen, who else would?"

"I would!" Lucas quickly responds.

"Yeah, I would too!" Stanley adds.

"And why would it matter to you two?" Sydney says, throwing in her two cents.

"Because we are your friends!" Lucas says, shocked at Sydney's behavior right at this moment.

This whole time, Emma has been wrapped up in the conversation and doesn't move the car, and Roscoe just stands glaring at them.

"Em?"

"Yes, Sydney?"

"Can we please just go?"

"Oh, yes. I am so sorry. I was just wrapped up in what y'all were conversing about. Let's get home, so we can get some dinner," Emma says as she pulls away from the school.

"Thanks, Emma. Roscoe was just staring at us back there, and I hope that he couldn't hear anything that we were saying," Sydney says, hoping she's right.

"So, Lucas, Stanley, can you elaborate on why you wanted to come over today? Not that you aren't welcome anytime. I was just wondering if there was a special reason or not?" Emma asks curiously.

"Well, I wanted to wait till we got to the ranch to say anything, but you will find out soon enough. So Emma, Stanley and I asked the girls to the homecoming dance."

"Oh, you did? How wonderful! Guess I will get to go dress shopping with the girls then."

"Well, that's what I actually needed to come by for."

"I'm sorry, Lucas, but how do you kids say that I'm not picking up what you are dropping?" Emma tries to remember.

"No, Em." Sydney giggles. "It's I'm not picking up what you are putting down."

"it's the same difference isn't it?" Emma asks confused.

"I guess kinda, " Sydney chuckles.

They all laugh, and Lucas continues, "Emma, remember when I said that I was took classes for manners and such?"

"Yes, I do, dear, but I still am very confused," Emma says, hoping he gets to the point soon.

"Well, I took a bunch of..." Lucas thinks how to word it right then continues, "I took life lessons or like life survival classes to teach me an array of things that could be useful someday. This one particular class I took I never thought I would ever get a chance to use, and I want to show off my talents, and so Stanley and I are coming to get measurements of the girls, so I can make them their dresses for homecoming."

Sydney and Sophie stop and look at each other like, *What did we sign up for?*

"Oh, how sweet, Lucas. So what style of dress will you be making for the girls?" Emma wonders.

"Well, that is a bit of a surprise, but I can assure them and you Miss Emma that they are very modest, unrevealing yet very beautiful." Lucas pokes Stanley then looks at the girls and back at Stanley to try to get him to tell them without telling them what they will be getting.

"Ah, yes. I can attest to this to comment they are very modest and should be very beautiful. I hope that I am not giving away too much info, but he took two very different but similar designs and redesigned them to be less revealing yet modest as we have already said. And even I was impressed with what he has drawn to demonstrate what it should look like. I think everyone will be pleasantly pleased with the final results." Stanley says as he looks at Lucas for approval.

Lucas gives him a thumbs-up and continues, "Yes, just like Stanley has stated everyone should be pleasantly surprised and possibly stunned not only at my abilities but the ladies' beauty with them on. Not that they are not already beautiful but these dresses should enhance their beauty."

"Very nicely stated, Lucas and Stanley. We cannot wait to see what you have in store for the young ladies," Emma says, excited to see what they have come up with. "So how long are you giving yourself to get these dresses made?"

"Actually, we will be leaving and headed for the fabric store just as soon as we get their crucial measurements that I need to make their dresses. And I am so sorry, but I will probably not be very reachable till I get them finished. Also, I or Stanley and I will also be providing the shoes and accessories for the ensemble. So that everything matches," Lucas also informs them.

"That is awesome, but when is the dance?" Emma wonders.

"It's in about two weeks. So I am not leaving myself much time to mess around," Lucas says, hoping that he can get everything he needs and get them finished in time.

"Okay, here we are, kiddos. Is there anywhere special that you need to be to get these measurements, Lucas?"

"Actually, Emma, if we could just be in the living room, that should be sufficient," Lucas states gratefully.

"Not a problem. We can definitely do that. Girls, go ahead on into the living room and help out Lucas and Stanley so they may go get started on these masterpieces for you ladies."

"Please don't give me that much credit. I am good, but I am not that good," Lucas humbly replies.

"Emma?" Sophie asks.

"Yes, dear?"

"My mom is coming over with Eliza, and I just wanted to let you know."

"Thank you, Sophie. I will watch for her."

Everyone gets out of the car and heads into the house at about the same time that Allison and Eliza are coming in the lane to the ranch.

"You kids go on in, and I will wait for Allison."

Just as all the kids have entered the house and shut the front door, Allison parks and Eliza gets out.

"Hi, Miss Emma," Eliza says, greeting Emma.

"Hello, little one. You may head inside. Everyone else has already gone in, and we can join them too, Allison."

"Why thank you, Emma! So what is going on here today?" Allison wonders.

"From what I gather, Lucas and Stanley are taking the girls to the homecoming dance, and Lucas will be making their dresses." "Really? How unique." Allison smiles.

Emma and Allison head into the house just in time to hear screaming. They go running to see what's all the commotion.

"Liz! Come on again?" Sophie says.

"Sophie Ann! What did I tell you?" Allison scolds.

"I'm sorry, Mom, but she's getting sick everywhere again."

"Everyone, just please calm down! Sophie and Sydney can you please come with me. Lucas, I am sorry can you just give us a few minutes?" Emma says, trying to get everyone in control.

"Sure, can I help with anything, Emma?" Lucas kindly offers.

"Actually, if you have time, sure, please come. I can give you something to do to help."

Lucas tugs on Stanley's shirt to follow him to help too! As they exit the living room, Emma is sending people all over to get supplies.

"Sydney, mop and bucket with hot, soapy water. Sophie, here, take this thermometer to your mother. Lucas, can you take this bucket into Allison please? Oh, and Stanley, thank you for offering to help. Can you please take these towels in to Allison?"

Everyone gets and takes all that Emma has instructed them to do, and she is headed for a drink for Eliza.

They get Eliza cleaned up. Lucas gets all the measurements that he needs from the girls and a few others just in case. Lucas and Stanley are just waiting for Oliva, Stanley's mother, to come pick them up to take them to the fabric store.

Page **361** of **374**

When Stanley remembers Lucas mentioning something about needing the girls' shoe sizes, so he whispers to Lucas about the shoes.

"Ah yes, thanks, Stanley. Just what would I do without you, my friend? Girls, I do need just one more thing from you, and that is your shoe size, so I can make sure I get the right sizes to match your dresses."

The girls give their sizes to Lucas and Stanley's mother pulls up out front and honks her horn.

"I'm sorry, everyone, but that is my cue to get the next step and get moving on this extravagant project," Lucas says as he tries to drag Stanley out the door with him.

"I'm sorry, but I know that you are in a hurry, but just how many other projects have you done on this magnitude that you seem to think this is going to be easy?" Emma asks.

"Sure, real quick. I have not done anything even remotely close to this, but I have much confidence in myself," Lucas says, smiling from ear to ear.

"Oh, okay, well, I wish you the best of luck. And please let me know if you need any pointers. I do happen to know a little bit about sewing," Emma adds as they head out the door, and to Oliva's car in quite the hurry.

"Okay, thank you, Emma. I will certainly do that if I need any help," Lucas says as they get in the car and slam the door.

CHAPTER 31
Day of the Dance

It's been a very hectic, busy, draining, eventful, and stressful two weeks. Finally, the day has arrived for the girls to get to see their dresses and show them off to the whole school. The girls are nervous, but Lucas is more nervous of what people will think of the bully jock turned Susie home and dressmaker.

Stanley meets Lucas at his house and helps him to carefully bring out the dress bags with the girls' dresses in and carefully put them in the car.

"So what time did you tell the girls we would be over today?" Stanley asks nervously.

"I told them we would message them when we leave here but that I was shooting for noon. I hope that's enough time for them because the dance starts at 4p.m.."

"Lucas, I think it should be plenty of time. I mean, we basically did everything that needed done for the girls besides actually dress them, so it will only be a matter of them getting dressed, Them doing their hair and make up and I am so sure that Emma will want pictures."

"And so do I, young man!" Claire adds.

"You and me both," Oliva adds too with her camera already in hand.

"Is Emma gonna be okay with all of us parents and kids at her house all at the same time?" Claire wonders.

"Yes, Mom, she will be just fine with it. Besides, it's just as big of a deal for them as it is for everyone else, and she loves big deals when it pertains to Sydney," Lucas assures his mother.

"Okay, well, should we be going then?" Oliva asks.

"Ah yes, please, Mom," Stanley says.

"Oliva, may I please ride with you since we are going to the same place?" Claire asks.

"Absolutely, I would not have it any other way," Oliva says happily.

They all climb in Oliva's car and head to the ranch.

Lucas texts Sydney and states that they are on their way and to be ready.

Meanwhile, at the Ashcraft Ranch

The anticipation is soaring. Everyone is there except for Stanley and Lucas and their moms.

The girls have already eaten so that they don't eat and mess up their dresses. Now they stand at the front door just staring out into the driveway looking and waiting patiently for Lucas and Stanley to get there.

When the girls see the boys coming up the lane, they are shrieking very loudly, and the excitement level just jumped like several notches at the Ashcraft ranch. They open the door and wait patiently for them to bring up the dresses. The boys get out of the car and carefully pull out the dress bags, shoeboxes, and one other little bag with goodies inside for the girls.

"Hello, ladies. I truly hope you are as pleased with the dresses as I am," Lucas says.

"No! As we are. Lucas did an amazing job with them!" Stanley says proudly.

"Thanks, Stanley."

"Yep, no problem."

"So we have them marked on the outside of the garment bags whose dress is whose. Here is a sneak peek at your colors, ladies," Lucas says as he opens up the shoeboxes to show the girls at least what color their shoes are so they are known before they leave that room.

"Wow, I love the colors, Lucas!" Sydney says as she reaches out to hug him before turning to head up to her room to change.

"Yes, definitely, I love the colors too! May we go see and try on our dresses?" Sophie eagerly asks.

"Yes, sure thing. Do you ladies need any help getting dressed?" Emma asks.

"Sure, you older ladies may come up and help us get ready," Sydney shares.

With that, all the females of the house have taken to the upstairs to Sydney's bedroom to help the girls get ready.

The males of the house just stand there, waiting to see if anything gets said that they can hear.

Sure enough there it is. "Agh!" Screams from the girls about the dresses. They hear the upstairs bedroom door open, and Sydney yells down the stairs, "Thank you. They are absolutely gorgeous!"

"Well, sounds like your dresses are a hit with the ladies, Lucas!" Parker adds, while trying to hide his excitement as long as he can.

It seems like hours pass when the girls finally open the door.

"We are about to come down. Can everyone please go to the living room?" Sydney asks politely.

Everyone makes their way into the living room as the girls come downstairs to show off their beautiful dresses.

As they enter the living room, Parker starts to tear up.

Greyson's jaw about hits the floor as he says, "No, seriously, Lucas, what store did you buy these at?"

"They are stunning!" Parker adds as he wipes his tears of joy away. "Boys, you may use my bedroom to change so we can get some pictures. Let me show you where it is. Follow me."

So while everyone is admiring Lucas's work, Lucas and Stanley make their way to Parker's room to change, so they can get pictures and get off to the dance.

"Here you are, boys. Take all the time you need."

"Parker?"

"Yes, Lucas?"

"There is one more surprise that I did not make clear just yet because I wanted to be the only one who knew, but the dance starts at four, and there should be the finishing touch arriving here by 3p.m.," Lucas informs Parker.

"Oh, okay, so I should keep an eye out closer to 3?"

"If you could please."

"Sure thing, Lucas. Okay, boys, get ready so we can get some pictures!" Parker says with excitement as he pulls the door shut and returns to the living room.

"Lucas, what did you do?" Stanley says, worried about what is showing up here at 3.

"You will see! I cannot tell you. I swore to myself I would be the only one to know till it happened."

"So not even your mom knows?"

"Not even my mother knows! It's not just a surprise for you and the ladies but everyone. So hurry, get dressed, I do not wanna be late!" Lucas says, trying to hurry along Stanley the slow poke.

In the living room, everyone is still so amazed at all the wonderful work, time, and effort that Lucas has put into the girls' dresses.

"Pardon me for saying so, but the girls are so sexy yet elegant-looking. It's crazy how fast they are growing up!" Greyson states as he sheds a tear.

"Oh, you old softy. Yes, they are so beyond beautiful!" Allison says as she rubs Greyson's back to show him support.

"I need to get my camera," Emma says as she leaves the room for a few minutes and returns with it on and ready to snap away.

"Why don't we get pictures of the girls awhile so when the boys come out, we can finish up with them?" Parker states as he excuses himself for a quick moment to check outside for the arriving surprise.

When Parker returns, they get pictures of the girls together, with their parents, separately, with Eliza. Everyone has their backs turned when Lucas and Stanley sneak back into the living room. When the girls look up and see Lucas and Stanley standing there all decked out in black tuxedos with long coattails and matching cummerbunds to the color of their dresses, they just get quiet and stop and look at each other then back at them.

"Girls, are you okay?" Emma asks.

"Yes, but I feel like I died and went to a fairyland," Sydney states.

"Why would you say that?" Emma asks curiously.

"Well, look behind you," Sydney points out.

Everyone turns to see Lucas and Stanley standing there all handsome looking and standing tall and proud.

"Well, come on, boys. Get over here so we can get some pics," Emma says to hurry them along so they aren't late.

As Stanley walks by his mother, she reaches out like she wants to hug him and not let go, but he puts up a finger asking her to wait.

"Okay, Lucas and Sydney, you are up first. Then Stanley and Sophie. Then can we get you all together as a group?" Emma says as she and everyone starts snapping away.

Parker sneaks out to see if the next surprise is here yet. He sees something coming very slowly in the lane. He returns and says, "Lucas, I think it is here."

"What is here?" Sydney asks.

"Follow me, and I will show you, but you have to keep your eyes closed," Lucas says as he reaches for Sydney's hand and walks her to the door.

Stanley shrugs when he looks at Sophie and reaches for her hand as she covers her eyes to be fair to Sydney.

When they get to the door, Parker opens it, and Lucas and Stanley lead the girls outside as everyone is shocked to see a limo sitting outside.

"Okay, girls, you may see your next surprise," Lucas says.

"A long white stretch limo? Oh, Lucas, you shouldn't have," Sydney says as she tries to hold back the tears of amazement and joy.

"Don't you cry, bestie, or you will mess up all that beautiful makeup I did for you."

"I'm trying not to," Sydney says as she dabs her eyes.

"Ladies, shall we?" Lucas says as he again reaches for Sydney's hand to walk her down the stairs and over to the limo.

"Kids, I would love some pictures by the limo, if you don't mind," Emma says happily.

"Sure thing, Emma," Lucas replies.

So the kids all line up together then each pair by themselves as everyone gets pictures. Then when the pictures are finished, everyone says their goodbyes.

"Have fun, kids. Be safe!" Parker says.

"Love you," everyone says in unison to the kids as they all load into the limo and it drives off.

"I just wish Ivy could have been here to see this," Parker says sadly.

"Oh, I am sure she was," Emma whispers.

"So would everyone like to come back in for a drink or a snack?" Parker asks.

So the adults go inside to mingle for a while as the kids are having a blast in the limo.

In the Limo

"So I know we are not old enough, so I just had them stock this with sparkling grape juice. I mean it looks like wine." Lucas chuckles.

"Oh, how sweet, Lucas, but I better pass till after the dance because I can be a klutz when I am dressed so fancy. But I absolutely love all the thought and effort that you have put into this." Sydney says as she pours out her emotions.

They arrive shortly at the dance, and the kids at the dance are shocked to see a white stretch limo show up and are all standing in amazement to see just who is inside of it.

When it parks and the limo driver opens the door and out comes Lucas and Sydney then Stanley and Sophie the crowd cheers.

They hear whistling and clapping, oohing and awing.

The girls start to blush as they enter the school dance.

During the first dance, they each dance with their dates, and they seem to be having a great time.

"Thank you, Lucas, for the amazing dress and evening. I could have never asked for something so beautiful. I am thankful to have you as my friend," Sydney states as she gives Lucas a kiss on the cheek.

"You are very welcome," Lucas says as he holds Sydney and dances with her around the room.

"Thanks for this wonderful opportunity, Stanley. It is so sweet of you and Lucas to do such nice things for Syd and me," Sophie says.

"You are welcome. I am just glad you said yes," Stanley says as they dance like nobody's watching.

ACKNOWLEDGMENTS

I would love to thank the following for all their love and support as I travel along this amazing journey: Allen, my hubby; Darlene, my best friend; Steve, my pre-reader assistant; my kids Brittany, Kristina, Amber, Brandon; Marsha, my mom; Mark and Lily, my dad and mom; Phyllis, my aunt; the rest of my family and friends; all my followers.

Thank you all for your patience and understanding as I write more books. I have shortened the lengthy publication process by self publishing. That in itself is a challenge that I have accepted and I am embracing more and more with each book I complete. I hope you all bare with me as I work out the kinks and get more proficient at the self publication process. It doesn't take away from the fact that everyone who reads my stories loves them, from the relatable characters, tons of emotion, plot twists and turns. If you see mistakes please understand I am only human. It means so much to me, and I appreciate you all! Thank you from the bottom of my heart. May God bless you as he has me and my family!

ABOUT THE AUTHOR

Susie is married to her amazing husband, Allen, 26 years this year. They are continuing to work together.

Susie's faith in God remains strong as she prays every day for guidance as to where he wants and needs her to be. She believes her calling is to write. She's always wanted to write, but coming up with an idea was a bit of a task. Now she has more things to write about than she had ever planned.

She has the Sydney's Passion series along with some but not limited to the following ideas: romance, sci-fi, murder, mystery, and yes, even an autobiography of sorts.

Susie is excited to make her move south with her husband one day soon to live by the beach and continue her writing. Crafts and a small thrift store may be in the works for her future.

Susie and her husband are excited and proud to announce that they are grandparents as of the fall of 2022.

Susie appreciates all her followers' love and support for her and her work. She asks that if you read her books to please leave a review for others to see. And always remember, "You will not be tested or tempted with something that another man has not experienced without a way out" (1 Corinthians 10:13).

Made in the USA
Middletown, DE
01 October 2023

39724594R00222